7⁹⁵

AN ADAMS BUSINESS ADVISOR

The Personnel Policy Handbook for Growing Companies

Other titles in
THE ADAMS BUSINESS ADVISORS

Bob Adams books are appropriate for professional development seminars, training programs, premiums, and specialized reprint activities. They can be ordered through retail outlets everywhere, or by calling the Special Sales Department at 800-872-5627 (in Massachusetts 617-767-8100).

AN ADAMS BUSINESS ADVISOR

The Personnel Policy Handbook for Growing Companies

**HOW TO CREATE
COMPREHENSIVE GUIDELINES,
PROCEDURES, AND
CHECKLISTS**

DARIEN McWHIRTER, J.D.

BOB ADAMS, INC.
Holbrook, Massachusetts

Published by Bob Adams, Inc., 260 Center Street, Holbrook, MA 02343

ISBN: 1-55850-465-6 (hardcover)
ISBN: 1-55850-430-3 (paperback)

Printed in the United States of America.

J   I   H   G   F   E   D   C   B   A (hardcover)
J   I   H   G   F   E   D   C   B   A (paperback)

Library of Congress Cataloging-in-Publication Data
McWhirter, Darien A. (Darien Auburn)
    The personnel policy handbook for growing companies : how to create comprehensive guidelines, procedures, and checklists / Darien McWhirter.
        p.   cm. — (An Adams business advisor)
    Includes bibliographical references and index.
    ISBN 1-55850-465-6. — ISBN 1-55850-430-3 (pbk.)
    1. Personnel management—Handbooks, manuals, etc. 2. Small business—Personnel management—Handbooks, manuals, etc. I. Title. II. Series.
    HF5549.17.M35   1994
    658.3—dc20   94-36545
                                                                                    CIP

Cover design: Marshall Henrichs

Table of Contents

Preface

While doing workshops for employers concerning the basics of employment law, I found that many of those in attendance wanted to go beyond basic concepts and get down to the nitty gritty. What should their policy be on a particular problem? What should their employee handbook say about this or that issue? Too often, books in this area say that employers should have a written policy, but make no effort to help employers write one that is both understandable and legal. This book does just that. It makes suggestions throughout concerning what an employee handbook might say on particular issues.

Nothing combines management theory and law like the need to write an employee handbook. At every step, the need to comply with the law and at the same time be concerned with the impact on employee relations must be considered. This book is intended to serve as an introduction and as a basis for discussion between an employer and the employer's attorney. While laws are discussed, it must be kept in mind that laws change and different judges interpret different laws differently. There is no substitute for legal advice from an attorney in your area.

The prime audience for this book is owners and managers of small and expanding organizations, who must consider what laws will apply to them as they reach the next rung on the growth ladder. At the same time, every effort has been made to provide information for organizations of all sizes and shapes. While state and local government agencies will of course have to go beyond what is said here, much of the discussion will also apply to them.

Employment law and employee relations have changed a great deal in the 1980s and 1990s, and any employer who wants to both stay out of the courthouse and have a good relationship with employees must be aware of these changes.

—DARIEN A. MCWHIRTER
Austin, Texas
August, 1994

Chapter 1

Why Personnel Policies and an Employee Handbook

Every business, no matter how small, should have some kind of personnel policy manual. Every business, no matter how small, should have an employee handbook. There are many reasons for this. Without a manual and a handbook, any business—or government agency, for that matter—will find itself wasting a lot of time reinventing the wheel every time a personnel issue comes up and answering the same questions every time a new employee is hired. Even a business with one employee will have to have policies on issues such as which holidays are observed and how much sick leave the employee is allowed.

At the same time, there are pitfalls. In most states a promise made in an employee handbook will be enforced by a court just as if it were contained in a written employment contract. The law considers an employee handbook given to employees to be a unilateral contract. That means that it is written by one side, the employer, and either accepted (by taking the job) or rejected (by not taking the job) by the employee. The problem comes when employers make promises in an employee handbook that they do not intend to keep. The legal system takes a dim view of people who make promises that they do not intend to keep, particularly employers who may have used those promises to entice an employee away from a competitor or used the existence of a "good" employee handbook as an argument why employees do not need a union to represent them.

Some employers have decided not to have employee handbooks because of this problem. This is certainly throwing out the baby with the bath water. An employee handbook is a valuable tool of personnel management and can be used as part of an employer's defense when it is sued in many different situations. Because of these advantages, every business and government agency should have a employee handbook. At the same time, any employee handbook should be written carefully, with an eye both to the law and to good management practices. No handbook should be given out until it has been reviewed by an attorney. At each stage in this book, I will suggest questions that should be asked of an attorney before that section of the handbook is completed. In some cases the answers can be gotten from the U.S. Labor Department or the state Labor Commissioner. However, employers must keep in mind that any law is capable of being interpreted in a number of ways, and only an attorney hired by you will be focusing on your particular situation.

Many businesses have both an employee handbook and a much more detailed personnel manual that is accessible only to managers. While a separate manual that is truly not accessible to the average employee will not be interpreted to be an employment contract, it can still be brought into court to prove a point. For example, in one case the fact that a company had not followed its own progressive discipline policy was used as evidence that the company had really fired the employees involved because they were union members, not for the reasons stated, which is a violation of federal law (*Wells Dairy*).

Throughout this book we will provide possible handbook entries. In many cases we will point out that some policies should not be part of the employee handbook unless you want to be bound to live up to the promises made. Whether or not they should be part of a separate personnel manual is a different question.

ADVANTAGES OF A HANDBOOK

Throughout this book we will be careful to use the word *handbook* to mean a document that is given out to employees and *manual* to mean a document that is given only to managers and executives. While a handbook can be dangerous, most of the pitfalls can be avoided by reading this book and consulting an attorney before giving the handbook out. An employee handbook has many advantages. In sexual harassment cases, for example, the handbook can be introduced into evidence to prove that the company has a policy against sexual harassment and that the policy was communicated to every employee (because every employee is given a copy of the employee handbook). This may reduce the damages and can even help to avoid liability completely. Without a statement concerning sexual harassment in the handbook, the judge and jury will assume that the employer condones or even encourages sexual harassment, and the employer will be considered guilty until proven innocent. That is not a very good position for anyone to be in.

Advantages of Having an Employee Handbook

1. It provides a uniform response to questions.

2. It saves time answering routine questions.

3. It helps to provide a basic orientation for new employees.

4. It increases compliance with legal provisions.

5. It helps to provide a defense against lawsuits.

6. It helps in recruiting qualified employees.

7. It helps to avoid confusion and charges of favoritism.

8. It eliminates having to reinvent the wheel over every issue.

Without a handbook, employees will assume that different employees are treated differently because of personal favoritism or, worse, because of factors such as race and sex. While some flexibility is acceptable, it should be recognized that any time two employees in the same situation are treated differently, an employer has at best a morale problem, and at worst a legal problem. Both problems are unpleasant and should be avoided whenever possible.

Every employee comes to any new job with dozens of questions. Throughout this book we will list questions employees might have and try to answer them in the handbook. To the extent that these common questions can be answered in the handbook, that reduces the amount of time some person has to spend answering them. In a small business that person is the owner, and the owner is usually too busy trying to run the business to answer these questions. It is usually less time-consuming to write an employee handbook once and have it available than to answer a hundred questions from employees in the course of a year. Also, as a business grows, the handbook will ensure that the same issue is dealt with in the same way in different locations.

Some management consultants argue that everyone is different and that every employee's situation is unique and should be treated that way. They complain that attorneys force managers to treat people in too rigid a fashion. The only answer to that is that every attorney involved in the personnel process has seen what can happen when an attempt to treat employees in a "unique" way turns into a lawsuit for discrimination. It is not pleasant. Of course exceptions can be made, but they should be made with an understanding of the potential legal and management consequences that might result.

ADVANTAGES OF A PERSONNEL MANUAL

Provisions in the handbook will generally be shorter than provisions in a personnel manual. The manual will spell out how a goal stated in the handbook is to be achieved or what detailed procedure should be followed. Generally, a very small business will not need a personnel manual. As the business grows and more than one manager and location are involved, a manual can help to keep calls back to the home office down to a minimum.

There can be no better way to minimize the expenditure of time and money in dealing with personnel problems than a good employee handbook and personnel manual. Too many smaller businesses feel that they cannot afford the time and money involved in preparing either a manual or a handbook. While a manual and a handbook may not make much sense for a business with one boss, most small businesses want to expand. If that is the case, then the manual and handbook will have to be prepared some day, so why not now? Once they are prepared, it will be much easier to review them once a year and update them than it would be to write them.

Even as they grow, many smaller businesses do not feel that they can afford to have a full-time human resources director. In many cases that function falls to the chief financial officer because personnel is considered to be simply "payroll and benefits." Most chief financial officers are not trained to deal with personnel issues and would benefit from having a well-written policy manual to provide them with guidance. An employee handbook would also save a great deal of time and eliminate the need to explain everything to each new employee.

It is amazing how much time and money some businesses spend writing annual reports to stockholders and how little time and money they are willing to spend writing an employee handbook. This communicates to employees that they are not valued by the organization, and that is exactly the wrong message to send.

STAGES IN COMPANY GROWTH

Because of the way federal and many state employment laws are written, there are essentially three stages in the growth of a business. In the first stage, the business has less than fifteen employees. There are many issues that need to be addressed, such as which holidays the business will observe and how much vacation people are allowed, but many federal and state laws do not yet apply. The most obvious example is the federal laws against race and sex discrimination. A business that is not yet subject to either state or federal discrimination laws must be careful not to make promises in the employee handbook that will be enforced against the business. If a business promises not to discriminate, then it will be held to that promise in most states, regardless of whether or not discrimination laws apply.

However, in many states, the state discrimination law applies even to small businesses. For example, in Iowa the state discrimination law applies to any employer with four or more employees, while Connecticut law applies to any employer with three employees. Once the state law applies, it may be advantageous to state in the handbook that the employer has a policy of trying to comply with these laws.

Once a business has fifteen employees, most federal laws dealing with discrimination will apply, as will a host of other federal and state laws. Any business with fifteen or more employees is asking for trouble if it is operating without some kind of employee handbook.

Another set of laws kicks in when a business has fifty or more employees. The federal Family and Medical Leave Act, for example, applies only to businesses and government agencies that meet this size requirement. In a very real sense, any business or agency with more than fifty employees needs the same kind of employee handbook and personnel manual as a giant corporation with thousands of employees. If it does not yet have a full-time human resources director, it may need them even more.

Of course, once a business has more than one location or more than one department or more than one manager dealing directly with employees, a handbook and manual of some kind become a necessity, not a luxury.

More and more laws assume or even require employers to either post policies in a number of areas or have an employee handbook or policy manual that deals with particular issues. For example, the federal Drug-Free Workplace Act of 1988 requires federal contractors to develop and communicate a drug awareness policy. The federal regulations under the Family and Medical Leave Act assume that every employer subject to the provisions of the act has an employee handbook and that particular questions are answered in that handbook. Other laws, both state and federal, dealing with everything from safety to discrimination assume that employers will either post certain policies or cover them in the employee handbook. The state of New York expects that "every employer shall notify his employees in writing or by publicly posting the employer's policy on sick leave, vacation, personal leave, holidays and hours" (Section 195.5, New York Labor Code).

BEING COMPETITIVE

An employee handbook serves a number of functions for any organization. It communicates information about the organization to employees and answers expected questions in a uniform way. It should be considered one of many tools that the organization will use to recruit and keep quality employees. It should be one of many reasons why a quality employee will want to join your organization instead of someone else's. Quality employees are hard to find and often harder to keep.

One thing any organization will want to do is find out what similar organizations in the area are saying in their handbooks. There are a number of ways to go about this, from contacting the local chamber of commerce to checking with the local office of the Bureau of Labor Statistics (a division of the U.S. Labor Department). The Bureau of Labor Statistics publishes a variety of reports that will give any employer an idea of what many other employers in the area are doing. A personnel management consultant who is familiar with the region can also be invaluable. In an ideal world, no organization would publish either an employee handbook or a personnel manual without first having it reviewed by both an attorney specializing in employment law and a management consultant that specializes in employment issues. While reading this book is a good beginning, every state and city is different, and these differences can be taken into account only by consulting local professionals. Usually it should be much less costly to ask these professionals to review a handbook than to ask them to write one. This review should be a part of the process. An expert personnel consultant should be familiar with what the competition is doing, and a review by such a person should save a great deal of time and money that would otherwise have been spent doing this research.

THE BENEFITS PROBLEM

One reason for having an employee handbook is to explain to the employees what employee "benefits" the company provides. Because of the way federal and state income tax laws are written, over the past few decades employers have been encouraged to provide more and more benefits instead of giving the employees the money and letting them buy their own benefits. The main reason for this is that if the employer provides a benefit, it is tax-deductible to the employer and does not count as income to the employee. If the employer were to instead pay the money to the employee, it would still be tax-deductible to the employer, but the employee would have to pay income taxes on the money before being able to buy the benefit. This would mean that twenty to thirty cents on the dollar would be "lost" to taxes. Whether or not this is a "good" way to conduct business, it is the way business is conducted in the United States, and it is unlikely that things will change any time soon.

Because it is cheaper for the employees if the employer provides many kinds of insurance, such as health insurance, most employers find that they must do so in order to compete for quality employees. If it does nothing else, an employee handbook should provide a clear explanation of what kinds of insurance and other benefits the employer provides. Often forms must be filled out and kept up to date, and this should be explained to employees in the handbook.

Conclusion

A business or government agency with even one employee can benefit from having an employee handbook and a separate personnel manual. An organization with more than three or four employees will find that a handbook can be a real timesaver simply by providing answers to frequently asked questions. An organization with more than fifteen employees is asking for legal and morale problems if it does not have an employee handbook. Throughout this book, we will discuss the legal and management implications of different handbook provisions. However, the law changes, and only an attorney can provide up-to-the-minute answers to important legal questions. Also, only a local management consultant can provide real insight into what "everyone else" is doing with regard to particular provisions. Hopefully, after reading this book, any employer will be better able to take full advantage of the advice these two professionals can provide.

Chapter 2

The Employee Handbook and Other Contract Problems

Until 1980, employers felt free to say anything they wished to in their employee handbooks. The legal principles that controlled the relationship between employers and employees had been developed during the previous century, when most judges felt it was their job to "protect" employers from employees. In the 1980s, that changed drastically in ways that we can only touch on in this book. The landmark court decision came in 1980 and was handed down by the Michigan Supreme Court.

The *Toussaint* case involved Charles Toussaint. When he was hired by Blue Cross/Blue Shield of Michigan, the employee handbook included a statement that employees would be disciplined or dismissed only following the procedures set out in the "progressive discipline" section of the handbook. When Blue Cross/Blue Shield dismissed Charles Toussaint without following those procedures, he sued. The Michigan Supreme Court ruled that when an employer passes out a handbook that spells out either the reasons why employees can be fired or the procedures that will be followed when employees are fired, the employer must live up to those promises. The court said that the handbook is a legally enforceable employment contract even though it is "signed by neither party" and "the employee does not learn of its existence until after his hiring." In 1983 the Minnesota Supreme Court agreed, ruling that an employer must follow disciplinary procedures contained in an employee handbook (*Pine River*).

In the decade that followed these two decisions, the majority of state supreme courts agreed with the courts in Michigan and Minnesota. Why would courts come to this conclusion? Because in too many cases employers were trying to have their cake and eat it too. For example, in the *Kenoshita* case, Canadian Pacific Airlines was trying to keep unions out of the company by having an employee handbook that looked a lot like a union contract. However, when the time came for employees to receive the benefits of the handbook, Canadian Pacific Airlines did not want to live up to the promises it had made. The Supreme Court of Hawaii said that a company could not use a handbook that looked like a union contract to keep unions out and then argue that a handbook is not a contract when it came time to live up to the promises.

State Supreme Courts that Have Ruled that
Employee Handbooks Are Legally Enforceable Contracts

Alabama	Idaho	Nebraska	Utah
Alaska	Illinois	Nevada	Vermont
Arizona	Iowa	New Hampshire	Virginia
Arkansas	Kansas	New Jersey	Washington
California	Kentucky	New Mexico	West Virginia
Colorado	Maine	North Dakota	Wisconsin
Connecticut	Maryland	Ohio	Wyoming
District of	Michigan	Oregon	
Columbia	Minnesota	South Carolina	
Hawaii	Montana	South Dakota	

In the *Duldulao* case, the Illinois Supreme Court found an employee handbook that looked a lot like a civil service system. The handbook called for a ninety-day probationary period. According to the handbook, when the probationary period was over, employees became permanent and could be fired only after specific procedures had been followed. The employer in this case was a private hospital, Saint Mary's, which had to compete for employees with government hospitals that provided a real civil service system. The Illinois Supreme Court assumed that Saint Mary's would have had to pay higher wages or provide other benefits if it had not provided its own private civil service system. The court enforced the handbook as written.

These cases provide several points that anyone writing an employee handbook should consider. First, there are three words that are dangerous and should not be used without careful consideration: probationary, permanent, and progressive. Employees should not be told that they are probationary unless the employer intends to set up something like a union or civil service system. Employees should not be called permanent unless the employer intends to fire them only for good cause. Progressive discipline should not be promised unless the employer actually intends to use progressive discipline in every case or spells out in detail when progressive discipline will and will not be used. If by "probationary period" the employer means the initial employment period during which certain benefits are not provided, then this period should be called the "initial employment period" or the "no-benefit period." If by "permanent" the employer means that employees will be working at jobs that are not temporary, then call them "nontemporary" employees. Progressive discipline is something that should be dealt with in a personnel manual, not in an employee handbook. There are too many situations in which progressive discipline is not appropriate, and employers should not promise employees that progressive discipline will be used in every case. What do you do with the employee who shoots a manager? Do you tell him or her to aim a little lower next time? And what is the appropriate first stage of discipline in such a case? Are you really going to give the employee a plan of improvement? Of course not. If a progressive discipline provision is going to be contained in the employee handbook, it needs to be carefully written to take these issues into account.

THE ORAL CONTRACT PROBLEM

Some employers have decided that, because of these decisions, they will just not have an employee handbook. That is certainly the wrong approach in most cases. An employee handbook can provide some defense in many situations. In one situation the handbook can be invaluable: where someone in the company has made oral promises that the company knows nothing about and would not wish to live up to. How does that happen? In a job interview situation, the recruiter wants to hire the best person. In an effort to make sure this particular person signs up, all too often the recruiter may say something like, "As long as you do a good job, you have a home at our company." Decades ago this was not a problem; today it is a very real problem.

In a case from Idaho, an employee was promised that he had a job as long as the factory was in operation (*Whitlock*). The court said that that was an enforceable oral promise and that the only way the company was going to get rid of that employee was by shutting down the factory or proving that the employee had done something bad enough to justify dismissal. In an Oregon case, an employee was told that he had a job as long as there was "production to run," and the Oregon courts enforced that promise as well (*Seibel*).

Employers with a written employee handbook can begin to deal with these problems by stating that no one in the company has the authority to promise anyone that he or she will be anything other than an at-will employee except the president, and the president must do so in writing.

AT-WILL EMPLOYEES

Under the ancient rules of English and American law, if there is no written, or more recently oral, contract setting out the length of employment, the law assumes that employees have been hired "at will." That means that they work at the will of the employer. The employer can fire the employee for any reason or for no reason at all. The employee can quit for any reason or for no reason at all. Of course, the employer cannot fire an employee for an illegal reason, and in the United States the list of illegal reasons has gotten quite long. If an employer wants to make sure that everyone understands that all employees who do not have a written employment contract are at-will employees, this can be spelled out at the beginning of the employee handbook.

DISCLAIMERS

Because of these potential legal problems, any employee handbook should begin with a disclaimer. The disclaimer should make it clear that all employees are at-will employees unless they have a personal written contract. The disclaimer should not attempt to do the impossible. For example, in the *Morriss* case, the handbook appeared to provide that employees would be fired only for good cause, but then had a disclaimer that said that "nothing in this policy manual should be construed as an employment contract." The Kansas Supreme Court ruled that an employer cannot make a bunch of promises in an employee handbook and then try to take them away with this kind of disclaimer. The disclaimer should instead state that all employees are at-will employees unless they are given a personal written employment contract, and then the handbook should avoid language that suggests that employees will be fired only for particular reasons or after particular procedures have been followed.

THE FAIRNESS PROBLEM

Courts in a few states, most notably California, have ruled that employers have a duty to treat their employees fairly. It is not exactly clear what these courts mean by this. In some cases it appears to mean that employees should be discharged only for a good reason following procedures that look a lot like a trial. This is not a burden any employer should put upon itself without knowing all the pitfalls. Generally, most employers will want to avoid telling employees that they will be treated "fairly" or using any other general term that looks nice on paper but may have unforeseen consequences.

Many organizations, particularly nonprofit corporations, often try to promise things in the handbook that look good on paper but can lead to problems. For example, in 1991 the Kansas Supreme Court was faced with a religious-affiliated nursing home that had an handbook that promised that employees would be treated in a "Christian" way (*United Methodist*). The Kansas Supreme Court sent the case back for trial, ruling that it would be up to a jury to decide what an average employee would think it means to be treated in a "Christian" way and whether or not this particular employee had been so treated.

WHAT NOT TO SAY

All of this means that there is a long list of things that employers should not say in an employee handbook.

1. Do not use the "P words": probationary, permanent, and progressive discipline.

2. Do not make any promise of job security or any promise to follow particular discharge procedures that appear to rule out firing except for good cause unless you intend to live up to this promise.

3. Do not state in the handbook that employees will be "subject to discharge" if they violate this or that provision. It suggests that they will be discharged only for things listed in the employee handbook.

4. Do not allow supervisors or recruiters to tell people that they are "special" or that normal procedures and handbook provisions will not apply to them.

5. Do not allow supervisors or recruiters to tell potential employees that they will have a job "for life" or "as long as they do a good job," or to use any other phrase that suggests that people will be fired only for good cause.

6. Do not tell employees that they will be treated "fairly" or "in a Christian manner" or anything else that suggests that you have given up your right as an employer to fire for no reason at all.

WHAT TO ASK AN ATTORNEY

1. How have courts in my state ruled on the question of whether or not employee handbooks are enforceable contracts?

2. What kinds of disclaimers have been held enforceable in my state?

WHAT TO ASK A MANAGEMENT CONSULTANT

1. Do most employers in this area have employee handbooks? If so, what kinds of promises are generally made?

2. Do any employers that I will be competing with for employees promise to fire only for good cause or make similar promises in their handbooks?

A SAMPLE EMPLOYEE HANDBOOK PROVISION

Welcome to the MNO Company. Employees at the MNO Company are at-will employees. That means that employees can be dismissed at any time for any reason or no reason and that employees can leave at any time for any reason or no reason. No one in the MNO Company has the authority to promise any employee that he or she will be employed for a particular or indefinite period of time except the president, and she must do so in writing. Any employee who feels that he or she has been promised that he or she will be employed for a particular length of time, or be fired only for good cause, should contact the human resources director immediately.

THE URGE TO SAY MORE

This sample beginning to an employee handbook is important for both what it says and for what it does not say. People tend to say things at the beginning of the handbook that they hope will make employees feel good about the company. Too often this amounts to a promise that employees will be treated "fairly" or "justly" or some similar phrase. Some employers want to say that the company is just one big happy family, and every employee will treated accordingly. This is a potential problem. Too often people who write employee handbooks try to put a statement similar to the above sample employee handbook provision in fine print at the end of the handbook. More and more judges are not willing to enforce such provisions. If you are an at-will employer, then say so up front in normal-size type. If you are not an at-will employer, then you should be proud of that and say so up front in normal-size type. There are a few companies in the United States that do intend to operate as if a civil service system were in place. They do intend to have a probationary period, and employees do have tenure once the probationary period is over. Employers who make these kinds of promises of job security should be able to get better-quality employees at a lower cost, and operating in this fashion may well be less expensive than paying higher wages and dealing with high levels of employee turnover. The point is, do not make such promises unless you intend to live up to them.

CONCLUSION

An employee handbook is potentially a two-edged sword. It can be used against the unwary or careless employer that has said things it does not intend to live up to, possibly without even realizing that such promises have been made. On the other hand, it can be used as a defense against employees who argue that they thought that particular promises had been made to them during the recruitment process. In this sample employee handbook provision, the argument can be made that any employee who thought he or she had been given an oral promise of lifetime employment should have contacted the human resources director immediately. If the employee did not do so, how can he or she complain years later when he or she is fired or laid off? Only a handbook provision such as this one can provide any real defense against claims that oral promises were made at the time of recruitment.

Chapter 3

Writing Manuals and Handbooks

The first question is: Who should write an employee handbook and a personnel policy manual? The answer is not simple. In a very small business, the owner or manager may be tempted to just sit down with this book and write them both, alone, without any input from the employees or advice from an attorney. Some employees may resent not being consulted about many of the policies we will be discussing throughout this book. Others will feel put upon if you ask them to participate. Still others may be resentful if other employees have more input than they have. There may be a temptation, even in small organizations, to turn this process over to a committee. That is usually a mistake.

There are a number of reasons why a committee should not be formed to actually write the handbook and manual. Committees have a tendency to take much longer on a project such as this and to expend too much energy on minor matters. Some committees will argue over items that the reviewing attorney will simply veto at the end of the process. Other committees will take it upon themselves to negotiate with the "boss" over provisions that might appear in the handbook.

There is a potential legal problem with anything that looks like a permanent employee committee. Section 8(a)(2) of the National Labor Relations Act makes it an unfair labor practice (and therefore illegal) for an employer to "dominate or interfere with the formulation or administration of any labor organization or contribute financial or other support." In 1959 the U.S. Supreme Court was faced with a permanent employee committee that dealt with issues such as job classifications, vacation policy, and employee grievances (*Cabot Carbon*). The Court ruled that the Cabot Carbon Company had violated the National Labor Relations Act by having such a committee because the committee performed some of the functions traditionally performed by a labor union, such as prosecuting employee grievances and negotiating over employment policies. The National Labor Relations Board has determined that permanent employee committees that meet regularly with management to discuss employee benefits issues are illegal employer-dominated "labor organizations."

In other words, there are many reasons why a committee is usually not a good idea when it comes to writing employee handbooks and personnel policy manuals. It is also not a good idea for the owner or chief executive officer to do it. If the task can be delegated to some other executive, that is usually the best approach. The boss, owner, or chief executive officer should be part of the group that reviews the final product, along with an attorney and a management consultant. Of course, when an organization hires its first human resources director, the first task of the new director will usually be to produce a new employee handbook and personnel manual.

The author of the employee handbook and personnel manual should, however, solicit the views of employees concerning many of the policies being considered. This is usually best done with a simple employee questionnaire. That way every employee has an opportunity to express an opinion without taking up a great deal of time. Some policies, such as which holidays the organization should take during the year, can almost be put to a majority vote. Other policies, such as whether or not employees are going to be fired only for good cause, should obviously not be part of the employee questionnaire. Throughout this book we will suggest issues that employers should consider putting before the employees either for a vote or for their input.

In many organizations, the corporate culture will require the use of a companywide committee of some type. If that is the case, then a number of steps can be taken to help the committee work effectively and avoid legal and morale problems. First of all, it must be made clear to everyone that the committee is not permanent. It has been formed to draft the handbook, and it will be disbanded when that job is finished. This helps to avoid the appearance of setting up some kind of company union. Speaking of unions, if employees are represented by a union, the union should be informed and someone from the union should be on the committee. Issues that are dealt with in the union agreement should not be in the handbook. The committee should make recommendations about what the new employee handbook should contain, but it should not have the job of coming up with a final version of the handbook. Of course, the employer should not appear to be negotiating with the committee or using the committee to get around any other policies or procedures that apply to the company.

TIME AND MONEY

Many owners and managers of smaller businesses do not think that much time or money should be spent on the process of writing an employee handbook or a personnel policy manual. However, studies suggest that the average employee lawsuit costs the average employer well over $100,000 in damages and attorney's fees. Once the process of writing an employee handbook is seen for what it really is, a combination of lawsuit prevention and good management practice, the organization should be willing to budget an adequate amount for its completion. An organization should not begin the process unless it is willing to have the final product reviewed by an attorney and an outside management consultant.

WHERE TO BEGIN

The first step for anyone who has been given the task of writing a personnel policy manual and an employee handbook is to figure out what the current handbook and manual say. Even if there is no formal handbook, employees have probably been given various pieces of paper over the course of several years dealing with everything from insurance to vacations and sick leave policy. There may be resolutions by the board of directors on personnel issues and memos from the chief executive officer to some if not all of the employees. There may be things posted on the bulletin board or taped to the wall that pertain to personnel policies. There may be letters to some of the employees that made promises or stated company policy that should be consulted and considered for inclusion into the handbook for everyone. There may be contracts signed with some employees, or a union contract, that should also be consulted.

It is important to make every effort to figure out what has been said orally or put in writing in the past. The new employee handbook will supersede all of that if it is written correctly, with some exceptions. If there will be differences between the new handbook provisions and promises made to some employees when they were hired, this will have to be dealt with. It can be argued that they were hired under the provisions of their employment letter and that it has the force of an employment contract and cannot be changed without their permission. This can get complex legally, and the advice of an attorney should be obtained if this is a problem.

In many cases there have been contradictory policies in the past, and a problem caused by these inconsistent policies has inspired the organization to finally write a handbook and a manual. This needs to be dealt with quickly, hopefully with a discussion that includes the employees who are involved.

ORGANIZATION

Generally, employee handbooks and personnel policy manuals are numbered or coded so that they can be discussed easily. This is a good idea. This book will not propose any particular numbering system, but one should be considered. Similar issues should be discussed in adjacent policies. For example, the holiday policy should be next to the vacation policy, if possible. While this book is organized in a particular way to suggest one approach to what should done in what order, there is no best answer.

WRITING STYLE

Before this project is begun, some fundamental decisions should be made about the style in which the handbook and manual will be written. Every effort should be made to make the handbook as understandable to the average employee as possible. If the two major goals of an employee handbook are to communicate with employees and to provide a possible defense in a lawsuit situation, neither goal will be satisfied if the handbook is written in such a way that most employees cannot understand it. Judges are no longer willing to enforce incomprehensible contracts against people who could not understand them, and the same is true for employee handbooks.

Throughout this book I will try to provide examples of different employee handbook provisions. Some people prefer calling the company "we" and the employees "you." This is informal and often can make complex issues more understandable. Others prefer to talk about the "company" and the "employees." Still others prefer to use words such as the "organization" and the "workers." This is not trivial. How the handbook is written will say a lot about the company and how it wants to be perceived by its employees. No one is going to believe that the "fun and friendly" company really wants to be fun and friendly if the employee handbook is written in legalese and discusses the "party of the first part."

The basic rules of good writing, particularly when writing for the average person, require short sentences, commonly used words, and active verbs. Writing with active verbs simply means putting the actor before the verb and the thing acted upon after the verb. The classic active verb sentence is: "John killed Mary." The classic passive verb sentence is "Mary was killed by John." Active verbs are easier to understand and minimize the chance for misunderstanding.

Of course, good grammar and punctuation should be used. In some cases it might be better to employ a professional writer to work with the person charged with coming up with the employee handbook.

Follow the Rules of Legal Writing

Over the centuries, attorneys and judges in the United States have developed some basic rules that will apply to an employee handbook to the extent that it constitutes a contract between the company and the employees. The first is that the word *shall* is a magic word. If you want to say that something must be done, use the word *shall*. If something does not have to be done, then *may* may be the appropriate word. Don't say that something *shall* happen unless you intend for it to happen all the time.

In the law, a *day* is a calendar day, not a work day or a business day. It is usually best to stick with this convention to avoid confusion, and perhaps explain that a day means a calendar day the first time the word is used in the handbook.

There are a number of terms that have a legal meaning because they are generally used by attorneys to mean something specific. For example, an "exempt" employee is an employee who is not covered by the overtime rules of the federal wage and hour laws. A "nonexempt" employee is entitled to overtime for every hour over forty worked during a week.

Generally the law assumes that if you have a list and then say "and so on," it is intended that only items that are similar to those on the list will qualify. For example, if a policy says that employees will be fired only for "gross incompetence, insubordination, or failure to follow safety rules" and then ends with "and other reasons that constitute good cause," the law assumes that the other reasons are of the same magnitude as those on the list.

Definitions Should Be Clear

Many contracts have a section for definitions. Since an employee handbook is a contract, the same should be true of employee handbooks. Some of the terms defined in the glossary of a handbook may be legal terms, such as exempt employee. Other terms will be concepts that the law allows the employer to define.

For example, a nonexempt employee is entitled to overtime pay for working more than forty hours a week, but the employer can define when the week begins. Generally, we assume that the week begins on Sunday if it has not been defined. As we go along in this book, I will suggest terms that you might consider defining in the employee handbook.

LEGAL REVIEW

The most important step in the writing of an employee handbook is the legal review. This should be done by an attorney who is a specialist in employment law and who is familiar with the employment laws of the state or states this handbook will be used in. Just as no one should write a contract without legal advice, so no one should write an employee handbook without legal advice. At the same time, it is waste of an attorney's time to have the attorney actually write the handbook. It is best to write the kind of handbook you feel you would like to have, then discuss with an attorney the potential legal problems with some of those desires. It may be that something can be written in a way that avoids a potential legal problem. It is important to remember that any ambiguities will be interpreted against the employer, the author of the handbook. The law says that if you cause the ambiguity, then you should pay the price. The answer to this problem is to avoid ambiguities as much as possible.

CONCLUSION

Writing an employee handbook and personnel policy manual will require some time and expense, but can save a significant amount of both time and money in the future. It should not be done without careful thought and real commitment. Once policies are laid out, particularly in the employee handbook, the company will be stuck with them until the next handbook is published or a supplement is issued. Many of the problems in the workplace involve mistaken expectations. Employees expect to be treated in a way that is different from the way they really are treated. Some of this can be avoided with a well-written employee handbook that is given to employees when they first come to work.

Chapter 4

Putting Company History into the Handbook

TELLING IT LIKE IT WAS

One of the things that drives new employees crazy is that they have come into an organization with a history that has an impact on them every day, but that there is no way to comprehend what that history is without asking a lot of questions of people who are too busy to answer. Every organization, no matter how old or how new, has a history that some of those in the organization know about because they lived it. This is often a morale problem for newer employees because they were not there and do not know what people are talking about when they refer to past events. This can be far more discouraging to new employees than most managers realize or are willing to admit. A great deal of this can be avoided with a history section in the employee handbook that is updated every few years as the organization grows.

In an ideal world, this section should be written by the founder of the company. The founder often does not believe that the employees would be interested in how the company got started, but most employees would be very interested. The American free enterprise system depends on new businesses being created every day to make up for the businesses that die each year. Without a steady stream of new businesses, American-style capitalism would be impossible. If employees are let in on the particular success story that they have become a part of, they may be motivated to work harder and smarter. If employees are allowed to feel a part of the American Dream, they may be encouraged to come up with suggestions for improvement that might make the difference between success and failure.

Every organization has a past that affects everything it does. When Mao Tse-tung led the Long March into the hills to save what was left of the Communist party in China during World War II, those who survived became the core of the new Communist party. The history of China for the next half century was shaped by that dramatic event. Every business has a similar story. The beginning, the long march to initial profitability, may be funny or it may be sad, but it affects the organization, and new employees would be better off knowing about it.

Every organization has had heroes that helped it to survive the rough spots when it was young. In Cuba, Che Guevara at first was Fidel Castro's good friend and then decided to lead his own revolutionary movement in South America. It would be impossible for anyone in Cuba to understand how things work there without knowing about Che. Every organization has had at least one Che, someone who was key to the organization's initial success and is no longer there. It often drives new employees crazy when they are told that "Bill" would not like the way they are doing things when they never knew Bill and resent being held to the Bill standard. Why keep who Bill was and what he did a secret from new employees? If they are going to be expected to do certain things a certain way because Bill set up the computer that way, then why not let them in on the Bill story?

The leader of every organization has what to new employees are quirks, strange ways of doing things that do not make sense when first encountered. Often, these strange procedures are the result of superstition. The leader did something a particular way once with great success, and he or she is afraid to do it a different way now for fear something will go wrong. New employees often find this difficult to deal with, and conflicts between new employees and the boss often arise from misunderstandings over what are really company superstitions. Much of this could be avoided, particularly in smaller organizations, if the leader would simply come clean and explain this to new employees. Of course, many leaders are not aware that these are superstitions. This is where circulating a draft of the handbook to employees can come in handy. New employees, particularly if they are allowed to respond anonymously, are a good source of information in this area. Many leaders are surprised to learn the extent to which superstitions rule their organizations. There is nothing wrong with this, but it can be a source of friction with new employees without some kind of explanation.

One of the problems with a growing organization is that as new employees are added, the wheel often is reinvented every few months, with a great expenditure of both time and money. This can be kept to a minimum by explaining why and how some of the standard operating procedures came about. For example, in most organizations there is a major supplier of something that is never considered because of some past event that new employees know nothing about. The new employee wants to buy a computer from XYZ Company or sign up for a long-distance deal with PQR Company, only to be told that "we simply do not do business with them." "Why not?" is the obvious question, and often the person telling the new employee this is not exactly sure of the answer. The reason lies somewhere in the dark history of the organization. Why not tell everyone about that dark history when they come on board so that they will at least understand why some suppliers are allowed and others are not?

Of course there are potential problems, but nothing that a review by a lawyer cannot avoid. The founder does not want to admit to violating the law, which he or she might inadvertently do without a review. The founder might suggest that the organization is biased because of the way a particular story is told in this section. This can also be avoided by a legal review. This possibility should not cause anyone not to take the opportunity an employee handbook provides to help with new employee orientation.

There are also potential negative effects on personnel administration. This can be avoided by having an outside management consultant review the handbook. The money spent on writing a good history section will be returned many times when the lost time and bad feelings that can result from not having such a section are taken into account.

Writing a real history section for the employee handbook can provide an excellent opportunity to review some of the standard procedures that have grown up over the years and probably need to be reexamined. Perhaps the "evil" supplier should be given another chance. Perhaps some of the superstitions should be abandoned in the light of modern history and technology. Perhaps the computer should no longer have passwords created by someone who has not been with the organization for over a decade.

QUESTIONS FOR AN ATTORNEY

1. Have I said anything in the history section that might appear to be a confession of a legal violation?
2. Have I said anything in the history section that suggests that I violate laws or legal principles?

QUESTIONS FOR A CONSULTANT

1. Have I said anything in the history section that might lead to bad employee relations?
2. Are there any procedures or superstitions that currently control the organization that should be reviewed?

Questions Employees Often Ask

1. What inspired the founder to start this business?
2. Why did the business move to its present location?
3. Who were the former heroes that are no longer here?
4. Why do we do strange things?
5. Why do we not use certain suppliers?
6. Why are some procedures set up the way they are?
7. What led the organization to stop doing things the way most competitors do and come up with the key innovations?
8. How did the products get their names?
9. How did the company get its name?
10. Why are some of the key employees no longer here?

SAMPLE EMPLOYEE HANDBOOK PROVISIONS

Welcome to the MNO Company. On behalf of myself and everyone here at MNO, let me say that after two decades of company growth, we are glad you are here. As the founder and current CEO of the company, I want to explain in a few pages where this company has been and where I hope it is going.

This company really began one day when Sue Jackson and I were sitting in a café discussing how crazy the company we worked for at the time was. We honestly believed that a few changes would result in major savings and much greater productivity. I had just inherited some money from my aunt, and Sue had saved a little over the years. We had heard that the company was going to discontinue a product line because it no longer felt it could keep up with foreign competition. Sue and I felt that it was a golden opportunity to begin a new business. We offered to buy the product line along with its trademarks and patents. The company had expected to just write it all off, so it was glad to help us. Our former employer also realized that if we could make a go of it, it would make money selling us some of the key components. That is part of the reason why we continue to buy those parts only from that company. While we might be able to save a little money if we shopped around, I feel duty-bound to continue to buy from that company as long as its prices are in the ballpark and its quality remains high.

When word got out that Sue and I were going to begin our own business, a dozen other women in the organization came to us and asked to be a part of the new venture. Some had money to invest, and others were willing to quit or retire and come with us for lower salaries so that the new business could have a fighting chance. We did not set out to exclude men during that initial period; it just turned out that our first two dozen employees were women. Of course, now many of our employees are men.

We leased an abandoned warehouse and set out to move the production out of the other company. There were a lot of problems, as you might imagine. The long-distance phone company gave us hell, and that is why we no longer take advantage of that particular company's services. We also needed to purchase a computer early on, and when the salesmen came around we were offended by their attitude toward us as women businesspeople. That is why we purchased the computer we have today and why we continue to use only that company's products. It was the only company that seemed to take a women's company seriously.

Sue was our computer genius. She set up the passwords and purchased the software. Two years after Sue and I started the company, Sue was killed in a car accident. That is why we call our headquarters "the house that Sue built" and why the computer is still referred to as "Sue's monster." Only Sue could tame it in the early days.

When we realized that we needed a larger facility, we began looking around for a new location. While we were doing that, Boston had the worst winter in history, and everyone expressed a willingness to move to a warmer climate. North Carolina seemed like the best location for many reasons, and that is why we ended up in North Carolina. The newspaper called us the "Babes from Boston" when we first arrived, and we decided to take that with pride instead of being offended. That is why when I address the troops, I call everyone "guys and babes." It is an inside joke. Since we became profitable six months after the move and soon put a major competitor out of business, we felt the babes were doing pretty well during those first few years.

The first time we sent a group to Washington, D.C., to make a sales pitch for a large contract, all of us showed up in blue suits. We did not plan it; it just worked out that way. The big brass in the Pentagon thought we must have a kind of uniform and, being people who spend their lives in uniform, thought that was a good idea. We got the contract. That is why the uniform of the day for salespeople is the basic blue suit and why we still expect everyone who represents the company to do so in basic blue. I guess it is a kind of superstition, but who can argue with success?

One of our competitive advantages in the beginning was our willingness to make full use of computer technology. It sometimes led us down rat holes, but we are still willing to work with computers because in the past we ended up saving a great deal of time and money in the long run by getting everything into the computer. We were the first company in town to put all new product development into workstations with high level graphics capabilities, and when our workstation supplier was in financial trouble, we invested in that business. We are proud of its continued success. It turned out to be a good investment from our point of view.

We now have locations in six countries and over 400 employees, but we still consider ourselves a bunch of transplanted New Englanders no matter where we go. When we first came to North Carolina, we found people expecting us to do strange things like have four o'clock tea, and we did not want to disappoint them. We still take a four o'clock tea break and try to have everyone sit down together for twenty minutes and talk about the day's work before getting ready to shut down. Some of our best ideas have come at tea time, and that is why even if we have to stay late and pay overtime to meet a deadline, I insist that we continue with the tradition.

Everyone in our organization during those early days was fond of travel. When we instituted our suggestion plan program, we decided to reward good suggestions with trips that would allow the person to combine business with pleasure and allow us to deduct the trip as a business expense. That is why to this day the suggestion plan winners get trips to places where they can see the sights and talk to possible new suppliers or customers at the same time. We found early on that some customers felt honored that we sent a delegation instead of just a salesperson, so we didn't tell them it was a kind of vacation. It's one of our best-kept secrets.

Because so many of the early employees were also investors, we tried to take advantage of the tax laws as much as possible. That is why lunch is free (subsidized by Uncle Sam) and why trips are made that combine business with pleasure. That is also why we currently have both a stock purchase plan and an employee stock ownership plan. You will read more about these plans later in this employee handbook.

We named the company the MNO company because someone said that if a group of women thought they could manufacture such a complex product and meet defense department specifications for quality, they must be headed for La-La Land. We thought about naming the company La-La, but we decided that that would put some customers off. MNO are the initials of my aunt, the one who died and left me the money to start the company. We work hard to avoid sexual harassment because many of us had experienced it in our lives before we began the company and felt that this was one problem we could solve right away. When the policy says that anyone who feels he or she has been the victim of sexual harassment should feel free to bring the problem directly to me, I mean it. I won't stand for it!

Of course, now we produce for both the public and private sectors and are continuing to expand into related products. We figure that if one new idea in ten pays off, we are ahead of the game. That is why we go to such lengths to get new ideas out of employees. Our most profitable product, the POPO machine, was literally the result of a dream Sue had one night right after we began the business.

During those early days we all had to perform every task at one time or another. It gave us a competitive advantage. That is why we spend so much time on cross-training. We don't have a union because our employees have felt they did not need one, not because we have done anything to prevent unionization. Many of our personnel policies are unique, but we stand behind them. Our goal is to have fun and make money at the same time.

We opened our second plant in Arizona because we couldn't afford California and our third in Ireland because of special tax breaks from the government. We decided on Australia instead of Indonesia for the fourth plant because none of us could speak anything but English. The plants in Turkey and Chile came on line next, and I hope we can move into South Africa in the near future. While we are a business, not a charity, we consider ourselves to be citizens of the world at this point, and we hope that we are good citizens. Every facility has adopted a local public school, and we mean it when we say that the future of the world begins in the classroom.

I hope this little history helps you understand us a little better. We do things a little differently around here because of who we are and how we got our start. I am proud of us, and I know I will be proud of you as you become part of our group.

Sincerely

Mary Wonderly
Founder and CEO

Conclusion

I have seen histories like this one, but never as part of the employee handbook. They are usually part of some research project by a business student at a local college or the local historical society. They get written up, passed around, and then forgotten. I believe that is a major missed opportunity. The chance to let all the employees in on some of the company secrets and make them feel like part of the team should not be missed. No one likes to feel like an outsider, and no organization should want its employees to feel that way.

Chapter 5

Putting Corporate Philosophy into the Handbook

THINKING ABOUT THE LONG TERM

It is amazing how much time and money some companies spend writing up a corporate philosophy for the annual report to the stockholders and how little time they spend communicating the same ideas to the employees. If capitalism is a game, too many players are expected to play without ever knowing the game plan. This can be avoided, of course, by placing a statement of corporate philosophy in the employee handbook.

What is a corporate philosophy? The best way to explore that is by looking at some classic examples from the past. The giant phone company, AT&T, was founded on one simple idea: that the main focus of the company should be high-quality service. If the company could provide high-quality service, other things, such as profitability, would fall into place. This idea was communicated to everyone in the company in a variety of ways and to the public at large. When AT&T asked for a rate hike, there were many arguments that could be made against it, but low quality of service was seldom one of them. When disputes arose in the company, those arguing for high-quality service had the upper hand. In fact, this simple decision rule accounts for much of AT&T's success around the world.

General Motors was founded on a different idea: that every customer is not the same. Henry Ford had built an industrial empire by building millions of copies of exactly the same automobile. The joke in the 1920s was that Henry Ford would provide you with any color automobile you wanted, as long as you wanted black. General Motors decided to build different kinds of automobiles for different segments of the market and paint them a variety of colors. Obviously, looking back on the middle of the twentieth century, it was a good philosophy. When disputes arouse in the company those who argued for the new and innovative had the upper hand. General Motors became the world's largest industrial company by building a variety of automobiles to fit every segment of the market. Today, at the end of the century, some critics of the company argue that this philosophy became a liability, that General Motors continued to build too many different kinds of automobiles when that was no longer profitable. Be that as it may, the strategy of segmenting the market worked for General Motors for many decades.

Other companies pride themselves on innovation. Some high-technology companies believe that the only way to stay in the technology business is to create new products. Their philosophy could be called "innovate or die." They call on all employees to bring forward any idea, no matter how far-fetched, for examination, and they communicate to their customers that they will consider any request for new products, even if nothing like them has ever existed. Near the end of the twentieth century, high-technology companies are having the same problems automobile companies faced at the beginning of the century: too many suppliers for the available customers. It seems clear that only the innovators will still be around at the end of the century.

Some companies have never thought about what their corporate philosophy is or should be. These companies are at a disadvantage in the competitive world. Some companies, such as General Motors, have forgotten what their successful philosophy used to be and suffered as a result. The old saying that it is easier to get somewhere if you know where you are trying to go is as true in business as anywhere else. However, deciding on a corporate philosophy is only half the battle. Some companies have a philosophy but have never made any effort to communicate that philosophy to the employees who are in the best position to bring it to life.

It could be said that some countries have embraced a kind of countrywide corporate philosophy. In Japan the corporate philosophy could be summarized as follows: Work toward long-term dominance in an industry, even if it means losing money in the short term; work to build the organization from within and provide job security to the employees; concentrate on quality even if it means short-term losses. The world has seen what these simple ideas have done to transform a devastated economy into one of the world's economic giants.

WRITING A STATEMENT OF CORPORATE PHILOSOPHY

How should this statement be written? Very carefully. No other part of an employee handbook is more important. A weekend retreat at which members of the board of directors, high-level managers, and randomly selected employees can meet in small groups to discuss what they think the current philosophy is and what it should be can be very productive. These three groups may be surprised to learn what the others in attendance think the current corporate philosophy is. Nothing generates more communication between these three groups than a frank discussion of their perceptions of the corporate philosophy. A consultant can help these diverse groups communicate with one another.

A corporate philosophy should consider a number of issues. The history of the company and the philosophy that got the company where it is today should be made explicit. The ways in which that philosophy no longer serves the company should be identified, along with any other disadvantages of the current philosophy. Where the company would like to see itself decades in the future should be spelled out. The philosophy should be a statement of where the company wants to go and how it intends to get there.

In an ideal world, the statement of the corporate philosophy should be the same whether it is in the front of an annual report to the stockholders or in an employee handbook. While some organizations have tried in the past to talk out of both sides of their mouth at once, this usually trips them up in the end. Employees can read the annual report just like anyone else. Stockholders talk to employees. There are few secrets in the real world of corporations that have more than a few dozen employees. Some private companies have learned that their competitors know more about their company philosophy than their own employees.

PROMISES AND PITFALLS

While some legal problems are certainly possible, very few lawsuits have resulted from statements of corporate philosophy in an employee handbook. Judges and juries generally can be expected to recognize that this is a general statement of views, rather than an attempt to make specific promises to anyone. That does not mean that an attorney should not review any such statement.

A corporate philosophy should be more than just a collection of platitudes and old wise sayings. A consultant familiar with these kinds of statements can be invaluable. The public relations department should be involved, along with the personnel department and everyone else.

Of course, some companies are tempted to write a corporate philosophy that bears no relation to what the company actually thinks and does. That is worse than no statement at all. We all know companies that, if they wrote a truthful statement of corporate philosophy, would find themselves on the front page of the *Wall Street Journal*. We can imagine the headlines: "Giant Corporation Admits Doing Work of the Devil," "Multinational Corporation Admits Exporting Substandard Products to the Third World," "Major Defense Contractor Admits Cheating the Federal Government whenever Possible." Of course none of these companies should consider having a statement of corporate philosophy.

QUESTIONS FOR AN ATTORNEY

1. Is there anything in our corporate philosophy statement that could get us into legal trouble?
2. Is there anything we can say in the corporate philosophy that might help us if we do get sued by someone?

QUESTIONS FOR A CONSULTANT

1. How does our corporate philosophy statement compare with what you think the average person on the street thinks of our company?
2. Do you think our corporate philosophy statement is really accurate?

Questions Employees Often Ask about Philosophy

1. What is the time focus of the company?
2. What is the major goal of the company in the long term?
3. What is the strategy for maintaining global competitiveness?
4. What will the company do if competition gets rougher?
5. Where does the company see itself a decade in the future?
6. How does the company hope to stay profitable in the face of drastic cost cutting by competitors?
7. What resources does the company expect to rely on in the future?
8. What markets does the company hope to enter in the future?
9. How will the philosophy change from what it was in the past?
10. Are you serious about this?

SAMPLE EMPLOYEE HANDBOOK PROVISION

There can be no better time than our hundredth anniversary to reflect on where we have been and where we are going. As is painfully clear to everyone, our once-great company has gone through some hard times recently. We have completed the elimination of over 100,000 employee positions and almost half of our product lines during the last decade. It is now time to focus on the future.

Our short-term goal is to show a profit during the coming years, although we may not show a profit every quarter. Our long-term goal is to return to a position of dominance in the industry. We recognize some major mistakes of the past. We hired far too many employees in anticipation of growth that was not forthcoming. We can only hope to avoid this by making more realistic predictions in the future. We created new competitors by contracting out work that we could have done ourselves, only to find that our subcontractors had jumped into the competitive world that we once dominated. We hope to do more work in-house to avoid this happening in the future. We did not listen to our customers when they told us they wanted major changes in our product mix.

Our major goal for the long term is to become *the listening company*. We intend to listen more to our customers and to seek out their advice about possible new products. We intend to listen more to our employees when they tell us how our products can be produced for less money with higher quality. We intend to listen to our stockholders when they tell us the kinds of financial returns they expect over the long term. We intend to listen to our competitors when they tell us what they are doing better than we are. We intend to listen to our suppliers when they tell us we have unrealistic ideas concerning what they can produce and at what cost. Management at this company has been too isolated in the past, and we hope to end that isolation.

In order to be more competitive in the world market, we intend to move more of our production and research facilities to other countries and to make more strategic alliances with other companies. These have proved successful for us in the past, and we expect them to help us regain profitability in the future. We hope this can be accomplished without further layoffs in the United States, but we will have to see what the future brings.

For too long this company rested on its past achievements. This led to complacency and a refusal to look at new possibilities. We hope to move forward by turning to our world-famous research centers for new innovations. Dozens of new products are in the testing stage as I write this statement of corporate philosophy, and we hope to bring many of them to market in the near future.

During the company's recent history we relied too much on centralized decision making. This led to long time delays that made it impossible for us to take advantage of innovations that we discovered. In order to avoid this problem in the future, we intend to decentralize decision making wherever possible. That means giving managers and employees more authority to act on their own.

As everyone knows, we spent millions of dollars on consultants' fees in an attempt to become a "total quality company," with little to show for it besides a few banners and silly signs. As the chief executive officer, I take full responsibility for that mistake. I was completely taken in by a group of con artists, and I can only hope that I won't make that mistake again. That does not mean that quality is not still at the top of our agenda. It does mean that we in upper management realize that a few slogans and pep rallies are not the way to achieve quality products. Quality products come only from highly trained and motivated employees.

As we enter the second century of this company's existence, we have a great deal to be proud of. We have played a major role in bringing the cold war to a close, and our defense work will continue, although at a lower level than in the past. Our innovations have become industry standards over the course of this last century, and I hope that will continue to be the case in the future.

Many of you remember my grandfather, the person who really built this business into the global giant it has become. He had a few principles that he tried to live by, and I can only hope that in the future we can remember those principles. He believed that salespeople are the eyes and ears of any company and should be given the chance to provide input wherever possible. He believed that the greatest product is not worth a dime if no one can afford it. He believed that research pays off only if researchers are given a chance to dream the impossible. Finally, he believed that if people are treated with respect, they will respond in kind. These were good principles in his day, and they are good principles today.

I hope we will return to the days when we set the industry standard. I hope we will return to the days when people looking for a job in this industry come to us first because they know how well we treat our employees. I hope we will return to the days when every quarter meant a dividend for our shareholders and a bonus for our employees. I hope we will again be the company my grandfather and thousands of others worked to build over the decades and that people will once again say, "Don't worry, it's a sure thing" when they talk about our products. I know it will take hard work and patience on the part of everyone involved in the company, but I think we will find the golden age again.

Conclusion

An attorney might suggest leaving out that bit about dividends for shareholders and bonuses for employees for fear someone will consider it a promise. Most judges would not, particularly if it were contained in a section of the employee handbook entitled "Corporate Philosophy." Of course, if dividends and bonuses are not a real possibility, then it should be left out.

The point is that the employees should not be left out. If times are going to be tough, they should be told. If changes are going to be made, they should be the first, not the last, to know. If the philosophy will mean changes in their everyday lives, then this should be brought home to them. Most of all, the employees should be let in on the goal, the game plan, the idea that will organize the company in the years to come. While some people do get places without knowing where they are going, it usually takes a long time, and often it was not worth the trip.

Chapter 6

Putting a Personnel Philosophy into the Handbook

PROMISES AND PITFALLS

Many employee handbooks begin with some kind of statement by the president or human resources director concerning the way employees will generally be treated. These statements are potential minefields. For example, many state that employees will be treated "fairly," "in a Christian way," or "like one big family." More and more judges are saying that it is up to the jury to decide what a reasonable employee might think after reading these kinds of promises. We can imagine the questions on cross-examination in the courtroom:

> *"Mr. President, do you really think it was fair to discharge my client without hearing his side of the story?"*

or

> *"Mr. President, do you really think it was a Christian act to discharge my client for such a minor infraction?"*

or

> *"Mr. President, would you have really treated a member of your family the way you treated my client in this case?"*

These are the kinds of questions attorneys love to ask. If the witness says no, then he or she is saying that the company did not live up to the promises made in the employee handbook. If the witness says yes then he or she sounds foolish and cold-hearted. How can anyone think it is fair not to let someone tell his side of the story or Christian to fire someone for a minor infraction? Isn't the basis of Christianity forgiveness for past sins?

Other statements in employee handbooks say that the company is committed to treat employees "with respect" or "as individuals." What does that mean? Is it respectful to charge someone with a crime without even listening to his or her side of the story? Does treating people as individuals translate into racial discrimination? The cross-examination might go something like this:

> *"Mr. President, in your introduction to the employee handbook, you say people will be treated with respect. What did you mean by that?"*

"What do you mean, what did I mean?"

"Well, I don't know how else to phrase it. Let me try again. Do you treat your mother with respect?"

"Of course."

"Would you fire your mother for stealing without even giving her a chance to tell her side of the story?"

"I don't know what that has to do with this case."

"I'll be glad to tell you. My client went to work for your company instead of another company because you promised him that he would be treated with respect. Then you fired him as a thief without even giving him a chance to tell his side of the story. Of course he did take home company property, but it was property that was about to be thrown away. Generally, the law does not consider it theft to steal garbage. Do you?"

You get the idea. You can imagine what is going on inside the head of the average juror. This employee was not treated with respect, and the company should pay for not living up to its promise to do so.

Does that mean that you should not put any kind of general statement concerning the relationship between the company and its employees in the employee handbook? Not at all, but the statement should focus on what the company expects from its employees rather than making promises about how it will treat its employees. There is a big difference between the president of a company telling potential employees that the company will treat them with respect and telling new employees that the company expects them to treat other employees with respect. It is the difference between a promise and a command. While both often have the same tone, the difference can be significant in the eyes of a judge and jury.

Imagine that the introduction to the employee handbook states that "employees will be expected to treat other employees as individuals and with respect." That is very different from a general promise that the company intends to treat its employees as individuals and with respect. We can imagine the cross-examination:

"Mr. President, what did you mean by this sentence?"

"I meant that I expected my employees to deal with one another in a respectful way without regard to their personal prejudices."

"Mr. President, how did you plan to treat them?"

"The purpose of that statement was to give new employees fair notice that I would not put up with prejudice and harassment. It was clearly not a promise to deal with employees in any particular way."

Quite a difference. The jury is looking at the statement as a command, not a promise, and that can make all the difference in the world.

The statement of a general personnel policy should provide the employer with grounds for dismissal, rather than providing the employee with grounds to challenge a dismissal. At the same time, it should avoid suggesting that dismissal will result only if particular infractions are committed.

GOALS FOR EMPLOYEES

The general personnel policy statement should provide employees with some idea concerning the general goals the company has for its employees. It should tell employees in general the kinds of support the company will provide to help them become better employees. As a general statement of hopes and goals, it should avoid making particular promises.

QUESTIONS FOR AN ATTORNEY

1. Have I made any promises in this statement that I might later regret on the witness stand?

2. How should some statements be reworded to make them general statements of principle instead of specific promises?

QUESTIONS FOR THE CONSULTANTS

1. What kinds of general statements of personnel policy will employees in this region find in the handbooks of other companies?

2. How should I modify the tone of my statement to make it sound friendly, yet avoid legal pitfalls?

Questions Employees Ask about General Personnel Policy

1. What is the general attitude of the company toward employees?

2. How concerned is the company with the problems of employees?

3. What is the company going to do to help employees improve?

4. Is the company concerned with the prejudice I see around me?

5. What can I expect from upper management if I have new ideas?

6. Will upper management always side against me in a dispute with my boss?

7. Does management understand that wages are low in this industry?

8. What kind of training support will I receive?

9. How does management think of workers in general?

PERSONNEL POLICY

Let's look at two different sample employee handbook provisions to bring home the point. The first is the kind of statement too many companies would write if they were being honest. Obviously, I do not recommend it. The second is an attempt on my part to write a general statement of personnel policy that avoids some of the legal pitfalls. As always, the potential dangers have to be weighed against the possible benefits of a statement like this.

SAMPLE EMPLOYEE HANDBOOK PROVISION #1

Welcome to the PQR Corporation. I think you will find here at PQR that upper management has managed to completely take over the company for its own benefit. We fly around in private jets while you work overtime for below industry-standard wages. We give ourselves bonuses while we lay off long-time employees. We cut stockholder's dividends while expanding our own expense accounts.

You might as well get used to this state of affairs right away and if you don't like it quit now and save us all a lot of trouble. This is a dictatorship of me, the chief executive officer. I control enough proxy votes to control the board of directors so what I say goes around here. I am famous for my strange habits and beliefs. I do not like black, so anyone caught coming to work with anything black, including black socks, will be dismissed immediately. I don't like fish so you will never find fish on the cafeteria menu.

I don't want to hear any of your stupid ideas. If I want ideas for product improvement I will hire an outside consultant. Your job is to get the product out on time and under budget. I'll take care of the rest. I am in complete control. If something goes wrong I will find the people responsible and make sure the blame is laid at their door.

We have just announced that we plan to layoff five thousand workers over the next two years even though we are a profitable company with good future prospects. I made that announcement to make sure none of you get complacent. You are the bottom of the totem pole around here and trying to increase your pay or protect your job security is the last thing on my mind. I know this kind of announcement encourages better quality employees to look for another job and lower quality employees to work less hard but that is a price I am willing to pay. I think most of you will stay right where you are, at least those of you with pre-existing conditions who can't get health insurance if you leave.

I expect absolute obedience to everything I say, without question. If I want a contradictory opinion I'll call my brother-in-law. What I want to hear from my employees is: "yes sir, right away sir." Any other response is just back talk as far as I am concerned.

I also do not appreciate your talking about me to anyone. Any employee caught talking to the media or anyone inside or outside the company about me will be discharged. Of course, that is just one of the thousands of reasons that I might discharge you, but it is one I want you to think about real hard. There are a lot of rumors about me, and most of them are true. I am a tough boss, and I run a tough company. That is why we are still here and a lot of our competitors are long gone. This is no business for pansies. If you don't think you can take it, quit now and save us both some grief.

Welcome to PQR, the heartless company. We don't know you and we don't want to know you.

SAMPLE EMPLOYEE HANDBOOK PROVISION #2

Welcome to the MNO Company. As president, I want to assure you that my door really is always open to you. The most difficult problem I face as president is getting information that is accurate and timely. If there is something you feel I should know, please tell me.

Here at MNO we face some tough competition, both here in the United States and from other countries. Sometimes this means cutting costs or trying to improve efficiency. I know, as someone who started on the shop floor, that you know more about the production process than anyone else. I want to hear your ideas. We have an extensive employee suggestion plan that you will read about in this handbook, and I just want to say that I am committed to getting as many good ideas from the employees as possible. Our three most profitable products all resulted from employee suggestions.

I wish I could promise you that we would never find it necessary to lay off employees, but I can't. The reality of the market is that if we are beaten in quality or price, we may have to lay people off. It is really up to you and to me to work hard to make sure we never have to face that prospect.

You will read in this handbook about our policies against harassment and discrimination. I want to assure you that I am committed to making sure that every employee in this organization treats every other employee as an individual and with the respect all people deserve, regardless of race, sex, or color. If you see any behavior that does not live up to that goal, I expect you to follow the procedures set out in this handbook to bring it to the attention of the Human Resources Department.

You know without my telling you that the name of the game is quality, and quality is the job of everyone in this company, from me, the president, right down to every man and woman on the shop floor. I expect you to do everything you can to help us maintain our high standards of quality. In this company, everyone on the shop floor has the power to pull the plug and shut down the facility if he or she sees a quality problem that warrants that action. While I don't always agree that this is the right course, I promise you that no one has ever been punished in any way for doing just that, and no one will be as long as I am president of this company.

Throughout this handbook you will read about our policies on everything from holidays to sick leave. Every even-numbered year we conduct an employee poll and ask everyone to provide input before we produce the next employee handbook. I hope you will give us your opinions when asked.

I try to make this a fun place to work, but I don't always succeed. I hope you will help me to keep a smile on everyone's face. We all know that the same task can be fun or boring depending on the attitude of the people doing it. I try to keep a smile on my face, and I hope you too will have a sense of humor as you become a part of our team.

Welcome to the company.

CONCLUSION

In both of these provisions, promises are being made. In the first, the promise is to be as mean as possible. Generally, employees will not sue if that promise is broken. They probably will sue if they can find any other reason to do so. In the second sample employee handbook provision, the company president is making promises about keeping the door open and getting input from employees when the handbook is revised. There is also the promise that no one will be fired or disciplined because he or she shut down the assembly line. Don't say something like that unless you really mean it. That is certainly a contract promise that most judges would enforce in court. At the same time, no other statement will have the impact that this statement by the company president has, and maybe that positive effect is worth the potential problems such a statement might cause.

Chapter 7

Antidiscrimination Policies and Job Descriptions

Everyone in the United States knows that there are laws commonly called civil rights laws. What most are not aware of is the number and complexity of these laws. First, there is a long list of federal laws dealing with discrimination. Second, every state has some kind of law touching on this subject. Because many of these state laws allow for greater damage awards than the federal laws, employees are going to file lawsuits under state law (in combination with federal law) whenever possible.

Most federal discrimination laws do not apply until the employer has at least fifteen employees. Many state laws, however, apply to much smaller employers. Anyone going into business should contact the state labor commissioner and the state human relations commission for information about state civil rights laws. Of course, you should also contact an attorney for guidance concerning which state and federal laws apply to you.

It is very important to be sure which laws apply to your organization. If you place a provision in the employee handbook that says that your company will not discriminate on the basis of "race, color, sex, religion, or national origin," then you have made a promise in a contract to your employees that will probably be enforced against you. In other words, even if the antidiscrimination statutes do not apply to you, you will be viewed as having created your own private antidiscrimination statute and will be held to that promise.

Once state or federal discrimination laws do apply to you, it would be to your advantage to place statements concerning antidiscrimination policies in the employee handbook and the personnel policy manual. If you are sued, you will want to argue that the employee who committed the discriminatory act was acting against your express orders as spelled out in the handbook.

While most federal antidiscrimination laws do not apply until the organization has fifteen employees, that is not uniformly true. For example, the Age Discrimination Act does not apply until there are twenty employees, whereas the Equal Pay Act applies to all employers regardless of size. For the sake of further discussion, we will assume that the employer has more than twenty employees.

Why would Congress exempt small employers from the force of most civil rights laws? There are a number of reasons. Most small businesses are going to be discriminatory almost by definition. People who begin a business are going to hire their friends and relatives, who will usually be of the same race and sex as themselves. Also, defending against charges of discrimination can be expensive, whether or not the charges turn out to be true. Congress apparently felt that small businesses have enough trouble surviving without having to face this expense. The legislators of many states have not accepted these reasons and have instead taken the view that all but the smallest businesses should be subject to civil rights legislation.

THE MAJOR FEDERAL ANTIDISCRIMINATION LAWS

The Reconstruction Civil Rights Acts

The Reconstruction Civil Rights Acts were passed in 1866 and 1871 to help prevent discrimination based on race only (42 U.S.C. sec. 1981 *et seq.*). These laws were virtually forgotten until the 1970s, when they were resurrected in a series of Supreme Court decisions. These decisions confirmed that these statutes still had the force of law and that they applied to some instances of intentional racial discrimination by business or government without regard to the size of the company (*Railway Express*). If the Reconstruction Civil Rights Acts apply, the employee can sue for full damages, including recompense for emotional distress and punitive damages. There is nothing in these acts to suggest that they would not apply even to the smallest employer.

The Civil Rights Act of 1964

The Civil Rights Act of 1964, the employment discrimination section of which is commonly referred to as Title VII, outlawed discrimination based on race, color, religion, sex, or national origin (42 U.S.C. sec. 2000e-2). Title VII applies only to employers with at least fifteen employees. The statute states:

> (a) It shall be an unlawful employment practice for an employer:
> (1) to fail or refuse to hire or to discharge any individual, or otherwise to discriminate against any individual with respect to his compensation, terms, conditions, or privileges of employment, because of such individual's race, color, religion, sex or national origin, or
> (2) to limit, segregate, or classify his employees or applicants for employment in any way which would deprive or tend to deprive any individual of employment opportunities or otherwise adversely affect his status as an employee because of such individual's race, color, religion, sex or national origin.

Title VII created the federal Equal Employment Opportunity Commission (EEOC) to enforce its provisions. Anyone beginning to hire employees in the United States should contact the EEOC and ask for a copy of any materials the EEOC has at the time concerning the rules and regulations it has developed over the years since the passage of Title VII.

The Civil Rights Act of 1991

The Civil Rights Act of 1991 was designed to address what Congress felt were some shortcomings of Title VII, based on the interpretation of Title VII by the Supreme Court. This act allows anyone suing for intentional discrimination to receive compensatory and punitive damages, whether he or she is suing for discrimination based on race, sex, religion, national origin, or handicap. At the same time, the act limits the amount of damages that can be awarded if the employer has fewer than 501 employees.

The Civil Rights Act of 1991 was particularly concerned with employment tests and job requirements that did not appear discriminatory on their face but that resulted in discrimination. This is called "disparate impact" discrimination because a test or job requirement is said to have a disparate impact on a particular group. The Civil Rights Act of 1991 states that the employee must prove that the test or job requirement in question has a discriminatory impact. If he or she can, then the employer must prove that the test or job requirement is necessary for the job.

The Equal Pay Act of 1963

The Equal Pay Act of 1963 applies to almost all employers regardless of size (29 U.S.C. sec. 206(d)(1)). It outlaws wage discrimination based on sex if the work being done "requires equal skill, effort, and responsibility" and is "performed under similar working conditions." The act allows unequal pay if the inequality is caused by a seniority system, a merit system, or a system that measures the quantity or quality of production or is based on some factor other than sex.

The Age Discrimination in Employment Act of 1967

The Age Discrimination in Employment Act applies to employers with twenty or more employees (29 U.S.C. sec. 631). While the original act outlawed only discrimination against people between the ages of forty and sixty five, it was later amended to remove any upper limit for most jobs. This federal law does not outlaw discrimination based on age for people below the age of forty, but many state age discrimination laws do.

The Americans with Disabilities Act of 1990

The Americans with Disabilities Act of 1990 applies to all employers with fifteen or more employees after July 1994. It outlaws discrimination against handicapped people who can perform the "essential functions" of the job and requires employers to provide "reasonable accommodation" in an effort to make jobs available to handicapped people. The act has a very expansive definition of disabled. Under the act, a disabled person is someone who has a "physical or mental impairment" that "substantially limits one or more major life activities," has a record of such impairment, or is "regarded as having such an impairment."

THE AFFIRMATIVE ACTION PROBLEM

Many employers have a sign over the door that says that the company is an "equal opportunity/affirmative action" employer. The problem is that in reality, a company cannot be both. Equal opportunity implies that everyone will be looked at in a way that does not take factors such as race and sex into account. Affirmative action means that factors such as race and sex will be taken into account. Given the current state of the law and regulations, there is nothing the average employer can do about this contradiction except speak to its U.S. senator or representative.

Writing Policies

Employment policies covering discrimination can help an employer in a number of ways. First of all, if the employer is subject to antidiscrimination laws, the policies should make it clear that every effort will be made to comply with the law. You want to order everyone to obey the law in this area, and a provision in the employee handbook is the best way to communicate such a standing order. Second, if policies are in place, they can be used to argue that if discrimination occurred, it was against company policy. In this case it will be argued that the person who violated the law should be punished, but not the company.

Sample Employee Handbook Provision #1

The RST Corporation believes that employees should be judged on their individual merit. It is the policy of RST Corporation to comply with all state and federal civil rights laws. All managers and employees are expected to be familiar with these laws and to obey them.

Sample Employee Handbook Provision #2

We at the PQR Corporation know that our success depends on the skill and commitment of our employees. We believe that every employee should be treated equally, regardless of his or her race, color, religion, sex, national origin, age, physical or mental disability, or status as a military veteran. We expect everyone at PQR Corporation to treat people as individuals without regard to these factors.

Sample Employee Handbook Provision #3

The MNO Company is committed to providing equal opportunity to all qualified employees without regard to race, color, religion, sex, national origin, age, physical or mental handicap, or status as a military veteran. All personnel decisions, including hiring, promotions, and compensation, should be made without regard to these factors. Anyone who believes that he or she, or anyone else in this corporation, has been the victim of discrimination should contact the human resources director immediately.

Writing a Handbook Provision

The handbook should have a list of factors that matches the requirements of federal and state laws that apply to the company. Other items that might be added to the list depending on the state include marital status, parenthood, sexual orientation, political affiliation, arrest record, smoking, and blood type, among others. Many cities have their own discrimination laws that also apply, which can make it difficult for a company with more than one location to write a handbook that complies with all the laws and ordinances that it might be subject to.

Sample employee handbook provision 1 is an attempt to provide a very general statement of intent without getting into specifics. It has the advantage of being applicable regardless of the state or city. It has the disadvantage that someone reading it is going to assume that the company is not very serious about preventing discrimination. Sample employee handbook provision 2 is an attempt to take things a step further. Sample employee handbook provision 3 tries to recognize that employee handbook provisions are a chance to give global commands to the entire workforce. In this case, employees are instructed to contact the human resources director if they feel that they or someone else has been the victim of discrimination. This kind of command in the handbook can also come in handy in court. If someone who has not contacted the human resources director files a discrimination complaint, your attorney can legitimately ask why the procedure in the handbook was not followed. The cross-examination might go something like this:

> *"Mr. Employee, you say you were the victim of race discrimination, is that right?"*
> *"Yes."*
> *"And you say it occurred six months before you left your job, is that correct?"*
> *"Yes."*
> *"And you were given a copy of the employee handbook when you went to work for the company, is that correct?"*
> *"Yes."*
> *"Then why didn't you follow the directions in the handbook and take your complaint to the human resources director?"*
> *"I don't remember seeing anything about that."*
> *"I see. So you did not read the employee handbook even though you were told to read it immediately and ask questions at your orientation?"*
> *"Well—"*
> *"So, you don't do what you are told, is that right?"*
> *"No one reads those dumb things."*
> *"I see, and what other orders did you decide not to follow?"*

You get the idea. If someone does not contact the human resources director immediately, his or her honesty can be questioned later, with good reason. This works only if the handbook has been given to everyone and everyone has been told to read it and ask questions about it at an orientation session.

WRITING THE POLICY MANUAL

The policy manual is not going to be given out to employees and can provide more detailed instructions. An employer can tell management that it wishes to comply with antidiscrimination rules that it is not strictly subject to under state and federal law. An employer can spell out the specific procedures it expects managers and the human resources director to follow. Too often hiring decisions are made by managers who have little knowledge or experience concerning employment law or good personnel practice. The manual can require anyone who will be hiring people to take a course in proper interview techniques or testing procedures. Employees should be questioned only about things that are relevant to the job. Generally, questions concerning such things as marital status, children, age, national origin, and religion are not relevant and can result in a discrimination complaint.

At the same time, too often the policy manual is filled with a lot of long-winded self-serving language that bores everyone and leads people who should read and follow the manual to ignore it. Often there is a lot of language concerning what the human resources director should or should not do. That should be in the human resources director's job description, rather than occupying a place in the personnel policy manual.

JOB DESCRIPTIONS

The best defense any company can have against a discrimination claim is a detailed job description showing exactly what kinds of skills and knowledge the job requires. The Americans with Disabilities Act of 1990 specifically states that if an employer has written a job description before advertising the job, that job description can be introduced into evidence at a trial. The act also says that the employer's judgment concerning what are or are not "essential functions" of the job will be given "due consideration." Generally a written job description can be used in other types of discrimination cases as well. Too many employers make little or no effort to write accurate job descriptions. This is very short-sighted. A good job description can serve as part of the employee's initial orientation and can help potential job applicants decide if this is really the job for them. The employee handbook should make it clear to everyone in the organization that written job descriptions are to be taken seriously.

SAMPLE EMPLOYEE HANDBOOK PROVISION

At the MNO Company we try very hard to develop a written job description for every position and to keep these job descriptions up to date. Every employee will be expected to help the human resources department keep job descriptions current and to make sure that job descriptions are accurate. It is important that job descriptions accurately reflect the work being done and that the essential functions of the job be listed.

FILING AND RESPONDING TO CHARGES AT THE EEOC

Anyone interested in pursuing his or her rights under federal civil rights laws must first file a "charge" with the local office of the EEOC or with the state human rights agency. Generally, a person will not be allowed to file a lawsuit under the federal law unless he or she has first filed a charge with the EEOC or the state agency. In most cases the charge must be filed with the EEOC within 180 days of the act of discrimination or with the state agency within 300 days. Employers will usually receive notice within ten days after the charge is filed. The EEOC or the state agency will then investigate to determine whether or not there is reasonable cause to believe that discrimination has occurred. This investigation may include visiting the employer's workplace, holding a fact-finding conference, or inspecting the employer's records. In most cases, the agency will issue a "no probable cause" determination. Soon after that, the agency will also issue a right-to-sue letter. At that point the employee has ninety days in which to file a lawsuit.

In a few cases, the EEOC or state agency will issue a "reasonable cause" determination. That means that the agency has reasonable cause to believe that illegal discrimination has taken place. In that case, the agency will try to eliminate the unlawful discrimination through conciliation and persuasion. If a reasonable solution can be achieved, a conciliation agreement that will protect the employer from being sued by the same employee over the same incident in the future will be signed by all parties. If agreement cannot be reached, the EEOC may decide to sue on the employee's behalf. If it does, the employee may not sue individually. Usually, the EEOC issues a right-to-sue letter, and the employee then has to find an attorney and sue.

CONCLUSION

In the 1960s some people hoped that America could put the race discrimination problem behind it in a few years. That has turned out to be impossible. Complaints and lawsuits based on race discrimination continue to be a part of the employment landscape in the United States. Employee handbook provisions and personnel policy manual provisions should be written to both further this important social goal and provide some protection for the organization when the almost inevitable complaint is filed. Every employer should be able to say with a straight face that it is against discrimination and that it has effectively communicated that policy to its employees at all levels of the organization.

APPENDIX: A Sample Job Description

The Human Resources Director

The Position

The director of human resources reports directly to the president of the company. The director is responsible for the planning, organization, and administration of the Human Resources Department. The director is responsible for all aspects of employee relations and related activities, including safety, civil rights enforcement, and communication between employees and administrators.

Duties and Responsibilities

The director will:

1. Develop, coordinate, and implement personnel policies and write and update an employee handbook that complies with the demands of the law and good management practice.

2. Coordinate all training programs and provide an orientation for all new employees.

3. Direct all employment and personnel operations.

4. Serve as the company's affirmative action officer. This will include making sure that the company's affirmative action plan meets government requirements and that proper reports are made to the proper government agency.

5. Operate a personnel records system that complies with the demands of the law and good management practice.

6. Coordinate all safety procedures and conduct safety training to the extent necessary to maintain a safe work environment for all employees.

7. Manage and communicate with employees about all employee benefit programs.

8. Coordinate and control the company's compensation program.

9. Coordinate and ensure compliance with workers' compensation insurance and unemployment insurance laws and regulations.

10. Direct and participate in negotiations and the collective bargaining process.

11. Supervise the internal grievance procedure.

12. Supervise all hiring and firing to make sure company practice complies with the demands of the law and good management practice.

13. Prepare materials for litigation and work with legal counsel on all matters relating to personnel.

14. Be familiar with all government policies, regulations, and laws that relate to personnel policies inside the company.

15. Work to make sure all employees feel that they are being treated fairly.

Qualifications

This position requires at least a master's degree and several years of experience in the field of human resources management. Applicants should have a demonstrated working knowledge of and experience with:

- Personnel management at a large organization
- The use of information technology in personnel administration
- Budgeting practices and the analysis of budgets
- Policies and procedures that relate to a large company
- The requirements of affirmative action
- The administration of salary and classification systems
- Computer programs relevant to human resource management

Applicants should have a demonstrated ability to:

- Prepare and present comprehensive and clear oral and written reports

- Establish and maintain cooperative and effective working relationships within an office
- Effectively interact with people of diverse socioeconomic and ethnic backgrounds
- Develop and implement personnel systems

Chapter 8

Sexual and Other Harassment Policies

The issue of sexual harassment grew out of the federal civil rights laws. Generally, under the law, a person who quit cannot sue for being illegally fired. There is a fundamental difference between being fired and quitting. However, there is also the legal concept of constructive discharge. The idea is that an employer should not be allowed to get around the antidiscrimination laws by making an employee's life miserable in order to force that employee to quit. If that has happened, the law looks upon it as a special kind of discharge, and the employee can still sue.

Also, under the Civil Rights Act of 1964, the law said that employers should not discriminate with regard to the "terms, conditions or privileges of employment." Beginning in the 1970s, federal judges began to use the idea of constructive discharge and the command that everyone should have the same conditions of employment to rule in favor of women who said they had been the victim of sexual harassment. In 1980 the EEOC defined sexual harassment as follows:

> Unwelcome sexual advances, requests for sexual favors, and other verbal or physical conduct of a sexual nature constitute sexual harassment when (1) submission to such conduct is made either explicitly or implicitly a term or condition of an individual's employment, (2) submission to or rejection of such conduct by an individual is used as a basis for employment decisions affecting such individual, or (3) such conduct has the purpose or effect of unreasonably interfering with an individual's work performance or creating an intimidating, hostile, or offensive working environment. (29 C.F.R. sec. 1604.11(a))

Telling women that they would get special treatment if they provided sexual favors came to be called *quid pro quo* sexual harassment, while simply making a woman's life miserable came to be called *hostile environment* sexual harassment.

THE SUPREME COURT AND THE NEED FOR A POLICY

In the *Meritor* case in 1986, the Supreme Court handed down its first decision in a sexual harassment case. The Court agreed that hostile environment sexual harassment did violate Title VII of the Civil Rights Act of 1964. The case involved a woman who was subjected to sexual harassment by her supervisor. A difficult issue for the Court was whether or not the company could be held liable for acts of a supervisor that were personal in nature and were not condoned or encouraged by upper management. The fact that the victim had not brought the harassment to the attention of upper management was also an issue. However, in this case these issues were swept aside when Chief Justice Rehnquist pointed out that this company did not have a policy against sexual harassment and had not provided potential victims with guidance concerning who to take this kind of complaint to. The company simply had a standard grievance procedure that required employees to bring their complaints regarding anything, including sexual harassment, to their supervisor. In this case the supervisor was the person who was doing the harassing, which left this employee with no other course of action except to sue. The justices of the Supreme Court agreed that it was not reasonable to expect someone to complain about sexual harassment to the person causing the harassment.

Justice Marshall, in a concurring opinion, also addressed this question of the lack of a sexual harassment policy. He stated that if a victim "bypassed an internal complaint procedure that she knew to be effective," a court would be reluctant to award much in the way of damages. This caused many employers to put special sexual harassment policies into place.

EXPANDING THE DEFINITION OF SEXUAL HARASSMENT

At the same time, the definition of sexual harassment seemed to be changing. With each passing year, conduct that had not been thought to rise to the level of sexual harassment was held to constitute sexual harassment. In October 1991 everyone listened to the charges of sexual harassment brought by Professor Anita Hill against Judge Clarence Thomas. While the nation listened to the charges, many attorneys were interested in the facts. Professor Hill charged Judge Thomas with telling her about his sexual prowess, discussing an obscene movie with her, and telling her that a Coke can had pubic hair on it. Many attorneys felt that this kind of conduct, over a period of years, did not rise to the level of sexual harassment. The nation and the national media seemed to take it for granted that it did. In a very real sense the definition of sexual harassment changed in October 1991.

In the years since Justice Thomas' confirmation hearing, judges have put this new definition into place with the idea that the new standard is the "reasonable woman" standard. The point is that sexual harassment should be judged not by what the average man might find offensive but by what the average reasonable woman might find offensive. Sexual harassment became more of a problem for employers around the country.

In the 1991 *Ellison* case, the federal Ninth Circuit Court applied the new reasonable woman standard for the first time. The case involved a female employee who became upset when she discovered that a male co-worker was leaving notes at her desk. The notes said things that frightened the female employee, such as, "I am watching you." She complained to her supervisor, who failed to reprimand the male coworker. The federal court ruled that this was sexual harassment because a reasonable woman would find that these notes created a hostile work environment. The employer was liable because it did not do enough to bring this hostile environment to an end.

In the same year, with the *Radtke* case, the Michigan Appeals Court came to a similar conclusion. A male veterinarian's female assistant objected to the veterinarian's putting his arms around her and trying to kiss her. The court ruled that even though this was only one incident, it was enough to constitute sexual harassment. The court felt that a reasonable woman would find this to be a hostile environment and that that was the main issue. She should not have to put up with this kind of behavior.

THE SUPREME COURT AND THE HOSTILE ENVIRONMENT

In the fall of 1993, the U.S. Supreme Court made another unanimous ruling in a sexual harassment case (*Forklift*). Teresa Harris was a manager for Forklift Systems Inc., and Charles Hardy was president of the company. Throughout Teresa Harris's time with the company, Charles Hardy made her the target of gender-based insults and unwanted sexual innuendoes. Charles Hardy called her a "dumb ass woman" and suggested that the company needed a man to do her job. At one point he suggested that the two of them should "go to the Holiday Inn" to negotiate her raise. Charles Hardy would ask women to get coins from his front pants pocket and would throw things on the ground and ask women employees to pick them up. In August 1987, Teresa Harris complained about this conduct to Charles Hardy, and he said he was only joking. He promised to stop, but by September the harassment began again. On October 1, 1987, Teresa Harris quit and sued.

Teresa Harris argued that Charles Hardy's conduct was sexual harassment and that her quitting was constructive discharge under the law. The federal district judge ruled that this kind of conduct would certainly offend a reasonable woman, but that it was not "severe" enough to cause serious psychological damage. In other words, the federal district judge did not believe that this environment was hostile enough to qualify as illegal sexual harassment. The Supreme Court unanimously ruled that "serious psychological damage" is not required. The Court ruled that when Congress said there should be no discrimination in the terms or conditions of employment, it meant to outlaw this kind of behavior.

Justice O'Connor, writing for the Court, made it clear that to qualify as legally actionable sexual harassment, the behavior must be more than "merely offensive," but it does not have to be so severe as to cause "tangible psychological injury." A woman does not have to wait until she suffers a nervous breakdown before quitting and asking for damages. Justice O'Connor said that judges must look at all the circumstances, including the frequency and severity of the harassing conduct. In this case, the Supreme Court ruled that Charles Hardy's statements and actions were enough to constitute sexual harassment.

PROMISES AND PITFALLS

It is clear from the Supreme Court's decisions in this area that a company is going to be better off with a policy that is not just stuck away in a policy manual. The policy should be placed in the employee handbook and communicated to every employee. However, there is no way to specify every kind of behavior that someone might consider sexual harassment. The policy has to be discussed in general terms. At the same time, something must be said to provide employees with some guidance as to what they can and cannot do. It is also clear that companies need some kind of special complaint procedure when it comes to sexual harassment. The normal grievance procedure will not work in situations where the person the employee is supposed to file a grievance with is the person doing the harassing.

Employers have to be careful not to make promises in the sexual harassment policy that they cannot keep. It may not be possible to resolve every complaint to the victim's satisfaction, and employers should not promise to do so. Things that were not considered sexual harassment a few years ago would probably qualify now. This includes everything from nude pictures to off-color jokes.

Questions Employees Often Ask

1. What kinds of behaviors are considered sexual harassment?
2. Who should a victim of harassment go to first?
3. Will charges be kept confidential?
4. Will the person making the charge be protected from retaliation by the person doing the harassing?
5. How will the investigation be handled?
6. What will happen if the charges are found to be true?
7. What will happen if the charges are found to be false?

QUESTIONS FOR AN ATTORNEY

1. Have I covered the necessary bases with the policy?
2. Have I promised to do too much?

SAMPLE EMPLOYEE HANDBOOK PROVISION

The MNO Company hires both women and men. We recognize that this can cause problems, and it is our hope that these problems can be avoided by having every employee make reasonable efforts to be sensitive to other employees. Sexual harassment is a violation of both law and company policy. Sexual harassment comes in many forms. It may be a supervisor promising to do an employee a favor in return for a sexual favor. It may be behavior that is unreasonable, such as touching someone in familiar and unwanted ways. It may be using language that causes offense to someone. Both men and women can be victims of sexual harassment.

The MNO Company usually will not be able to do anything about sexual harassment until it is brought to the company's attention. Any employee who is the victim of sexual harassment, or who witnesses what he or she believes to be sexual harassment, should contact the director of human resources immediately. This is true regardless of who the harasser is, including suppliers and customers. Our employees should not have to tolerate inappropriate behavior at the hands of supervisors, suppliers, customers, or fellow employees.

Every effort will be made to conduct an investigation as quickly and as confidentially as possible. All employees will be expected to cooperate with any investigation of sexual harassment. No one bringing a sexual harassment complaint to the attention of the human resources director will be punished in any way even if it is decided that that person was mistaken. The human resources director will decide what action to take if sexual harassment is found to exist.

We expect everyone working for the MNO Company to recognize that what one person sees as harassment may have been innocent and unintentional. Nevertheless, behavior that makes a fellow employee uncomfortable should be avoided. We expect employees to bring any problems in this area to the attention of the director of human resources rather than trying to solve the problem themselves. While it may simply be a case of misunderstood communication, the director of human resources is trained in this area and needs to know of any potential problems.

GOING BEYOND THE HANDBOOK

Sexual harassment is one area where simply having a handbook provision is just the beginning. Any company of any size should consider routine training for every employee on the issue of sexual harassment. One day a year might well be devoted to discussing this issue with the assistance of outside consultants or using video aids. Many companies have well-written policies against sexual harassment but hire strippers for a sales meeting. That certainly sends the wrong message.

The above sample handbook provision asks employees to contact the director of human resources rather than trying to solve the problem informally. This is to protect the company from the charge that employees were expected to solve such problems themselves. It is to the company's advantage to have one person keep up with problems of this nature. There may be a common misunderstanding that should be dealt with. It may be that someone is causing a problem and that the company is only now becoming aware of it. It may be that corrective action taken in the past has not worked. Employees cannot know what has gone on before and should not be expected to.

At the same time, every effort should be made to keep an investigation confidential and to work the problem out to everyone's satisfaction if the complaint is minor or based on a misunderstanding. Again, this can usually be handled better by a human resources professional than by the employees on their own. Obviously, cases of gross behavior or requests for sexual favors will require a response that may range from a warning to dismissal. Employers should avoid saying that a particular type of conduct will result in a particular type of punishment. In no other area is it more true that every situation is different. There will not be any universal punishment that fits every situation.

CONDUCTING THE INVESTIGATION

Every complaint of sexual harassment should be investigated in a professional manner. The person making the complaint should be asked to provide as much detail as possible, including listing witnesses and discussing any other incidents that might explain this one. The who, what, when, and where questions should all be asked and answered. Every effort should be made to keep the investigation confidential to avoid disruption of the workplace and to avoid saying things that may turn out to be untrue.

Some employers have two types of sexual harassment complaints with two types of investigation: formal and informal complaints. An informal complaint is investigated quickly by talking to the victim and the person who is engaging in the offensive conduct. It is understood that what is requested in an informal complaint is a resolution of a probable misunderstanding. The formal procedure involves a written complaint signed by the victim and a full-scale investigation that may involve interviewing witnesses and may result in termination of the offending employee. Having two types of procedures has its advantages and disadvantages. On the one hand, it may encourage employees to bring problems to the Human Resources Department before they get out of hand. On the other hand, it may result in placing employees who bring formal charges in a bad light and may limit the employer's actions unnecessarily.

OTHER RELEVANT POLICIES

Of course, the sexual harassment policy is only one of several policies that bear on this problem. The person charged with harassment may point to the kind of clothes worn by the victim and argue that "she was asking for it." This means that a dress code policy may be needed. Problems often arise because supervisors date their subordinates. The *Meritor* case involved a women who had an affair with her boss for four years and then quit and sued for sexual harassment. The Supreme Court said that it did not matter that the affair went on for four years. If she had agreed to have sex with her boss in the beginning out of fear for her job, she was the victim of sexual harassment. Even an affair that begins with both parties agreeing to it can become the basis for a lawsuit when the affair ends. A company can provide itself with some protection by making it as clear as possible to everyone that supervisors are not allowed to date their subordinates and by taking immediate action when this kind of policy is violated. Companies should consider adding something to the sexual harassment statement such as the following.

SAMPLE EMPLOYEE HANDBOOK PROVISION

Charges of sexual harassment often arise because of romantic relationships between supervisors and subordinates. Such relationships are strictly forbidden here at MNO Company. Anyone who is aware of such a relationship should report it at once to the director of human resources.

STOPPING OTHER TYPES OF HARASSMENT

While sexual harassment has gotten the most press attention, it is also illegal to harass an employee because of the employee's religion, race, color or place of national origin. Such harassment can result in a lawsuit for the same reason sexual harassment does: because it might constitute constructive discharge or because it means that people are discriminated against in the conditions of their employment. An employer subject to the provisions of state or federal civil rights laws should also consider a general harassment policy. Because sexual harassment has gotten so much attention, it should have its own provision in the employee handbook, but the handbook should also outlaw other kinds of harassment.

SAMPLE EMPLOYEE HANDBOOK PROVISION

The MNO Company hires people of all races, colors, places of national origin, and religions. We recognize that this can cause problems, and it is our hope that these problems can be avoided by having every employee make reasonable efforts to be sensitive to other employees. Any kind of harassment is a violation of company policy, regardless of the reasons for it. Harassment comes in many forms. It may be a supervisor or employee using a racial term that is generally considered offensive. It may be telling jokes that belittle or intimidate the members of some group. It may mean making fun of particular religious practices. Anyone can be the victim of harassment.

The MNO Company usually will not be able to do anything about harassment until it is brought to the company's attention. Any employee who feels that he or she has been the victim of harassment, or who witnesses what he or she believes to be harassment, should contact the director of human resources immediately. This is true regardless of who the harasser is, including suppliers and customers. Our employees should not have to tolerate inappropriate behavior at the hands of supervisors, suppliers, customers, or fellow employees.

Every effort will be made to conduct an investigation as quickly and as confidentially as possible. All employees will be expected to cooperate with any investigation of harassment. No one bringing a harassment complaint to the attention of the human resources director will be punished in any way, even if it is decided that the person was mistaken. The human resources director will decide what action to take if harassment is found to exist.

We expect everyone working for MNO Company to recognize that what one person sees as harassment may have been innocent and unintentional. Nevertheless, behavior that makes a fellow employee uncomfortable should be avoided. We expect employees to bring any problems in this area to the attention of the director of human resources rather than trying to solve such problems themselves. While it may simply be a case of misunderstood communication, the director of human resources is trained in this area and needs to know of any potential problems.

SOLVING THE PROBLEM AND AVOIDING LIABILITY

The *Bennett* case points out what a company can and should do in order to avoid liability. The case involved a female employee who quit and sued when she learned that she was depicted in an obscene drawing in the men's restroom. She did not complain or follow the sexual harassment procedure. Her employer fired the executive who saw the drawing and did nothing about it. Her employer also paid her salary in full until she found another job, paid her psychiatric counseling bills, and begged her to come back to work. The federal district judge ruled that the female employee was not entitled to anything in the way of damages because the company had done everything it could to minimize or eliminate the damage caused by the incident. That is the kind of decision attorneys love judges to come to. It is possible only if the company has a policy against harassment and makes it clear to everyone that it is serious about enforcing it.

CONCLUSION

Harassment is a very difficult problem for employers because one person's innocent comment or touch is another person's harassment. More and more judges are allowing the victim to decide what is and what is not harassment. From the employer's point of view, it is more important to provide a procedure to investigate complaints than to try to predict what is or is not illegal harassment. With all the publicity given to sexual harassment, it is often forgotten that other kinds of harassment, such as racial or religious harassment, are also illegal and that the same kinds of procedures and policies should be instituted when such harassment is involved. This is one area where employers can protect themselves with a policy and procedure as long as the policy is communicated to everyone and the procedure is fair and honestly attempts to solve the problem.

If the employer does not really intend to solve the problem, then it might be better off without a policy. This is illustrated by the case of Leta Fay Ford (*Ford*). Ms. Ford went to work for Revlon as a secretary in 1973 and worked her way up to buyer. Revlon then hired Karl Braun as her supervisor. One of the first things Braun did was to explain to Leta Fay Ford that he expected to sleep with her. When she refused, he told her she would regret it. His harassment of her got worse and worse. At the company picnic, he actually attacked her in front of witnesses. Leta Fay Ford complained to upper management, who took six months to investigate her case. Meanwhile she developed high blood pressure, a nervous tic, and other symptoms of stress. Finally Revlon put a letter of censure in Karl Braun's file. Ms. Ford then tried to kill herself, and ultimately Revlon fired Braun. Leta Fay Ford sued both Braun and Revlon not just for sexual harassment but also for assault, battery, and intentional infliction of emotional distress. The jury found Braun guilty of assault and battery and Revlon guilty of intentional infliction of emotional distress. To sue someone for intentional infliction of emotional distress, the victim must prove that what happened to him or her was outrageous. The judge and jury agreed that what Revlon did in this case—waiting six months and then responding with a letter of censure—was outrageous. The jury awarded Ms. Ford $10,000 in compensatory damages and $100,000 in punitive damages against Revlon.

Revlon could have avoided liability in this case, but it had to do more than just have a policy against sexual harassment. It also needed to quickly investigate harassment and take appropriate action.

Chapter 9

Affirmative Action for Race and Sex

There is probably more confusion over the issue of affirmative action in the American workplace than over any other issue. This confusion is exemplified by the statement many employers make that they are "affirmative action/equal opportunity" employers. One employer cannot be both. Affirmative action suggests that factors such as race and sex will be taken into account when personnel decisions are being made. Equal opportunity suggests that all personnel decisions are made without regard to issues such as race and sex. Of course employers make this nonsensical statement because—you guessed it—federal regulations require them to.

To compound the problem, the term *affirmative action* is used by different people to mean different things. We can conceive of four different uses of the term. The first use is to suggest that the employer will seek out women and minorities and encourage them to apply for job openings. It would be better if people who meant this used some term such as "affirmative outreach" because this is not what most lawyers mean by affirmative action. Employers have a right to cast as wide a net as they wish to in seeking job applicants. This should not cause either a legal or a morale problem for any employer.

The second meaning of the term affirmative action might better be called "diversity plus." People sometimes mean that factors such as race or sex will be taken into account once it is determined that two or more candidates for a position are essentially equal in terms of background and job qualifications. Once this essential equality has been determined, then the employer turns to factors that would help the workforce better reflect the society. President Clinton has apparently been using a diversity plus plan in making appointments to the top positions in the federal government.

The third meaning of affirmative action is the meaning most attorneys have in mind when they use the term, and it is the meaning we will have in mind when we use the term in this book. For most lawyers, affirmative action means that reasonable minimum qualifications have been established for a position, and that if any of the candidates who have those minimum qualifications is a member of a targeted group, such as a racial minority, that person will get the job rather than someone else. In a very real sense this kind of affirmative action, true affirmative action, is a violation of the general principles of the civil rights laws, which require employers to ignore factors such as race and sex in making employment decisions.

The fourth meaning of affirmative action is that a quota has been established and only people who fit the quota requirements will be given the job. If no such people apply, the job will stay open until they do. This kind of affirmative action is rare, and is generally the result of a court order after an employer has been found to have engaged in intentional discrimination in the past. We will call this *quota affirmative action*.

QUOTA AFFIRMATIVE ACTION

Generally, no organization should set up rigid quotas for hiring unless it is operating under a court order requiring it to do so. The Supreme Court has spent many years trying to set out when quota affirmative action plans may be ordered by judges. In the case of one union, a federal judge found that it had engaged in "egregious" intentional racial discrimination in the past and ordered the union to set up and meet racial quotas in finding new members (*Local 28*). The judge ordered the union to take a variety of steps until union membership was 29 percent nonwhite, the percentage of nonwhites in the relevant labor pool, New York City. In 1986 the Supreme Court approved of this plan because it was the only real way to correct past intentional discrimination; it would not result in the firing of any white members; and the judge could waive the quota if necessary. The next year, 1987, the Supreme Court approved a quota plan for the Alabama Department of Public Safety after a federal judge found past intentional racial discrimination (*Paradise*). The plan required the department to promote one black state police officer for every white officer promoted until 25 percent of the corporals were black. Again, the judge could waive the quota requirement if necessary, and the plan had a definite ending point once the quota had been reached.

As a general rule, employers should not try to operate quota affirmative action plans unless they have been ordered to do so by a judge. This kind of plan causes resentment among the other employees and is, in a very real sense, a violation of the civil rights laws in that it discriminates against some job applicants because of their race or sex.

AFFIRMATIVE OUTREACH PLANS

At the other end of the spectrum, affirmative outreach plans seldom cause either legal or morale problems. Every employer should, both as a matter of good business and in an attempt to provide opportunities for minorities, try to inform as many potential employees as possible about job openings. At the same time, no employer should say it is trying to do this if it is not.

SAMPLE EMPLOYEE HANDBOOK PROVISION—AFFIRMATIVE OUTREACH

The DEF Corporation is an affirmative outreach company. We try whenever possible to advertise any job openings widely throughout the region. We notify the state employment commission and advertise in a number of periodicals when we have job openings. We also post all job openings on the bulletin boards. We encourage our employees to help us in this effort. Any suggestions concerning ways in which we can make job openings known to the widest possible audience will be considered to the extent that they are cost-effective. We also encourage our employees to notify anyone they feel might be interested in working here at the DEF Corporation about relevant job openings.

DIVERSITY PLUS PLANS

The Supreme Court has looked at diversity plus plans only once, in the 1987 case of *Johnson v. Santa Clara County* (*Johnson*). In this case, the county had an opening for a new road dispatcher and found that of 238 people in the skilled-craft job category, none were women. A promotion panel conducted interviews with the job candidates and gave each applicant a number score. Seven applicants scored above 70, with Paul Johnson, a white man, scoring 75 and Diane Joyce, a white woman, scoring 73. Santa Clara County, California, was not operating under a court-ordered affirmative action plan, and there was no reason to think that the county had engaged in intentional racial or sexual discrimination in the past. At the same time, the county felt that it should try to have a more diverse workforce and to have workers that better reflected the very diverse makeup of the region. Therefore, the county did have a written plan that could be called a diversity plus plan. The plan stated that factors such as race and sex should be taken into account when applicants for jobs or promotions were essentially equal in qualifications. A majority of the Supreme Court justices approved of this plan as a way to create greater diversity in the county workforce.

Diversity plus plans should be in writing, and of course should be discussed with an attorney. There should also be an employee handbook provision to make it clear to everyone in the organization what is going on. One of the major problems with any kind of "affirmative action" plan is that rumors spread that this or that decision was based on factors other than merit and "isn't that the pits?" These rumors can cause very real morale problems in any organization. Some organizations have tried to deal with that problem in part by holding diversity training sessions. Many of these sessions consist of people from outside the organization lecturing to the employees about what they should and should not think and feel in this area as if they were bad little children. This often makes matters worse. Many organizations would be better off simply explaining the policy and the reasons for it to the employees.

SAMPLE EMPLOYEE HANDBOOK PROVISION—DIVERSITY PLUS

The GHI Corporation believes that it can benefit from having employees with diverse backgrounds. While we of course seek only qualified employees, when many candidates are qualified for a position, we do take factors such as race, sex, and life experience into account. We provide goods and services for a very diverse population, and we believe that it is to our advantage to have a workforce that reflects that diversity. We do not have quotas, and we do not consider people for positions for which they are not qualified.

TRUE AFFIRMATIVE ACTION PLANS

A true affirmative action plan is a plan that requires anyone meeting the minimum qualifications for a job to get the job if he or she is a member of a target group. While these plans do not have rigid quotas, they do have goals based on the makeup of the relevant workforce. The general goal is that over time the employer's workforce should better reflect the diversity of the relevant labor pool.

Congress has never passed a general statute dealing with this kind of affirmative action plan. The 1991 Civil Rights Act stated that nothing in the act should be interpreted to affect affirmative action plans that were "in accordance with the law." That is a strange statement, since there is no general federal statute on the subject of racial or sexual affirmative action plans.

There is an executive order. After the passage of the Civil Rights Act of 1964, President Johnson signed Executive Order 11246 (41 C.F.R. 60). This executive order requires businesses that do business with the federal government (including most public agencies that receive federal funds) to institute affirmative action plans that benefit racial minorities and women. It is interesting that this is simply a presidential order and could be rescinded at any time by any president. While President Reagan talked a great deal about the evils of affirmative action, he did not rescind Executive Order 11246.

This executive order affects businesses that have at least fifty employees and have contracts with the federal government that total at least $10,000. The order also applies to subcontractors of businesses that do business with the federal government. The Office of Federal Contracts and Compliance Programs (OFCCP) enforces this and other affirmative action requirements that will be discussed in the next chapter. Generally, a written plan will not be required until the contractor has a contract for over $50,000. Any employer who does business with the federal government or subcontracts with a company that does should contact the OFCCP for information.

An affirmative action plan under Executive Order 11246 can be viewed as a combination of outreach and affirmative action. An employer is expected to seek out minorities and women to the extent that they are underrepresented in its workforce and to consider their race or sex to be a positive factor if they actually apply. This causes a problem for many employers in that for the first time they must keep track of the race and sex of the people that apply for jobs. While the company must ask for this information, the applicant is not required to give it. This means that many job applicants are given a form that asks questions concerning race and sex and also says that the answers will not have any negative effect on their job prospects. Of course, that is not exactly true if the applicant is a white male.

An affirmative action plan worked out in collaboration with the OFCCP will have five parts: workforce analysis, availability analysis, utilization analysis, goals, and timetables. For a large company, it can be a very large book in its own right. The workforce analysis shows the number of women and minorities currently working for the company in every job category. The availability analysis shows how many women and minorities are available in the relevant labor pool to fill these positions. The utilization analysis compares the current workforce with the available labor pool for each job category. The company then sets goals and a timetable for reaching those goals. Goals are not quotas. If a goal is not met, the OFCCP will want to know what has been done and why the goal has not been met. The best reason for not meeting the goal is that not enough people with minimum job qualifications and the right race or sex applied for the available jobs. The timetable will reflect the fact that no organization can come into compliance overnight.

Companies with affirmative action plans are expected to actively recruit women and minorities for job classifications where they are underrepresented. This may mean recruiting at colleges further away than would otherwise be the case or advertising the opening in journals or newspapers further from the facility.

Federal affirmative action plans do not require anyone to hire someone who is not minimally qualified for the position. It may require a company to hire someone other than the person it believes is the very best in order to meet the affirmative action goals.

After more than a quarter century of affirmative action mandated by the federal government, we have no way of knowing how many women and minorities have been employed in good jobs that would not have gotten those jobs without affirmative action. It is impossible to compare companies that have affirmative action plans with companies that do not have affirmative action plans because most companies in the same business and of a similar size will either all have or all not have such plans.

If an employer does have an affirmative action plan mandated by the federal government, it is important to communicate that fact to the employees. It is better that accurate information about the plan come from the employer than that it become the subject of rumor. At the same time, the entire affirmative action plan cannot be placed in the employee handbook.

SAMPLE EMPLOYEE HANDBOOK PROVISION—AFFIRMATIVE ACTION PLANS

The MNO Company is a contractor with the federal government and several states that require affirmative action in the areas of race and sex. In conjunction with the Office of Federal Contract Compliance Programs, we have developed an affirmative action plan, which is available in the Human Resource Department for any employee who wishes to read it. It contains goals and a timetable for meeting those goals. It does not require us to hire people who are not qualified for any job. It does require us to make reasonable efforts to reach out to women and minorities in job categories where we have a low percentage of women or minorities and to offer them the job if they meet the minimum qualifications. We are also required to reach out and hire the disabled and Vietnam veterans.

CONGRESSIONAL AFFIRMATIVE ACTION PLANS

While Congress has never passed a general statute dealing with affirmative action, it has passed several laws that do contain affirmative action components. The Rehabilitation Act of 1973 requires federal contractors to work to hire the disabled. There are no required goals or timetables. Instead, contractors are urged to hire and promote as many disabled people as possible and to reach out to the disabled whenever there is a job opening.

The Vietnam Era Veterans Readjustment Assistance Act of 1974 is similar. No specific goals or timetables are required, but federal contractors are expected to reach out to Vietnam veterans and hire or promote as many as possible.

The Public Works Employment Act of 1977 requires that at least 10 percent of federal funds used for public works projects must be used to procure the services of businesses owned or run by minorities. There is a very specific definition of what constitutes a public works project. This is unique among the federal affirmative action programs because it is a quota plan that requires what has come to be called the 10 percent minority set-aside. In 1980, with the *Fullilove* case, the Supreme Court upheld this statute as constitutional by a vote of 6 to 3.

AUDITS

Either the EEOC or the OFCCP may wish to audit your affirmative action plan. It will be much easier to deal with this audit if you have planned for it in advance. The auditors will wish to see your written affirmative action plan, the personnel policy manual, and of course the employee handbook. They will also want to see the job application form and any job advertisements or recruitment materials. Testing and training materials will also be of interest to them. They will want to know what the current composition of the workforce is in terms of race and sex at each level or type of employment. The auditors will also want to see the applicant flow data, showing how many women and minorities applied for jobs. They will be particularly interested in employees hired over the last year. They will want evidence of real progress and a real commitment on the part of management to the goal of creating an integrated workplace.

JOB ADVERTISEMENTS

Any employer subject to the affirmative action requirements of the OFCCP should contact that office to make sure current regulations on job advertisements are being followed. You may be required to state that you are an equal opportunity/affirmative action employer. You may be required to state that you are actively seeking women or minorities for the position. This is of course tricky, because in a sense an advertisement that suggests that a company is seeking one type of employee is stating that other types of employees may be discriminated against. Also, as a general rule, employers who are subject to federal affirmative action supervision must do much more than simply rely on word-of-mouth advertising when recruiting new employees.

City and State Affirmative Action Plans

Many cities and states also require the companies they do business with to have an affirmative action plan. Companies that already have such a plan because they do business with the federal government will usually not be expected to formulate a new plan for the city or state. However, in some cases, the city or state plan requirements will be more extensive than the federal requirements.

In 1989 the Supreme Court threw out the affirmative action plan required by the city of Richmond, Virginia (*Richmond*). The plan required contractors with the city to hire 30 percent of their subcontractors from businesses that were at least 51 percent owned by blacks, Spanish-speakers, Orientals, Native Americans, Eskimos, or Aleuts. Contractors objected to this rigid requirement, pointing out that there were no Eskimo or Aleut subcontractors in Richmond. The justices of the Supreme Court found this plan objectionable for many reasons. Affirmative action is generally supposed to make up for past discrimination, yet there was no evidence that Orientals or Native Americans had ever suffered discrimination in Richmond. Also, because there were no Eskimo or Aleut firms operating in Richmond, the plan would have given a special benefit to any such firms that moved into Richmond, without there being any historical justification for such a special benefit based on race. In throwing out the Richmond plan, the Court did not make it clear when such city and state affirmative action plans will be considered legal. Of course, anyone doing business with a city or state that has an affirmative action requirement will have to comply until a judge declares the plan to be illegal or unconstitutional.

Conclusion

Affirmative action for women and minorities has never been debated by the U.S. Congress, and no federal statute requiring this kind of affirmative action has ever been passed, except for the Public Works Employment Act of 1977, which requires that at least 10 percent of federal funds used for public works projects must be used to procure the services of businesses owned or run by minorities. The current law is based on a very old executive order signed by President Johnson. It is impossible to know whether the extensive paperwork required by these plans has actually brought about integration in relevant job categories any faster than would otherwise have been the case. Employers that are required to institute such plans, or that wish to do so on their own, must contact an attorney who is familiar with this area of the law. Because affirmative action is by definition a violation of the basic principle of equal opportunity, there are many potential problems that must be dealt with. The best way to deal with the issue of employee morale is to communicate to the employees exactly what is going on in this regard and why.

Chapter 10

Reasonable Accommodation and Affirmative Action: Religion, Disability, and Veterans

A number of federal and state laws require reasonable accommodation rather than, or in addition to, affirmative action. This means that employers are expected to make changes to make it possible for people to work who would otherwise not be able to hold a job. The idea is that some employees need special treatment not because they are not able to work, but because the average job has been structured with the average worker in mind without thinking about minor changes that could open up the job to millions of other workers. The idea of reasonable accommodation is that the law should encourage and require employers to make changes in jobs to help people join or stay in the labor market.

RELIGION

Federal and most state civil rights laws prohibit discrimination based on religion. Title VII also requires employers to reasonably accommodate people of different religions. The statute says that employers must reasonably accommodate people of different religions if doing so will not cause "undue hardship." The Supreme Court has handed down one decision in this area.

When Mr. Hardison became a member of the Worldwide Church of God, he accepted the religion's rule that he could not work from sunset Friday to sunset Saturday (TWA). At the time of his conversion this was not a problem because his high level of seniority enabled him to have himself moved to the 11:00 P.M. to 7:00 A.M. shift. Then he bid for and got a transfer to a different building. Under the terms of TWA's seniority plan, he now went to the bottom of the seniority list, and he could not get on the graveyard shift in the new building. The union refused to waive the terms of the collective-bargaining contract, and TWA refused to violate the terms of the contract. Mr. Hardison sued, arguing that Title VII required both the union and TWA to reasonably accommodate his religion and move him to a shift that allowed him to not work on Saturday. The Supreme

Court did not agree. The justices felt that Title VII was not intended to supersede union contracts and that it was not reasonable to ask an employer to do so. The justices also felt that it was not reasonable to ask the employer to pay overtime so that someone else could take the Saturday shift. Mr. Hardison had been discharged for not working on Saturday, and the Supreme Court refused to order him reinstated.

The question of how far an employer has to go to reasonably accommodate someone because of his or her religion is a difficult one for the courts. On the one hand, the goal of preventing religious discrimination is a valued one, but the First Amendment to the U.S. Constitution requires that government not "establish" religion, and too much of a government requirement that employers accommodate religion could run afoul of this provision. At the same time, the First Amendment also requires that people be allowed to freely exercise their religion, and it could be argued that not being able to get a job would interfere with that right of free religious exercise.

As in the TWA case, employers who operate under union contracts have less freedom to accommodate their employees' religious practices. Employers who are required to reasonably accommodate their employees' religion should consider making that fact known to the employees in the handbook.

Sample Employee Handbook Provision

The MNO Company is required by federal and state civil rights laws to avoid discrimination against people because of their religion and to reasonably accommodate any employee who could otherwise perform the job but who cannot because of his or her religion. This most often means allowing some employees to take their Sabbath day off and allowing them to observe their religious holidays. The MNO Company is able to accommodate diverse religious practices only to the extent that our employees are willing to switch shifts and work overtime on occasion. The MNO Company hopes that all employees will be understanding when they are asked to make it possible for other employees to observe their religious practices.

Handicapped and Disabled

In 1973 Congress passed the Vocational Rehabilitation Act (29 U.S.C. 701 *et seq.*). This law requires federal agencies and federal contractors to implement affirmative action plans for handicapped people. It also requires organizations receiving federal funds not to discriminate against the handicapped (which extends the law to state and local governments and many nonprofit organizations). In 1990 Congress passed the Americans with Disabilities Act (42 U.S.C. sec. 2101 *et seq.*). As of July 1994, employers with fifteen or more employees are required not to discriminate against disabled people and to "reasonably accommodate" the handicaps of people who can perform the essential functions of the job if they are given reasonable accommodation.

Both of these federal laws have a very expansive definition of what constitutes a handicap or a disability. While most employees in the United States were already covered by state laws barring discrimination against the handicapped, these state laws have much more limited definitions of handicap in most cases. The federal laws say that someone will be considered handicapped (disabled) if he or she has a physical or mental impairment that substantially limits one or more of the person's major life activities, has a record of such an impairment, or is regarded as having such an impairment. This definition is very broad. For example, many state courts have ruled that simply being overweight is not protected by the state law barring discrimination against the handicapped, but federal courts have uniformly ruled that this is protected by federal laws as a disability. The federal laws also apply if someone is discriminated against because of a perceived disability that he or she does not actually have. Someone thought to have AIDS would be protected whether that person actually had AIDS or not. Someone with a contagious disease may or may not be protected depending on the circumstances of the job and the disease.

Regulations have been written by the federal government to help define handicap under the Vocational Rehabilitation Act and disability under the Americans with Disabilities Act. Generally, a physical impairment of short duration, such as a broken arm or influenza, would not be considered either a handicap or a disability. A number of disorders are specifically not considered disabilities under the Americans with Disabilities Act, including homosexuality, transsexuality, pedophilia, exhibitionism, voyeurism, compulsive gambling, kleptomania, pyromania and disorders resulting from the current use of illegal drugs. People who are recovering from past drug or alcohol use are protected. People who are currently suffering from alcoholism must be able to perform the job without any additional accommodation to be protected by the federal law. Some state statutes do protect alcoholics and current illegal drug users, so legal advice must be sought before discriminating against such people.

The Americans with Disabilities Act allows employers to determine the "essential functions" of the job if this is done in advance of any job advertisement. This is another reason to write detailed job descriptions for every position.

Reasonable Accommodation of the Disabled

The amount of money and effort that an employer is expected to put into accommodation of the disabled depends on a number of factors, such as the size of the employer and the degree of the disability. Smaller employers are not expected to do as much in this regard as large employers. Large employers will be expected to spend significant sums of money to make their facilities and jobs more accessible to the disabled.

Accommodation can mean anything from making a door wider to changing a job description to fit the skills and limitations of a disabled employee. It may mean buying a piece of equipment that makes the job more accessible, but it usually will not mean paying for glasses or a hearing aid. It may mean changing the work schedule or hiring a reader or assistant. It does not mean accepting work that is of a lower quality or quantity than would be expected from an employee that was not disabled. The whole point of accommodation is that the disabled employee is put in a position where he or she can do as good a job as someone who is not disabled. If that is not possible, then accommodation is not possible.

Reasonable Accommodation for the Disabled

Steps that employers may be required to take to accommodate the disabled include:

1. Altering existing buildings to make them accessible
2. Assigning nonessential functions to another employee
3. Restructuring jobs
4. Modifying work schedules or creating part-time jobs
5. Rewriting tests or using readers or interpreters
6. Buying special equipment
7. Providing assistants or interpreters on the job

Employers are not required to accommodate disabled employees if it would cause an undue hardship to their business. In determining whether or not a particular accommodation would be an undue hardship for a particular employer, the size and financial resources of the employer will be taken into account along with the cost of the accommodation. If the accommodation would result in a major disruption of the employer's business, then it is not required. Generally, the larger the employer, the more the employer will be expected to spend in time and money to accommodate the disabled.

SAMPLE EMPLOYEE HANDBOOK PROVISION

The MNO Company, as part of a general effort in American society, is trying to provide reasonable accommodation for disabled individuals. All employees are expected to help with this effort. This may mean restructuring a job or altering a work process if it does not affect the quality or quantity of the work performed. It may mean altering a work schedule or asking for help from fellow employees.

AFFIRMATIVE ACTION

The Vocational Rehabilitation Act of 1973, as amended, requires employers who have contracts over $2,500 with the federal government to take affirmative action to hire and accommodate the handicapped. These employers must place an affirmative action clause in the contract and inform employees of their obligation to provide affirmative action for the handicapped. Contractors with fifty or more employees and contracts of $50,000 or more must have a written affirmative action plan. This plan must be available for inspection by any employee or job applicant. The law requires handicapped individuals who are "otherwise qualified" for the job to be beneficiaries of affirmative action. Whether or not the person is "otherwise qualified" will take into account the effect of reasonable accommodation. If the accommodation requires changing the essential nature of the job or imposes an undue burden on the employer, it is not required. This plan will not have goals and timetables like plans developed for race and sex. It is impossible to know how many handicapped people there are in the relevant labor pool who would be able to do the job with reasonable accommodation. Instead, the plan will state the general goal of seeking out, hiring, and promoting as many handicapped people as possible.

There are a wide variety of sources of funds to help employers accommodate handicapped individuals. There are also special tax deductions that may apply to an employer that has to spend money to accommodate a handicapped person.

SAMPLE EMPLOYEE HANDBOOK PROVISION

As a contractor with the federal government, the MNO Company is required to provide affirmative action and reasonable accommodation for handicapped individuals who can perform jobs here at MNO. The written affirmative action plan is in the Human Resources Department and can be read by any employee or job applicant who is interested. We believe that we have a good record of hiring and accommodating the handicapped here at the MNO Company, but we are always trying to improve on our past performance. Employees here at MNO are expected to work with the Human Resources Department when a handicapped individual is hired to help with accommodation and possible job restructuring. We are confident that all of our employees will use their best efforts to make accommodation successful.

VIETNAM-ERA VETERANS

Section 402 of the Vietnam Era Veterans Readjustment Act of 1974 requires companies that contract with the federal government (and their subcontractors) and public employers to take affirmative action to hire veterans of the Vietnam War (amending 38 U.S.C. sec. 219 *et seq.*). A veteran of the Vietnam War is anyone who served in the American armed forces between August 1964 and May 1976.

After the Vietnam War some people discriminated against veterans, feeling that they had fought in an unjust war or were likely to be suffering psychological disorders because of their participation in the war. The readjustment act was an attempt by Congress to combat this discrimination and provide Vietnam veterans with a chance to enter the workforce. Federal contractors and public employers must treat Vietnam veterans the same way they treat any other job applicant or employee.

The act also requires federal contractors and public employers to have a written affirmative action plan concerned with the recruitment, hiring, and promotion of Vietnam-era veterans. This plan will not have goals and timetables like plans developed for race and sex. It is impossible to know how many Vietnam-era veterans with the necessary job skills there are in the relevant labor pool. Instead, the plan will state the general goal of seeking out, hiring, and promoting as many Vietnam-era veterans as possible.

Of course, some veterans will also qualify as handicapped under federal law and may require various kinds of accommodation in order to be able to perform the job. There are many organizations, including the Veterans Administration, that will help disabled veterans gain and keep a job and help employers accommodate them at the workplace.

SAMPLE EMPLOYEE HANDBOOK PROVISION

As a contractor with the federal government, the MNO Company is required to provide affirmative action and reasonable accommodation for Vietnam-era veterans who can perform jobs here at MNO. The written affirmative action plan is in the Human Resources Department and can be read by any employee or job applicant who is interested. We believe that we have a good record of hiring and accommodating Vietnam-era veterans here at the MNO Company, but we are always trying to improve on our past performance. Some veterans may be disabled and require accommodation or job restructuring. We are confident that all of our employees will use their best efforts to make accommodation successful.

SEEKING OUT THE DISABLED AND VETERANS

For most employers, the major affirmative action effort will be taking affirmative steps to seek out job applicants who are handicapped or Vietnam-era veterans. This will mean posting job openings with organizations in the community that work with these two groups of potential employees. It will also mean recruiting from training programs and schools that help the disabled integrate into society. Accommodation at work may mean training current employees about the special problems the disabled have at work. Often the biggest problem is the attitudes of fellow employees. This may require the services of an outside consultant to help employees discuss their feelings and overcome them.

CONCLUSION

Affirmative action and reasonable accommodation require employers to do more than just not discriminate against some potential employees. Affirmative action means taking positive steps to recruit people and help integrate them into the workforce. This can mean spending more money than would otherwise be the case. Affirmative action plans for the handicapped and Vietnam-era veterans will not have the goals and timetables of other affirmative action plans. They will require employers to take reasonable steps to find and hire the disabled and veterans.

Reasonable accommodation will mean spending more time and money than would otherwise be the case to fit the job to the employee rather than fitting the employee to the job. This is not what employers generally do in the United States. In most cases, reasonable accommodation for the disabled will come about because a current employee has become disabled. In that situation, there is an existing employer-employee relationship and the employer can look at a very specific job to see how it could be changed to accommodate a disability. Over time, it is hoped that employers, particularly large employers, will become more comfortable with the idea that some jobs can be changed without much expense to allow the disabled to have a place in the American workforce.

Chapter 11

Testing

When World War II broke out, the United States found that it had to mobilize an entire nation for war in a very short time. Millions of men and women had to be placed into jobs to serve the war effort as quickly and efficiently as possible. The only way to accomplish this with any hope of success was through a massive testing program. Intelligence tests, aptitude tests, and agility tests were quickly created and put to use. The goal was to find tests that could be administered easily and that held some hope of finding something close to the right person for every job. There was little concern that some people might not perform on these quick-and-dirty tests. After all, the fate of democracy hung in the balance. After the war, the thousands of experts who had created the thousands of tests went out to sell their tests to private businesses and state and local governments. Americans came to believe in the cult of the test. Experts armed with the right battery of tests would be able to find just the right person for every job. By the 1960s, some were beginning to question both the efficacy and the efficiency of many of the standard tests.

THE DISCRIMINATION PROBLEM

Soon after the passage of the Civil Rights Act of 1964, judges began to develop a distinction between disparate treatment and disparate impact. By *disparate treatment* the judges meant that an employer intentionally discriminated against a job applicant or employee. By *disparate impact* the judges meant that the discrimination might not be intentional. A test or job requirement was having a negative (disparate) impact on a particular minority group, whether or not that was the intent of the employer. The landmark case in this area came to the U.S. Supreme Court in 1971.

In *Griggs v. Duke Power Co.*, the Supreme Court was faced with a Duke Power Company requirement that all job applicants have at least a high school diploma and passing scores on two standard intelligence tests before the company would consider them for a job—any job. Statistics showed that these requirements had a disparate impact on black applicants. This was particularly obvious where the high school diploma requirement was concerned because only a small percentage of black workers in North Carolina had graduated from high school at the time (12 percent of working-age blacks had a diploma, compared with 34 percent of working-age whites). The district judge did not find the high school diploma requirement or the intelligence tests to be a violation of Title VII because there was no evidence of an intent to discriminate on the part of Duke Power Company. The company argued that it was simply trying to hire only reasonably well educated workers with reasonable intelligence.

The justices of the Supreme Court pointed out that Title VII was intended to prohibit more than just obvious and intentional discrimination. It was also intended to prevent job requirements that appeared reasonable on the surface but had the effect of discriminating against minority groups. While Title VII specifically allows employers to use tests, it states that the tests must not be "intended, designed or used" to discriminate. In this case, the Supreme Court found that the tests and requirements in question were being used to discriminate because they had a disparate impact on a particular group.

Over the years that followed the *Griggs* case, judges and attorneys debated who had the burden of proving what in these kinds of cases. Finally, in 1989, the Supreme Court cleared up the confusion in the case of *Wards Cove Packing Co. v. Atonio*. This case involved a suit by salmon cannery workers in Alaska. These workers pointed out that most of the blue-collar jobs in the cannery were held by minorities, while most of the higher-paying white-collar jobs were held by white employees. The Supreme Court ruled that simply finding such a disparity did not prove that the company engaged in illegal hiring practices. The Court then ruled that to prove a case of disparate impact, the employees and job applicants that sued would have to prove two things. First, they would have to prove that a specific test or job requirement had a discriminatory effect on their particular group. Second, they would have to prove that the test or requirement was not job-related.

It was principally this decision that led Congress to revise the civil rights laws with the Civil Rights Act of 1991. This act states that if employees are suing for disparate impact, they must point to particular tests or job hiring criteria and prove that these tests or criteria have a negative impact on a particular group. However, if the employee or job applicant can demonstrate to the judge that the decision-making process cannot be separated out, the process may be analyzed as a whole. That means that in some cases employees or job applicants will be able to sue for discrimination based only on the fact that there is a low percentage of minority employees in a job category.

The Civil Rights Act of 1991 also dealt with the question of burden of proof. The act states that it will be up to the employees or job applicants to prove that a particular test or job criterion has a disparate impact on a particular group. Once the employees or job applicants have met that burden, the burden will then shift to the employer to prove that the test or job requirement is job-related. If the employer can prove that the test or requirement is job-related, the employees may still win if they can prove that a "less discriminatory alternative practice" was available to satisfy the employer's legitimate needs and that the employer refused to adopt that less discriminatory alternative.

This means that after 1991, employers that are subject to the federal civil rights laws must be careful when they use any test for job selection, promotion, or any other purpose. Employers will want to know from the company selling the test if it has a disparate impact on any minority groups (or women). Equally important, the employer will want to know if the test really does test for some knowledge or skill that is required on the job.

Before 1991, it was a common practice for companies to use certain standard tests and then adjust the scores to try to eliminate the disparate impact. This might mean adding points to the scores of some job applicants if they belonged to particular minority groups. This seemed to some like a unique type of racism, assuming that just because someone belonged to a particular minority group, he or she needed an increase in a test score. Women argued that they were usually put at a disadvantage because of this practice. The Civil Rights Act of 1991 outlaws this kind of score adjustment. From now on, either the test is not discriminatory or it has a disparate impact. It cannot be adjusted to get around its disparate impact.

It is important to realize that even if a test has a disparate impact, employers may use it, as long as it is job-related and there is no less discriminatory alternative. For example, even if a typing test discriminated against a group, it would be allowed in hiring a secretary who was required to type as part of the job.

RELIABILITY AND VALIDITY

Employers must be careful to look at two factors before using any test: reliability and validity. A test is reliable if it comes up with the same score every time it is used to measure the same thing. For example, if you got a significantly different number every time you stepped on a bathroom scale, even though only a few minutes had passed and you knew that your weight had not changed, you would say that that scale was not reliable. If a test is not reliable, it should not be used, no matter how good it looks. We know that a test that is not reliable is measuring nothing.

Validity is the second criterion any test should meet. A test is valid if it measures what it says it measures. This is a simple matter with skills tests. A typing test clearly measures the ability to type. A spelling test clearly measures the ability to spell. This becomes more difficult when the test is supposed to measure things such as personality or integrity.

Once a test is shown to be both reliable and valid, the third criterion it must meet is that it must be job-related. A typing test makes a lot of sense when hiring a secretary. It would not be job-related in hiring a janitor.

LIE DETECTOR TESTS

Lie detector tests were once popular across the American employment landscape. That is no longer the case. These tests were resented by employees for many reasons, not the least of which was that after almost a century of use, there was still no scientific evidence that lie detectors detected lies. Over the years more and more states passed laws to control the use of lie detectors, particularly in the workplace. Finally, in 1988, Congress passed the Employee Polygraph Protection Act (29 U.S.C. sec. 2001). This law makes it very difficult for private companies to use lie detectors. It does not affect local, state, or federal government.

Private employers may not use a lie detector on an employee unless they believe that the employee has caused "economic loss," such as taking something of value. Even if the employer believes this, the employee may stop the test at any time. Special rules apply to private security firms and companies that make drugs, but even these companies may not use the results of a lie detector test, or the refusal to take such a test, as the only basis for a decision to fire or not hire someone.

The Employee Polygraph Protection Act has a set of strict rules that must be followed, including requiring the person giving the test to give the employee advance notice of the time and place of the test and warning the employee that he or she has a right to consult an attorney before taking the test. Employees must sign a statement saying that they understand that they can refuse to take the test and that they can sue both the employer and the test giver if the laws are violated. Employees must be allowed to review all questions before the test is given, and the test must last at least ninety minutes. Also, the person giving the test may not ask questions about religion, race, politics, unions, sex, or lifestyle. Employers risk being sued if anyone outside of the company finds out about the results of the test.

The federal Employee Polygraph Protection Act is not the end of the story. Most states also have laws on the use of lie detector machines, and many state supreme courts have handed down decisions that make it easy for employees to sue for invasion of privacy if they are subjected to these tests. The net result of all this is that no employer should use a lie detector test without legal advice. Some attorneys suggest that any employer considering using a lie detector test should take two aspirins and lie down until the urge passes.

While the federal Employee Polygraph Protection Act does not apply to government workers, these workers are protected by the Fifth Amendment to the U.S. Constitution, which protects everyone from forced self-incrimination. Because there is no evidence that a lie detector test will actually detect lies, people taking such a test are in danger of incriminating themselves and should consider refusing to take the test.

In response to these legal problems, many employers turned to paper-and-pencil honesty tests. In 1991 the American Psychological Association issued a report on these tests entitled *Questionnaires Used in the Prediction of Trustworthiness in Preemployment Selection Decisions: An A.P.A. Task Force Report* (copies available from the American Psychological Association in Washington, D.C.). Few of the companies that sell honesty tests responded to the task force's request for information. The report found that some honesty tests are valid in that they will distinguish between a group of average citizens and a group of convicted felons. However, the report did not specify which honesty tests demonstrated this validity. It is important that any employer using such a test ask the company selling the test for information about both the test's validity and the impact that the test has on minority groups. In many cases honesty will not be related to the job. In that case, if the test does have a disparate impact on a group of potential employees, the employer will be in violation of antidiscrimination laws if it is used.

PERSONALITY TESTS

Another popular group of tests is personality tests. Of course, such tests should be used only if they are reliable and validly test for the personality traits they say they test for. Also, any employer using these tests should be able to prove that these particular personality traits are job-related. That is often difficult to prove when personality tests are used.

One example of a test that should not be used is the Minnesota Multi-Phasic Personality Inventory (MMPI). In one case, when Target stores were using the test to screen job applicants, one of the applicants took the test to a copy machine, copied the questions, and then sued for violation of his privacy rights under the California constitution (*Soroka*). He won. What kinds of questions did this test ask? People were expected to answer yes or no to questions such as: "I go to church almost every week," "I believe in the second coming of Christ," "I believe my sins are unpardonable," "I am very strongly attracted by members of my own sex," and "Many of my dreams are about sex matters."

The MMPI was created early in the twentieth century by giving thousands of questions to people who were diagnosed with mental illness and asking the same questions of people who were thought to be normal. The major issue was whether or not a particular question could distinguish between these two groups. It is doubtful that it can be useful in selecting employees for particular jobs today.

In selecting a personality test, an employer should ask if there is evidence that the test has a disparate impact on minority groups. Also, an employer using such tests may have to prove that the particular personality trait tested for is actually required to do a particular job.

APTITUDE AND INTELLIGENCE TESTS

Many standard aptitude and intelligence tests have been found to have a disparate impact on minority groups and not to be a valid predictor of quality job performance. That means that employers using such tests should assume that they have a disparate impact and should be prepared to prove that the test actually measures what its creators say it measures and that this trait is actually related to the job. Generally, employers are going to be better off using tests that measure a particular aptitude that is obviously needed on the job. For example, people working with numbers will need to be able to do mathematics. A test that was designed to test for the exact types of mathematical calculations the person will be doing on the job would be best. People who write need to have a reasonable English vocabulary. Many employers routinely use spelling tests to screen applicants. Given the ability of computers to check spelling, it could be questioned whether these tests are really the least discriminatory way of screening job applicants.

DRUG TESTING

Drug tests are very controversial in America society. At last count, fifteen states had laws controlling the use of drug tests in the workplace. These laws range from Utah's, which is a license to drug-test employees as long as all employees are subjected to the same test, to Rhode Island's, which prohibits drug testing unless the employer "has reasonable grounds to believe, based on specific objective facts, that the employee's use of controlled substances is impairing his ability to perform his job." If the employer does have such "reasonable grounds," it must follow the drug-testing procedure set out in the statute and offer any employee flunking the test a chance to join a "bona fide rehabilitation program."

The story gets more complex. While the Americans with Disabilities Act specifically states that people currently using illegal drugs are not protected by its provisions, some state laws barring discrimination against the handicapped may protect current drug addicts. Also, the Americans with Disabilities Act states that employers may not discriminate against people who have stopped using drugs and are currently in rehabilitation programs. That might allow someone who tested positive to claim that he or she had just given up drugs and joined a rehabilitation program.

Anyone running a drug-testing program should use a second test if someone tests positive using less expensive and less reliable tests. Also, anyone running a drug-testing program should consider using a different kind of test that did not invade privacy and tested more directly for the qualities needed on the job. A drug test is a bad test for most purposes in that it does not catch many people who may not be capable of doing the dangerous work they are about to engage in. Someone who has not slept in days or is upset over personal problems will pass a drug test but may not be capable of driving a bus or operating heavy machinery. Employers should consider using one of the mechanical tests that have been developed to test for reaction time, visual acuity, and other clearly job-related skills. These tests are usually cheaper and easier to administer, and do not involve invading the employee's privacy.

Federal Drug-Free Workplace Act

The federal Drug-Free Workplace Act of 1988 requires employers that have a contract with the federal government for $25,000 or more to certify that they have a drug-free workplace. This also applies to entities that receive federal grants. The act does not require these contractors to institute a drug-testing program. It does require employers to distribute to their employees a policy statement that they are required to comply with the Drug-Free Workplace Act. This policy statement should notify employees that it is unlawful to manufacture, dispense, possess, or use controlled substances in the workplace and spell out what will happen if an employee is caught violating the drug laws. Employers are also expected to establish a drug awareness program that informs employees about the dangers of illegal drugs and notifies them about any drug counseling or rehabilitation programs that are available.

SAMPLE EMPLOYEE HANDBOOK PROVISION

As a federal contractor, the MNO Company is required to comply with the federal Drug Free Workplace Act. This act requires us to notify you that the manufacture, distribution, dispensation, possession, or use of controlled substances is illegal and is prohibited at any of our facilities. If an employee is found to be manufacturing, distributing, dispensing, possessing, or using any controlled substances either at work or while on company business, he or she will be subject to disciplinary action, which may include termination. The MNO Company cannot afford to pay for a drug rehabilitation program, but the Human Resources Department will provide any employees who request it with a list of available rehabilitation and counseling services in the community. Any employees who are convicted of violating the drug laws while at work or on company business are required to notify the director of human resources within five days after the conviction. If you must manufacture, distribute, dispense, possess, or use controlled substances, please do so somewhere else besides work so that we do not lose our federal contracts, which could result in layoffs of employees for lack of business. Because of this potential terrible consequence, we expect all of our employees to be on the lookout for the violation of this policy and to report such violations immediately to the director of human resources or their immediate supervisor. We also hope that anyone currently manufacturing, distributing, dispensing, possessing, or using any controlled substance will stop and seek help immediately.

PHYSICAL EXAMINATIONS

The Americans with Disabilities Act makes it illegal for employers covered by the act (most employers with fifteen or more employees) to require a physical examination before offering someone a job. Once a person has been offered a job, the offer can be made contingent upon passing a physical examination that will be conducted to see if the person is capable of doing the work. The Americans with Disabilities Act requires employers who conduct physical examinations to examine everyone, not just those with disabilities. Any medical information obtained from the examination or from any other source, such as from the employee, must be kept in a separate file and treated as confidential. It may be released only to supervisors and managers to the extent that the employee will need accommodation, to health services and safety personnel so that they will know how to help the employee in case of an emergency, and to government officials who need to know. There is no restriction on the use of regular or voluntary medical examinations, but presumably disabled people may not be singled out in any examination process.

SAMPLE EMPLOYEE HANDBOOK PROVISION

The MNO Company conducts physical examinations before hiring new employees and requires regular physical examinations of all employees. Medical information is kept in a confidential file separate from other personnel information. This information is released only to supervisors to the extent that they need to know about job restrictions that might apply and to health services and safety personnel so that they may respond appropriately in the case of an emergency. It is also released to government officials who investigate our compliance with law. Employees who have a medical condition that should be brought to the attention of emergency personnel are urged to inform the appropriate person in the Department of Human Resources. Employees who have a physical or mental condition that may affect their ability to do their job are also urged to inform the appropriate person in the Department of Human Resources. The MNO Company does not discriminate against disabled people. However, we cannot accommodate disabilities we do not know about, and we cannot be responsible for emergency treatment in situations where employees have withheld information about their physical condition.

GENETIC TESTING AND THE RISK OF FUTURE HARM

With each passing day we are getting closer and closer to the time when a full battery of genetic tests will tell us a great deal about everyone. They will tell us if particular people are more susceptible to certain illnesses or more sensitive to certain substances. Science already suggests that genetic factors are significant in a number of diseases, such as many kinds of cancer and blood diseases. Mental illness and drug or alcohol dependency may also be influenced by heredity. Also, a predisposition to some diseases may be linked to certain racial or ethnic factors.

Why would employers want to engage in genetic testing? The main reason will be to reduce workers' compensation claims and health insurance premiums by reducing the probability of some illnesses that might be caused by exposure to some substances at work. There are, of course, potential problems. If employers do conduct genetic tests, they will have a duty to inform employees about the results if those results suggest that the employees are more likely to contract an illness. Failure to do so might result in legal liability.

The real question, to which we do not yet have an answer, is the extent to which federal and state laws barring discrimination against the handicapped will apply to people who "flunk" genetic tests. Will this mean that the employer considers the person handicapped, and will this then entitle the person to the protection of the law? To what extent may employers argue that it is reasonable to exclude someone from a job if he or she is more likely to contract an illness at work than the average worker? In one case, Mr. Crosby, a thirty one-year-old carpenter, applied for construction work in Hawaii (*Crosby*). A physical examination revealed that he had a congenital back defect and had previously suffered two back injuries. The company rejected him because of a fear of future injury. Crosby sued, but the judge in this case ruled that it was not illegal to reject a qualified handicapped applicant if the rejection was based on "the likelihood of injury, the seriousness of the possible injury or the imminence of the injury." The judge ruled that the likelihood of a serious injury was high enough in this case to justify not hiring him.

In 1988 the West Virginia Supreme Court allowed a coal mine to reject a female applicant with psoriasis (*Ranger*). Her preemployment examination revealed that her psoriasis would be aggravated by work in the mine and that there was "a high likelihood" that it would lead to a "secondary infection that would require extensive treatment." The West Virginia Supreme Court ruled that "the fact that an applicant's handicap creates a reasonable probability of a materially enhanced risk of substantial harm to the handicapped person or others is a legitimate, nondiscriminatory reason for an employer to reject the applicant." At the same time, the court pointed out that in coming to this conclusion, employers must not rely on "general assumptions or stereotypes" but must consider the actual condition in relation to the actual conditions of the job. The employer must also be able to demonstrate that no "reasonable accommodation" could eliminate the risk.

Presumably, similar concepts will apply to someone who flunks a genetic screening test. As this kind of screening becomes common in the twenty-first century, employers will have to be sensitive to the legal precedents in this area.

CONCLUSION

Testing is big business in the United States. For more and more employers, it is becoming a dangerous business. Tests may result in a variety of discriminatory effects, and they may or may not actually help select better employees. Lie detector tests created so much resentment that Congress finally passed a law all but eliminating them from the American workplace. Whether other types of tests will generate that degree of resentment remains to be seen. Employers should try so far as possible to use tests that do not have a disparate impact and that actually do measure skills, knowledge, and personality traits that are necessary for the job in question. Employers must keep in mind that they may test people for a job, but they may not test people in general. Whether or not a test was job-related will be the main issue in most cases if the test is challenged in court.

Chapter 12

Interviews and Advertisements

The two major steps in the hiring process for most jobs are advertising the position and interviewing some of the applicants. Both of these steps can lead to potential legal liability. The first step in the process should be analyzing the job, and the next step should be writing a job description.

WRITING A JOB DESCRIPTION

Before placing an advertisement in a newspaper or conducting any job interviews, a detailed job description should be written. This is very important because this job description may be introduced in court if there is a legal challenge to the hiring process. The description should list all the areas of knowledge that the person will actually need to be acquainted with in order to do the job. It is important to make sure that the job description is up to date. It should not be the same description used decades ago. People who are currently doing the job should be asked to participate in the job description process.

The description should list all the "essential functions" of the job. This list should not be written with an eye to changing the job description to accommodate people with disabilities. The job may be altered later to accommodate a particular disabled individual, but job descriptions should accurately reflect what the job as currently structured actually entails.

The description should list all the skills that are needed to perform the job well. Remember, the whole point of the hiring process is to find the very best person for the job. While you do not want to discriminate against anyone, and you may be able to accommodate disabled people, it should usually be in a situation where the person accommodated will be able, with accommodation, to perform as well as the best other person you can find.

AFFIRMATIVE ACTION INFORMATION

For affirmative action employers, the hiring process begins with the creation of a form to give to job applicants. This form should ask for all the characteristics you are trying to act affirmatively about. A typical form for a company that contracts with the federal government will ask for sex, race, disability, and Vietnam veteran information. This form should be given out with each job application and should contain a basic statement about why this information is being gathered. It should indicate that submission of the information is voluntary and that the information supplied will not be used to adversely affect the hiring process or the terms and conditions of employment. This information should usually come into play after people who do not meet the minimum requirements have been eliminated but before the final hiring or promotion decision has been made. At that point someone who does not have the major responsibility for hiring the particular person, such as the director of human resources, should look at the applications of the remaining candidates and compare them with the list of applicants from groups that the company is trying to hire. Some intervention into the hiring process may be called for at this point.

The form asking for information about disabilities should point out that the Americans with Disabilities Act will be complied with, which means that the information will be kept confidential, except that (1) supervisors and managers may be informed regarding restrictions on work duties and necessary accommodations, (2) health services and safety personnel may be informed, when and to the extent appropriate, if the disabling condition might require emergency treatment, and (3) government officials investigating compliance with the law may be informed.

A current problem is people who claim to be members of a racial minority or a Native American tribe but really are not. Some people, by marriage, have Hispanic last names, but their own ethnic origin is not Latin American or Spanish. Some people may have a black ancestor, but they are not black and would not be subjected to discrimination because of the color of their skin. Many people in the United States have some Native American ancestry, but they no longer maintain an affiliation with a tribe. There is at present no affirmative action law for the people who were once called half-breeds. As the United States becomes more and more ethnically and culturally mixed, it becomes more and more difficult to say who is what.

ASKING THE WRONG QUESTIONS

Interviews are potential minefields for two main reasons: An illegal question might be asked, and an oral promise might be made. Let's examine a typical interview to see where mistakes are usually made.

> "Hello, Ms. Johnson, is that Miss. or Mrs.?"
> "Miss."
> "Let's see, you are about five feet tall, and I would guess you weigh over 200 pounds. Is that right?"
> "Yes, about. I haven't weighed lately."
> "Fine. Now, are you a U.S. citizen?"
> "Yes."
> "And have you ever been arrested for anything other than a traffic violation?"
> "No."
> "Fine. What about military service?"
> "No, I have never been in the military."
> "O.K., and what is your religion?"

"I'm a devout atheist."

"I see. I'm a devout Catholic myself, as are most of the people who work here. Are you pregnant, and do you have any children?"

"I have one child, age two, and I am pregnant."

"I see. Well, I guess I've heard enough. Don't expect a call."

This interviewer has violated every rule in the book. First of all, while federal civil rights laws do not outlaw marital status discrimination, many state civil rights laws do. Even in states that do not outlaw this kind of discrimination, a question concerned with marital status may violate federal civil rights laws if only women are asked about their marital status. While the interviewer can obviously see how tall and fat the person is, asking about it suggests that these factors will be used in hiring. Height restrictions usually discriminate against women, and weight restrictions may violate the Americans with Disabilities Act and other laws barring discrimination against the handicapped. While companies are not allowed to hire illegal aliens, they are also not allowed to discriminate against legal aliens in most cases. Some government jobs may require U.S. citizenship, as may jobs that require a security clearance. However, for most jobs, asking if the person is a U.S. citizen is illegal. Asking about children is usually discriminatory because these questions are usually asked only of women, not of men, and constitute sex discrimination. Of course, asking about religion also violates federal and most state civil rights laws.

The best approach to avoiding most of these problems is to discuss the actual job, with the job description in front of the interviewer. While the interviewer should not ask directly about disability, it is acceptable to point out that the job involves lifting heavy objects and ask if the applicant is able to perform that essential function of the job. While you should not ask about children, it is acceptable to point out that the job requires working late some days, and ask if that is a problem for the applicant. While you should not ask about religion, it is acceptable to point out that the job entails working on Saturday or Sunday and ask if the applicant will be able to do that. Generally interviewers should avoid asking about arrest records because minorities tend to be arrested more often than white applicants. You may ask if the applicant has been convicted of a felony, although some state civil rights laws require that if you do this, you must also state that this may not necessarily disqualify the applicant. Asking about military service discriminates against women, who have not served in the military at the same rate as men.

It may seem strange that the interviewer is avoiding questions that the affirmative action form specifically asks for, but that is the world in which we live. The person with primary responsibility for hiring should be trying to hire the best person for the job without regard to such issues as race, sex, or irrelevant disability. Someone else in the organization should have the responsibility for following the process and stepping in to achieve the goals of the affirmative action plans.

Some questions that would be illegal during the hiring process are of course necessary after the person has been hired. People should not be asked who to contact in an emergency when they are being hired. This might indicate marital status discrimination. Of course, after hiring, this information becomes necessary. Group insurance forms will require information on issues such as sex, age, marital status, and dependents. At that point, gathering this information is of course legal. Any medical problems or disabilities that might require special emergency treatment or job accommodation should of course be discovered after the person is hired and before he or she begins work. The person will have to prove, before beginning work, that he or she is either a U.S. citizen or a legal alien with the right to work in the United States.

ASKING THE RIGHT QUESTIONS

Asking the right questions means explaining the job and asking about knowledge, skills, and experience that are relevant to the job. Can the applicants perform the essential functions of the job; can they operate the necessary machines; can they speak the language that is spoken at the workplace well enough to communicate with supervisors and coworkers? Employers often forget that the interview itself can be viewed as another test that applicants are given before being hired. It is legitimate for people to ask if this test has a disparate impact on a particular group. If it does, then the employer will have to show that the interview is job-related. A written interview form with the questions asked and the answers given will help to prove that the interview is job-related because the information solicited was job-related. Generally, anyone conducting an interview is also looking for a number of intangible factors that will influence the hiring decision. Insofar as possible, these intangible factors should be listed on the interview form so that their job relevance can be demonstrated. Basic interpersonal skills are often being measured in a job interview. These skills should be listed on the interview form. Is the person at ease talking with other people? Does the person communicate well orally?

I once discussed this with a man who hired hundreds of employees a year for a large manufacturer. The jobs were low-skill and had little in the way of essential functions. The interviewer said that he talked with each applicant for ten minutes and then gave the applicant a number from one to ten. If an opening came up, he called back only those with an eight or above. There are two problems with that process. First, does this number giving process discriminate against any group? I presumed that it did because it sounded so totally subjective. Second, if it does discriminate, is there any reason to think that this number giving process is actually predicting who will do well on the job? In most cases that will be impossible to prove in a court of law.

The second problem to be avoided in the interview is the problem of offering someone an oral contract of employment. Offers of employment should be made in writing, and that should be made clear to any job applicant. The interviewer should avoid saying that this will be a "permanent job" or that the applicant will have the job as long as he or she "does a good job." Words such as *career* should also be avoided. Much of this can be avoided by giving the person a copy of the employee handbook at the same time he or she is offered a job. A well-written handbook should clear up any confusion concerning the length of the promised employment.

Do's and Don'ts of Job Interviewing

- Do hand the applicant a copy of the job description and ask if he or she can perform the functions required.
- Don't ask the applicant about personal characteristics, such as marital or parental status, religion, race, or disability.
- Do make written notes of the interview and the traits you are looking for.
- Don't make written notes of irrelevant information that might be discriminatory, such as weight and height.
- Do ask the applicant to discuss his or her past work experience.
- Don't tell the applicant you are looking for people with limited experience.
- Do explain both the positive and the negative aspects of the job.
- Don't tell some applicants the positive aspects of the job while telling others the negative aspects of the job.
- Do explain company policy on things such as receiving personal phone calls at work or smoking at work.
- Don't ask about child care arrangements.
- Do tell the applicant the good things about the company.
- Don't lie to the applicant about the bad things about the company.

A good job interviewer should be looking for particular experience and traits that are necessary for the job. If the person will be part of a team, it would be good to discuss any other times in the person's life when he or she was part of a team. If the job requires working directly with customers, then asking about past experience working with customers would of course be relevant.

ANSWERING THE APPLICANT'S QUESTIONS

Part of any interview is answering the applicant's questions. Many interviewers believe that they can find out a great deal about an applicant in this process. At the same time, there are potential legal problems. Employees who have been lied to in a job interview have sued and won. In one case, Roberta Berger asked in the job interview about the current financial status of the company (*Berger*). She was told that the company had many customers, and that everything was fine. In fact, the company had few regular customers and was already in financial trouble. Roberta Berger moved to Denver in February, only to find the company going out of business in March. She sued for fraudulent concealment and won. Interviewers should answer questions truthfully and admit it if they do not know the answer to a question.

ADVERTISING THE POSITION

The same problems that can arise in the interview can also come up with the advertisement. The point that has to be kept in mind is that the advertisement will be in print for all the world to see. There will be no question of who said what in a job advertisement. The advertisement should concentrate on telling about the job rather than stating job qualifications. There is generally no better, and no safer, job advertisement than one that accurately spells out what the job is and what the person doing the job will be expected to do. Remember, any job qualifications stated in the advertisement will have to be supported later. Do you really need people with a high school diploma for this job? How much experience is really necessary? Sexist language should be avoided: It is salesperson or draftsperson, not salesman and draftsman.

Generally the major problem with advertisements concerns age discrimination. The advertisement says that the company wants someone who is young or who has between two and three years' experience. Older workers are going to have more experience, and most employers are going to have a hard time explaining why that is a bad thing. The general response is that employers expect older workers to want more money. This problem can be solved by stating the salary range in the advertisement. In fact, any negative aspects of the job should be stated in the job advertisement. This keeps the number of applicants down and should help avoid job turnover. If the job has problems, the best time to deal with them is in the beginning.

JOB POSTING

Companies operating under affirmative action plans are required to post any job openings internally in the organization. This is, of course, a good idea for any employer, regardless of the legal requirements. The employees of a company know about the company, and they may even know about the specific job. They can be a source of potential employees who have been told the positives and negatives of working for this organization. Also, internal candidates for any job should be seriously considered. Promotions from within help to boost employee morale and usually provide a job candidate that the organization knows a great deal about. At the same time, the goal should remain finding the best person for this particular job, and that will often mean going outside the organization.

CONCLUSION

Advertising and interviewing are the major way in which many job openings are filled. At the same time, they are potentially the point at which illegal discrimination is revealed. Employers should work to make sure interviewers have been trained in good job interview techniques and that advertisements are not discriminatory.

Chapter 13

Older Workers and Age Discrimination

Congress passed the Age Discrimination in Employment Act in 1967 (29 U.S.C. sec. 631). Originally it protected only people between the ages of forty and sixty-five from age discrimination. Over the years, Congress first raised the upper limit to seventy and then eliminated it completely. The federal law applies only to employers with at least twenty employees; however, many states also have age discrimination laws that apply to smaller employers. Also, some state laws protect even younger workers from age discrimination.

The federal Age Discrimination in Employment Act protects older workers against discrimination in the terms, conditions, or privileges of employment. It prohibits discrimination in wages and salaries and discrimination in all employment decisions from hiring to firing and from promotions to layoffs. The federal law did not originally apply to state and local governments, but it was amended to cover these entities in 1974. Federal laws and regulations specifically exempt some occupations, such as air traffic controllers, but very few occupations are exempted. The act also allows for age discrimination in apprenticeship programs if the programs meet federal guidelines. At one time colleges were allowed to force professors to retire at the age of seventy, but that special exemption from the provisions of the act was eliminated in 1994. The Age Discrimination in Employment Act was amended in 1991 to cover American employers who employ Americans outside of the United States unless this would violate the laws of the country in which the employee is working.

Employers are prohibited from segregating older workers or classifying older employees in a way that is different from the way in which other employees are classified. Employers may discriminate against older workers if this is part of a bona fide occupational qualification, such as the need to hire someone to play a young person in a play. Employers also may discriminate if this is based on reasonable factors other than age, such as a bona fide seniority system. Courts have ruled that bus drivers and airline pilots and copilots may be discriminated against because of age, but for most other job classifications, age discrimination has not been allowed.

Generally older workers are subject to different treatment because the employer believes older people cannot perform the essential functions of a job. In some of these cases, the older worker may also be protected by the Americans with Disabilities Act because the employer is assuming that the worker is not capable of doing a job because of physical or mental disability.

In a suit for age discrimination, it is up to the employee to prove that he or she is protected by the law (old enough), that he or she was adversely affected (fired or not hired), that he or she is qualified for the job, and that a younger employee was treated better. Then it is up to the employer to prove that the action taken was required for legitimate business reasons. Then the burden shifts back to the employee to prove that this stated business reason is simply a pretext for discrimination. Generally a worker who is replaced by someone who is at least five years younger will be able to sue for age discrimination even if both workers are over the age of forty.

Often older workers are rejected because they are considered to be overqualified. Federal courts have ruled that overqualification is usually not a legitimate reason for not hiring an older worker (*Taggert*). After all, if the person is better qualified than needed, shouldn't that be a plus? Some people argue that people who are overqualified will not be happy in a lesser position or will be more likely to leave the job when something better comes along. Generally these reasons will be seen as simply an excuse not to hire older workers.

Often older workers do not have a college degree but have the equivalent in experience. Because a college degree requirement will usually discriminate against older workers, employers need to be able to justify this requirement by showing concrete aspects of the job that really do require a college degree.

Some employers assume that older workers will not stay on the job as long as younger workers because of retirement or illness. This is usually an unreasonable assumption. Young workers will not be retiring soon, but they are usually more likely to move to another city or find a more promising job.

When laying off employees, employers often lay off the older workers because they have higher salaries. This can constitute age discrimination. Older workers should be given a chance to take a cut in pay before being laid off.

Some employers try to reorganize older employees out of a job. In one case, an executive found, at the age of sixty, that the company was reorganizing his work to take staff away from his department. New positions and new divisions were created over the years, and his job was given away to younger workers. Finally, when he was sixty-seven, there was nothing left for him to do, so he was fired. The court said this was age discrimination (*Ewing*). The company had created a number of new jobs during the intervening seven years and had made no effort to place this older employee in any of them.

FILING AND RESPONDING TO CHARGES AT THE EEOC

Anyone interested in pursuing his or her rights under the Age Discrimination in Employment Act must first file a "charge" with the local office of the EEOC or with the state human rights agency. Generally, a person will not be allowed to file a lawsuit under the federal act unless he or she has first filed a charge with the EEOC or the state agency. Generally, the charge must be filed with the EEOC within 180 days of the act of discrimination or with the state agency within 300 days. Employers will usually receive notice within ten days after the charge is filed. The EEOC or the state agency will then investigate to determine whether or not reasonable cause exists to believe that age discrimination has occurred. This investigation may include visiting the employer's workplace, holding a fact-finding conference, or inspecting the employer's records. In most cases, the agency will issue a "no probable cause" determination. Soon after that, the agency will issue a right-to-sue letter. At that point, the employee has ninety days in which to file a lawsuit.

In a few cases the EEOC or state agency will issue a "reasonable cause" determination. In that case, the agency will try to eliminate the unlawful discrimination through conciliation and persuasion. If a reasonable solution can be achieved, a conciliation agreement will be signed by all parties that will protect the employer from being sued by the same employee over the same incident in the future. If agreement cannot be reached, the EEOC may decide to sue on the employee's behalf. If it does the employee may not sue individually. Usually, the EEOC issues a right-to-sue letter, and the employee then has to find an attorney and sue.

BENEFIT PLANS

The Age Discrimination in Employment Act allows for discrimination as part of a "bona fide employee benefit plan," but this has caused some confusion. It does not mean that older employees may be discriminated against when hiring or promotion decisions are being made. Employers are not allowed to use the possibility of an increase in group insurance premiums as an excuse for not hiring an older worker or as a reason to fire one. It does mean that employee benefits for older workers may be reduced because the premiums would otherwise go up. Older workers may not be forced to pay employers in order to make up the difference in premiums.

In 1990 Congress passed the Older Workers Benefit Protection Act. This Act was passed to make sure that older workers were not discriminated against simply because of their age. For example, in one case the employer provided different profit-sharing plan provisions for employees over the age of sixty-five. The federal court ruled that this was illegal (*AARP*).

Federal law now requires employers to treat older workers the same way they treat young workers when it comes to contributions to pension and retirement plans. This means with a defined benefit plan that older employees continue to accrue benefits just like younger workers at the same rate younger workers accrue benefits. With regards to a defined-contribution plan, older workers continue to receive company contributions just like younger workers, and these contributions accrue at the same rate as they do for younger workers.

REDUCTION IN FORCE

As far as the law is concerned, an employer is not required to use reverse seniority in implementing a reduction in force. An employer is free to lay off employees with less skills or lower levels of work performance. However, if this results in laying off more older workers than young workers, the probability of a suit for age discrimination is very high. Employers with well documented performance appraisals will be in a much stronger position when it comes to defending such lawsuits.

Employers who do not have good records of performance may fall back on seniority as a neutral decision rule that should not discriminate against older workers.

MANDATORY RETIREMENT

While it was common in the United States for most companies and governments to have mandatory retirement ages most of these are no longer allowed under the Age Discrimination in Employment Act. Even seventy may no longer be used as a mandatory retirement age even for formerly exempt classifications such as college professors. Any employer wishing to force a particular group of employees to take retirement at a particular age should consult an attorney. The Act does allow mandatory retirement for executives who are at least sixty-five years old, worked as a high level executive for at least two years before reaching age sixty-five and who will receive a pension of at least $44,000 a year.

Many employers once had mandatory retirement policies and have not revised them since the law was changed in 1986. It is high time to make the change.

SAMPLE EMPLOYEE HANDBOOK PROVISION

The MNO Company does not have a mandatory retirement age for any of its employees. Employees in safety related occupations may be tested on a uniform basis to make sure they are able to perform their jobs, regardless of age. Employees who are planning to retire should inform the Director of Human Resources as soon as possible after making that decision. The MNO Corporation expects all employees to treat all other employees with respect, regardless of age. At the same time, all employees are expected to report any employee who is a danger to himself or other employees because of an unwillingness or inability to perform job tasks in a safe way.

EARLY RETIREMENT

The Older Workers Benefit Protection Act was also passed to deal with what Congress considered to be a major abuse of older workers in the area of early retirement incentive plans. These plans offer older workers a chance to retire early and receive special benefits, such as more years of credit on the pension plan. Employers are allowed to set a minimum age requirement for such early retirement incentives without violating the Age Discrimination in Employment Act. In return for the special incentives of the early retirement plan, older workers are usually expected to sign a release giving up the right to sue their employer for anything that might have happened while they were employed, including age discrimination. Federal law now requires employers to give employees at least twenty-one days to decide whether or not to sign the release (forty-five days if releases are given to a group of employees). Also, any employee who signs a release must have seven days in which he or she can revoke the signature. The release must be written in plain English and may not cover any claims that might arise after the date the release is signed. The employer must advise the employee in writing to consult an attorney prior to signing the release. The release must specifically refer to the Age Discrimination in Employment Act if it is to effectively release the employer from liability under the act. If early retirement is offered to a group of employees, the employer must explain how it determined who would be in the group, the names and titles of those in the group, and the ages of the employees in the same job class or unit who were not selected to be included in the group. In any dispute over the release, the employer has the burden of proving that the release was signed voluntarily by employees who understood what they were doing. Releases signed as part of the settlement of an age discrimination lawsuit must also meet these requirements.

Guidelines for Releases of Liability for Age Discrimination

1. The release must be in plain English.
2. The release must specifically mention the Age Discrimination in Employment Act.
3. The release must not apply to actions taken after the release is signed.
4. Something must be given in exchange for the signing of the release that the employee would not otherwise have been entitled to receive.
5. The employee must be told, in writing, to consult an attorney before signing the release.
6. Employees must be given twenty-one days (or forty-five days for a group) to consider whether or not to sign the release.
7. Employees may revoke the release for seven days after signing it.
8. In any dispute, the employer must prove that the employee knew what the release contained and signed it voluntarily.

Even if an employee has signed a release, he or she may still file a complaint with the EEOC to inform the EEOC of illegal age discrimination or to challenge the legality of the release. The burden is on the employer to prove that the provisions of the Older Workers Benefit Protection Act were followed.

STATE LAW

Employees who have been victims of age discrimination may also sue under state law. Employees suing under state law may sue for violations of the state common law as well as the state age discrimination statute.

In one case, a sixty-year-old employee who had worked for the company for thirty years was demoted from an executive position to warehouse supervisor in an attempt to force him to quit. He ultimately became very depressed because of this demotion. The jury awarded the employee $300,000 for age discrimination and over $3 million for intentional infliction of emotional distress (*Monarch Paper*).

CONCLUSION

Judges and jury members usually have sympathy for people who sue for age discrimination because they themselves either are already over forty or soon will be. This makes it difficult for an employer who does not have a good reason for treating an older job applicant or employee differently. Because of the complexity of the various laws in this area, including the Older Workers Benefit Protection Act, care must be taken before reductions in force or early retirement offers are instituted.

Chapter 14

Family and Medical Issues

During the 1970s, 1980s, and 1990s, legislators in both state capitals and Washington, D.C. became more and more concerned about the need to protect workers, particularly female workers, from discharge or discrimination caused by the need to deal with family issues such as ill children or pregnancy. As more and more women entered the workforce, many with families to take care of, it became more and more apparent that some kind of protection was needed. Congress made the first move in 1978 with the Pregnancy Discrimination Act.

PREGNANCY

The Pregnancy Discrimination Act of 1978 amended the 1964 Civil Rights Act to make it clear that sex discrimination included discrimination against women because they were pregnant (42 U.S.C. sec. 2000e(k)). The initial impetus for the law was the realization on the part of women that pregnancy was not being treated in the same way as other temporary disabilities. Women who had to leave work temporarily because of pregnancy came back to find their seniority gone, while men who took temporary disability leave kept their seniority. The act made that kind of discrimination against pregnancy illegal. It also made illegal any policies that treat pregnancy leave differently from other temporary disability leave in any way. For example, if people who take temporary disability leave have the time counted toward retirement, then pregnancy leave must also count toward retirement. The law does not require companies to have a temporary disability leave policy, but if they do, they must treat pregnancy the same as other temporary disabilities. Also, a medical insurance policy that covers the spouses of employees must cover the pregnancy of those spouses. That does not mean that policies may not favor pregnancy. In 1987 the Supreme Court said that what the Pregnancy Discrimination Act did was to set "a floor beneath which pregnancy disability benefits may not drop—not a ceiling above which they may not rise" (*Guerra*).

FETAL PROTECTION POLICIES

For many years after the passage of the Pregnancy Discrimination Act, many companies continued to deny women who might become pregnant certain jobs, using the theory that the jobs might be hazardous to the health of a fetus. Companies argued that they were not violating the Pregnancy Discrimination Act because they had a right to discriminate against pregnant women in these kinds of occupations and that to discriminate against women who might become pregnant was not, technically, discrimination against the pregnant. Critics pointed out that only women get pregnant, so that any policy that kept people who might someday become pregnant out of certain jobs, usually high-paying jobs, discriminated against women.

Finally, in 1991, the Supreme Court dealt with this issue in the *Johnson Controls* case. The Johnson Controls Company made batteries and refused to allow women who either were pregnant or might someday become pregnant to work in areas where they might be exposed to lead. This kept women out of many high-paying jobs at the company. The company felt that it had to institute such a policy because of the fear that eventually a child would be born with birth defects and sue the company for exposing it, while still in the womb, to dangerous levels of lead. Women protested that this policy put them in the position of having to decide between not working in high-paying jobs and undergoing sterilization. The Supreme Court struck down the policy. The Court pointed out that the Pregnancy Discrimination Act specifically deals with this issue by saying that pregnant women may not be kept from particular jobs unless being pregnant actually prevents them from doing the work. No one disputed that women, pregnant or not, could do the work in this case.

What should employers do who have pregnant employees working in dangerous areas? The only sensible answer is: Do everything possible to protect yourself in the event of a lawsuit later by the child. Remember, no one, not even the mother, can sign away the rights of another person, in this case a person to be. Employers should do all they can to inform pregnant employees, or employees that might become pregnant, of the potential dangers and get a signed statement from all employees, men and women, that they understand the potential risk to an as yet unborn child of working with certain chemicals. Of course, the best course of all is to make the workplace as safe as possible.

MATERNITY LEAVE

Whether or not employers can force pregnant employees to take maternity leave is another difficult area for the courts. For example, in the case of airline stewardesses, one federal court ruled that the airline could force an employee to take maternity leave the moment she found out she was pregnant, while another federal court ruled that mandatory maternity leave for stewardesses could not begin until the twenty-eighth week of pregnancy (*Harriss, Burwell*). The only safe approach is to treat maternity just like any other temporary disability. When the pregnant employee can no longer do the work, she can be required to take leave under the company's temporary disability leave policy. For most employers, that temporary disability leave is going to meet the provisions of the federal Family and Medical Leave Act of 1993.

FEDERAL FAMILY AND MEDICAL LEAVE ACT OF 1993

Horror stories from people who lost their jobs because they had to take a few weeks off for temporary disability or to care for a sick child ultimately led to passage of the federal Family and Medical Leave Act of 1993. The act applies to employers, public or private, with fifty or more employees. Smaller employers that expect to grow and that already have some kind of temporary disability leave policy should consider modifying the policy to comply with this act to save confusion in the near future. The regulations for this act are contained in Publication 1419, available from the wage and hour division of the federal Labor Department (29 C.F.R. part 825). These regulations assume that employers large enough to be covered by the act already have employee handbooks and suggest that certain items should be covered in employee handbooks.

The act requires covered employers to grant up to twelve weeks of unpaid leave per year for the birth or adoption of a child; to care for a spouse, child, or parent with a serious health condition; or when the employee has a serious health condition. Employers must maintain any group health insurance coverage during the leave period, and must reinstate the employee in the same or an equivalent job when the leave is over. The act applies to an employee only if the employer employs at least fifty employees within a seventy-five mile radius of the worksite where the employee works. In other words, even an employee working for a large employer may not be covered if that employee is working out in a small field office. This means that employers might consider limiting the impact of the family and medical leave policy to those employees covered by the act. For employee morale purposes, however, most employers will not do that. Under the law, employees must have worked for the employer for at least twelve months and for at least 1,250 hours during the year preceding the start of the leave.

The act allows employees to take up to twelve weeks' leave during a twelve-month period, but it is up to the employer to decide when the twelve-month period will begin and end. Most employers will simply select the calendar year. The act allows employers who employ both the husband and wife to limit their total leave for the birth or adoption of a child to a total of twelve weeks. This would provide an incentive for married couples not to work for the same company so that they can have a total of twenty four weeks of leave between them. This combination rule applies only to the birth or adoption of a child, not to any other uses of the leave, including caring for a sick child. In that case, each employee could take up to twelve weeks of unpaid leave during the year.

The regulations allow employees to take leave in short spurts if it is for any purpose other than the birth or adoption of a child. An employer can require employees to take their leave all at once if it is to care for a newly born or adopted child. Employers may transfer employees who anticipate the need to take intermittent leave to another position that offers the same pay and benefits if that other position would make it easier for the employer to deal with the intermittent leave.

The act allows employers to dock the salaries of employees who are exempt from the wage and hour laws even though this would usually not be allowed under that law. Normally, docking the salaries of exempt employees for any absence of less than a day would violate the Fair Labor Standards Act, but the Family and Medical Leave Act specifically allows this. Of course, employers do not have to do this, and many won't if the leave is for less than a day. Employees are allowed to substitute any paid leave they have saved up, and employers are allowed to require employees to do just that. In other words, employers can require employees to use up their paid vacation and personal leave before taking unpaid family and medical leave.

The act requires employers to maintain any group health insurance coverage while the employee is on family and medical leave. If the employee usually pays part of the premium for this insurance, then the employer may require the employee to continue to do so. The regulations allow for a thirty-day grace period after the date the employee was supposed to pay. If the employee has not paid his or her share of the premiums at the end of that time, the employer may drop the employee from the policy.

When the leave is over, the employee must be returned to the same or an equivalent position. An equivalent position is one that has similar duties and terms and conditions of employment. The work must involve substantially similar duties and responsibilities and substantially equivalent skill, effort, responsibility, and authority. Simply having the same pay is not enough. The employee must be restored to the same level of benefits when he or she returns. If the employer has had a reduction in force or eliminated a shift and it affected the employee, then the employee will not have a right to return to work. The point is, the employee is to be treated just as if he or she had never left.

Special rules apply to "key" employees. A key employee is salaried and is among the highest-paid 10 percent of the employees employed within a seventy-five mile radius of the worksite. An employer may deny restoration to a key employee, but only if reinstating the employee would result in substantial and grievous economic injury to the operations of the employer. Employers must tell people that they are key employees before they begin the leave.

Of course, employers are required to post a notice telling employees about the provisions of the act and to explain the company policy in this regard in the employee handbook if there is an employee handbook. If there is no employee handbook, then employers must provide written guidance to an employee requesting leave. Employees must give thirty days' notice if the leave is foreseeable for the birth or adoption of a child or for planned medical treatment. If it is not practicable to give such notice, then notice must be given as soon as it is practicable. The regulations urge employees to work with their employers whenever possible to schedule leaves so that they will not unduly disrupt the employers' operations. Employers may require medical certification of the need for the leave from a health care provider. Employers may require employees to get a second medical opinion concerning the need for the leave at the employer's expense. Employers may require employees who have taken leave because of their own serious health condition to present a certificate from a health care provider that the employee is "fit for duty." Of course, employees must be told in advance that they will be expected to provide such a certificate. The following is one possible approach to placing a policy statement in the employee handbook.

Sample Employee Handbook Provision

The MNO Company is subject to the provisions of the federal Family and Medical Leave Act. This act allows employees to take up to twelve weeks of unpaid leave a year because of the birth or adoption of a child; because of the serious health condition of a child, parent, or spouse; or because of their own serious health condition. For the purposes of this policy, a year will be a calendar year. Only employees who have been employed for at least a year may take unpaid family and medical leave. Employees are asked to provide notice as soon as possible if unpaid leave will be required. Employees will be required to take any accumulated paid vacation leave and paid sick/personal leave before taking unpaid family and medical leave. Health insurance coverage will be continued through the leave period. Employees returning from family and medical leave will be returned to the same or an equivalent position unless a reduction in force or other layoff has eliminated their job.

STATE LAWS

At least eighteen states also have family and medical leave acts, and the provisions of these state laws are different from those of the federal law. Some of these state laws apply to smaller employers. The Minnesota family and medical leave act, for example, applies to employers with twenty-one or more employees. Most state laws apply to employers with either fifty or one hundred employees.

MARITAL STATUS DISCRIMINATION

There is no federal law prohibiting discrimination based on marital status, but many states have such a law. Employers in those states may not hire or fire people because they are married. The difficult question is whether or not these laws apply to policies that prevent people who are married to each other from working for the same employer. In some states, such as New Jersey, New York, and Michigan, the courts have ruled that these laws do not prohibit such nepotism policies. Courts in other states, such as Hawaii, Washington, Minnesota, and Montana, have ruled that they do. Any employer who wishes to prevent anyone who is married to an employee from coming to work should consult an attorney before implementing such a policy. Generally, policies that prohibit a person from supervising his or her spouse or relative are not going to run afoul of the law.

States that Outlaw Marital Status Discrimination

Alaska	District of	Michigan	New York
California	Columbia	Minnesota	North Dakota
Colorado	Florida	Montana	Oregon
Connecticut	Hawaii	Nebraska	Washington
Delaware	Illinois	New Hampshire	Wisconsin
	Maryland	New Jersey	

SAMPLE EMPLOYEE HANDBOOK PROVISION

The MNO Company does not prevent people who are related to each other or married to each other from working here. However, no one may directly supervise his or her spouse or relative. If a supervisor and a subordinate get married, one of them must resign if there is no reasonable way to transfer one of the two to a different division. If they cannot decide between them which will go, then the lower-paid employee will be fired.

CONCLUSION

In many countries in Europe, the benefits provided to working mothers under the law far exceed those mandated by American law. The average European working woman expects to receive paid maternity leave lasting several months and paid child care when she returns to work. Nothing like that is yet available in the United States for most workers. Federal and state laws have been passed to help make it easier for working people to care for their families. Since the burden of family usually rests more heavily on women, these laws have generally been seen as an effort to provide working women, particularly working mothers, with some protection. While some employers object to laws such as the federal Family and Medical Leave Act, this is an insignificant provision when compared with what companies in many countries around the world are expected to provide.

Chapter 15

Privacy

Employee privacy is one of the fastest-growing areas of legal dispute between employers and employees. More lawsuits are being filed about more issues with each passing day. Yet most of this litigation could be avoided by employers. This is one area where a few common sense actions and a few well-written employee handbook provisions can both clear up confusion and provide a real defense against employee lawsuits. To understand why requires a step back into history.

THE BEGINNINGS OF COMMON-LAW PRIVACY

Until the end of the nineteenth century, there really was no such thing as a lawsuit for privacy invasion in the United States. There were lawsuits for trespass on private property and for assault, but not for the kinds of privacy invasions for which lawsuits are routine today under the American legal system. This all began to change in 1890 with the publication of an article by Louis D. Brandeis (who would go on to become a Supreme Court justice) and Samuel Warren, "The Right to Privacy," in the *Harvard Law Review*. The main motivation for the writing of this article was their feeling that the press was going too far in prying into the private lives of prominent people. Samuel Warren had been the target of this kind of prying.

Over the decades that followed the publication of this law review article, the courts developed four basic kinds of common-law privacy rights. They are called common-law privacy rights because they have generally been discovered by judges, rather than being spelled out by legislatures. These privacy rights usually control the relationships between private people, absent any agreement between those private people concerning what their relationship will be. Invasion of privacy became a kind of tort, meaning an injury that the law will allow people to sue to recover damages for.

The first type is the right of any individual to commercially exploit his or her own name or likeness for commercial purposes. The second type is the right to keep potentially embarrassing facts secret. The third type is the right to keep facts that might be misunderstood and lead someone to get the wrong impression of the person secret. The courts say that such facts would put the person in a "false light" and consider this a first cousin to a defamation lawsuit. The fourth is the right to be free from unwanted invasions of physical privacy, such as being spied on or searched.

It is important to realize that as far as a relationship between private individuals is concerned, a person may consent to all four of these types of privacy invasions. However, the law says that absent an agreement between the parties, someone may sue for these kinds of activities. This is where a well-written employee handbook can be invaluable. Employers should be able to gain their employees' consent to privacy invasions with well-written employee handbook provisions that point out the kinds of privacy invasions that might occur and state that anyone coming to work for that employer understands and consents to these privacy invasions. We will explore this idea as we discuss each type of privacy invasion.

COMMERCIAL EXPLOITATION OF NAME AND LIKENESS

In the course of American legal history, the first area in which the judges had sympathy for people who had experienced an invasion of privacy was the commercial exploitation of a person's name and picture. Some people refer to this as the "right of publicity" because it is the legal right to exploit your own name and picture for publicity purposes. At the beginning of the twentieth century, a young woman named Roberson found her picture on boxes of flour. (Actually, it was more of a silhouette.) She sued and took her case to the highest court in New York, only to be told that New York common law did not recognize this as something people could sue for (*Roberson*). This decision was handed down in 1902, and in 1903 the New York legislature passed a statute barring the "unauthorized use of the name or picture of any person for the purposes of trade" and allowing the injured person to sue for damages and receive a court order stopping any further unauthorized use of his or her name or picture. Other state supreme courts did not wait for their legislatures to act. For example, in 1905 the Supreme Court of Georgia ruled that a man who found his name being used to advertise an insurance company could sue for invasion of privacy, even without a statute (*Pavesich*). Other state supreme courts followed suit.

What does this have to do with the relationship between employers and employees? Take the *Staruski* case. Ms. Staruski woke up one morning to find her name and picture in the local newspaper. It had been included in a advertisement by her employer, the Continental Telephone Company, without her knowledge or permission. She sued and took her case to the Vermont Supreme Court, which ruled that her right to privacy had been violated. The court agreed that she had not agreed to have her privacy invaded in this way simply by coming to work for the Continental Telephone Company. Of course, when she came to work, or at some later time, the company could have obtained her permission to use her name and picture in advertisements. It could have had her sign a consent form. Better yet, it could have had her sign a consent form for the particular advertisement, and it could have included a provision in the employee handbook (handbooks are contracts in Vermont) stating that anyone coming to work for the company agreed to have his or her name and picture used in company advertisements.

Sample Employee Handbook Provision

Here at the MNO Company we are constantly taking pictures and making commercials of various kinds. Anyone coming to work for us consents, by accepting the job, to participate in these commercials and agrees that the MNO Company may use his or her name and picture for the purposes of commercial advertisement. We consider making commercial advertisements for the company to be part of everyone's job description, and part of everyone's pay is compensation for this activity. While in some cases we may undertake to pay employees who must spend a great deal of time in this activity a special bonus, whether or not we do so is strictly up to the discretion of the MNO Company. Anyone coming to work for the MNO Company agrees to allow the company to continue to use his or her name and picture for commercial purposes even after he or she leaves the company if such pictures were taken or advertisements constructed while the person was employed by the MNO Company.

Publication of Embarrassing Facts

The second area of American privacy law is concerned with the revelation of embarrassing, but perfectly true, facts. This is what Louis Brandeis and Samuel Warren were most concerned about when they published their famous article in the *Harvard Law Review* in 1890. Throughout the twentieth century, celebrities of various kinds have tried to stop the press from publicizing various embarrassing facts about their lives. The problem for them is that at the same time the courts in the United States were expanding the concept of the right to privacy, they were also expanding the protection of the rights of freedom of speech and freedom of the press, and in most cases these rights took precedence over the right of celebrities to keep embarrassing facts out of the press. The most difficult cases involved people who found themselves in the limelight through no fault of their own. For example, in the *Florida Star* case, a woman sued a newspaper for revealing that she had been the victim of a rape. Revealing this kind of information was a violation of a specific Florida statute. The U.S. Supreme Court overturned the verdict, ruling that the right of a free press included the right to reveal this kind of information, even if it embarrassed the person involved.

This can be a problem for employers because they may find themselves in possession of a wide variety of embarrassing facts about their employees, some of which get revealed for one reason or another. Take the case of Betty Dee Young (*Young*). While she was working for the Grand Gulf Nuclear Power Station in Mississippi, she left work to have a partial hysterectomy and tried to keep the reason for her hospital visit a secret. She told her supervisor about it when requesting leave, but asked that it be kept private. The supervisor revealed the reason for her stay in the hospital after other employees expressed concern that she might be suffering from radiation poisoning. In order to alleviate their fears, the supervisor explained that Betty Dee Young had gone to the hospital for a hysterectomy and that there was no reason to think that her problems were in any way job-related. The Mississippi Supreme Court ruled that people such as Betty Dee Young had a right to expect that this kind of private information would be kept private. However, the court also ruled that employers have a right to reveal this kind of information when reasonably necessary, and the Court felt that it was reasonably necessary in this case.

Technically, the Mississippi Supreme Court ruled that an employer in this situation has a conditional privilege to reveal information in circumstances where it seems reasonable to do so. This is a common idea in the law: that in some situations some people are given the right, the "privilege," to violate the common law because of some higher good that might be served. In this case, the court felt that the higher good of furthering communication between an employer and its employees overrode Ms. Young's right to keep this kind of information confidential.

Today much of this is controlled by the Americans with Disabilities Act and other state and federal statutes that require that medical information be kept confidential. The Americans with Disabilities Act requires employers to keep information about the disability confidential, except that (1) supervisors and managers may be informed regarding restrictions on work and possible accommodation, (2) first aid and safety personnel may be informed to the extent appropriate, and (3) government officials investigating compliance with the law may be informed.

In writing a provision for the employee handbook, employers face a dilemma. On the one hand, the attorney would like a straightforward statement that the employer reserves the right to reveal any information it has about the employee. On the other hand, the management consultant points out the possible morale problems such a statement would cause if it were really included in the employee handbook. The management consultant would like assurances from the employer that the company will make an effort not to reveal private information unless there is a need to do so. One solution to this dilemma is not to put anything at all about this subject in the handbook. Another option is to write a provision that tries to satisfy the concerns of both the attorney and the management consultant.

SAMPLE EMPLOYEE HANDBOOK PROVISION

While you are employed at the MNO Company, you may have reason to provide confidential personal information about yourself to your supervisor, medical personnel, or the Human Resources Department. All supervisors, managers, and employees are expected to keep such information confidential and reveal it only to those who need to know it. At the same time, it is important for all employees to realize that this kind of information must be revealed in some circumstances and will be revealed in situations in which some employees will feel it should not have been revealed. By coming to work for the MNO Company, you agree to leave the question of when personal information known by those in the company will be revealed to others in the company and to whom it will be revealed to the discretion of the company and its managers and employees. The MNO Company expects all of its managers and employees to use good judgment in this regard. Generally, confidential information concerning medical issues and disabilities should be revealed only to supervisors and others who must know in order to work effectively with the person involved or to accommodate a disability, to emergency and medical personnel who may be called upon to provide emergency treatment, and to government officials investigating our compliance with law.

FALSE LIGHT PRIVACY INVASION AND DEFAMATION

The third area of privacy invasion is called "false light." This means that someone has revealed something about someone that is true but that puts the person in a false light, meaning that someone hearing the information is probably going to get the wrong impression of the person involved because of this information. The *Mendez* case illustrates the point. When Mr. Mendez was told to clean up a work area, he took home a small number of nails instead of throwing them away, which was the usual practice. His employer, the Diamond Shamrock Company, fired him and told everyone that he had been fired for theft of company property. While that was technically true, it certainly gave anyone hearing that story the wrong impression about Mr. Mendez. A Texas court ruled that Mr. Mendez could sue for false light invasion of privacy in this case.

Of course, most conflicts between employees and employers concerning the revelation of information involve suits for defamation of character. Generally, anyone who reveals facts about someone that are damaging to that person's reputation and are also untrue can be sued, even an employer talking about an employee or former employee. Courts do grant employers a conditional privilege to say defamatory things about their current and former employees, but only if they do so in a situation in which it was reasonable for the employer to be revealing the information. This usually means that employers may reveal potentially defamatory information only to people who need to know. For example, in one case an Exxon auditor accused an employee of stealing from the company in front of a restaurant full of people (*Exxon*). None of these people had a need to know about the possible theft. This turned out to be a false accusation, and Exxon ended up paying damages for defamation.

One case in particular shook up employers around the country when it was decided by the Minnesota Supreme Court in 1986 (*Equitable*). This case involved several employees of the Equitable Life Assurance Society who had been sent to Pittsburgh on a temporary assignment. When they left the St. Paul office, they were not told about the company's travel policies. They were each given a $1400 advance for travel expenses, and they spent all of it. When they returned to the St. Paul office, having done a good job, it was explained to them that the manager had not expected them to spend all the travel money. They were asked for the first time to account for their expenses, and they were ultimately fired when they could not do so to the satisfaction of their boss. The reason for their firing was listed as "gross insubordination." When these employees went looking for work, they were asked on job application forms why they had left their last job. When they put down that they had been fired for gross insubordination, they did not get the job. Ultimately these employees sued Equitable for defamation of character. Usually, before someone can be sued for defamation of character, the person claiming injury must prove that the defamer said something defamatory and "publicized" it to people who had no need to know. In this case the publicizing had been done by the employees themselves, so the company argued that it could not be held liable. The Minnesota Supreme Court ruled otherwise. The judges ruled that by telling this lie to the employees knowing that they would have to repeat it, the company had engaged in a kind of publication. The court called this a situation of "compelled self-publication."

This and similar cases have led more and more companies to stop listing any reason for discharge and to stop giving out any information to other people or companies except the title the person had while working at the company and the beginning and ending dates of employment. Others object that this is going too far, and that it makes life much more difficult for everyone. The only response to that is that one defamation lawsuit, even if you win, can ruin your whole day, not to mention your whole budget.

While people can generally consent to having torts committed on them, it is doubtful that they would agree in advance to being defamed. Also, one has to wonder what the impact on employee relations would be if a company said in the employee handbook that anyone coming to work for the company agreed to have his or her character defamed and not sue for defamation. At the same time, it has to be made clear to everyone that false light and defamation are very real problems and that the company is doing everything it can to avoid liability. The argument can then be made in court that anyone who made a defamatory statement violated a clear company policy, and therefore the company should not be held liable.

SAMPLE EMPLOYEE HANDBOOK PROVISION

Because of the problem of making potentially defamatory statements about current and former employees, it is the policy of the MNO Company not to give out any information about current or former employees except to government officials who are authorized to receive such information. Any manager or employee who is approached for information about any current or former employee should refer the matter to the human resources department.

SEARCHING EMPLOYEES

In more and more situations, employers are finding it necessary to search both their employees' lockers and desks at work and their purses, briefcases, and clothing. There are two issues involved in these cases. The first is whether or not the employee had a reasonable expectation of privacy when the search took place. The second is whether or not the employee knowingly consented to the search. A Texas case illustrates the first problem. When Ms. Trotti came to work for KMart, her employer told her that her locker at work was her private place (*Trotti*). She was told to bring her own lock from home and lock it up. The employer then searched her locker, and a Texas jury awarded her $100,000 in damages for invasion of privacy. This was, of course, completely avoidable. In a similar case involving the U.S. Mint, government officials searched the locker of an employee and found freshly minted quarters. When the employee objected to the search, the federal judge ruled that he had no expectation of privacy in his locker at work because the Mint regulations specifically stated that "no mint lockers in mint institutions shall be considered to be private lockers" (*Donato*). Because of that regulation, the court ruled, it was unreasonable for the employee to have an expectation of privacy in a locker at the U.S. Mint.

The lesson of these two cases is simple and obvious. Every company or government agency should have a provision in the employee handbook that deals with the issue of searching desks and lockers at work and makes it clear that the employer reserves the right to search them at any time. The more difficult issue is the extent to which an employer can reserve the right to search briefcases, purses, and clothing. Whether or not employers may search employees' automobiles when they are parked in company parking lots is also an issue. The first general rule is that employees may consent to these kinds of activities. The second general rule is that the expectation of privacy can be taken away with sufficient notice. Employers must weigh this against the morale problems that might be caused by trying to take away all expectations of privacy.

SAMPLE EMPLOYEE HANDBOOK PROVISION

The MNO Company engages in a significant amount of confidential research, both for itself and for the United States government. Also, the MNO Company has experienced a significant amount of theft over the last few years. Every employee coming to work at the MNO Company is on notice that anything inside a company facility is subject to search at any time for any reason or no reason. This means that all company property, such as desks and lockers, is subject to search at all times. It also means that the personal belongings of employees, such as purses and briefcases, are also subject to search, as is the clothing of employees. All automobiles on company property are also subject to search by the company at any time. Anyone entering or leaving an MNO facility is subject to inspection and search. We are a drug-free workplace, and we have a responsibility to maintain a drug-free atmosphere, which can be accomplished only by periodic searches. All employees are expected to cooperate with any manager or security guard who is conducting a search.

MAIL

As a general rule, employers are well within their rights to assume that all mail that arrives at their place of business is concerned with business. However, if mail is addressed to a particular person and says on the envelope that it is "personal" or "confidential," it should be assumed to be just that. This kind of mail should not be opened by anyone other than the person it is addressed to. At the same time, employers should inform employees in the employee handbook that they should not have personal mail delivered to the office and that they should expect that all mail arriving at the office may be opened by someone else.

SAMPLE EMPLOYEE HANDBOOK PROVISION

It is the policy of the MNO Company to assume that all mail arriving at an MNO facility is related to company business. All employees should know that any mail arriving at an MNO facility may be opened by someone other than the particular person it is addressed to. Employees are expected to receive personal or confidential mail at their homes, not at work.

SURVEILLANCE

As a general rule, employers have a right to observe their employees at the workplace and outside the workplace in any area open to the public. For example, in one case, an employee receiving workers' compensation payments reported that he was unable to return to work. The company then hired private detectives, who observed the employee engaging in activities such as mowing his yard and rototilling his garden. The employee sued for invasion of privacy, but the judges ruled that being observed in public was not an invasion of privacy (*McLain*).

The same rule generally applies to the use of undercover agents at work, such as spotters and shoppers (people that pretend to be shoppers in order to check up on salespeople). Employers are generally regarded as being within their rights in using other employees to observe their employees. However, a number of lawsuits are currently pending in this area that may change this. Also, some states have statutes that deal with this issue. For example, in California, before an employee can be disciplined or dismissed based on a shopper's report, the employee must be given a copy of the report and a chance to explain. Generally employers who wish to use spotters and shoppers will be on firmer legal ground if they make it clear to employees when they are hired that the company makes use of such people.

SAMPLE EMPLOYEE HANDBOOK PROVISION

The MNO Company prides itself on maintaining a good relationship with customers. In order to assure that all employees conduct themselves in an professional manner at all times, the MNO Company does use undercover agents and has employees or agents that pose as suppliers or customers from time to time. While some may be offended by this, it is the only way we can maintain our high standards of performance.

ELECTRONIC SURVEILLANCE

Electronic surveillance is becoming more and more common in the American workplace. Employers who wish to use electronic surveillance techniques need to be familiar with both the relevant federal and state statutes on the subject and will usually be better off if they are up-front with employees about the surveillance methods used. Also, because of the times in which we live, any company that does not make use of electronic surveillance might want to point that out to employees as well.

Title III of the federal Omnibus Crime Control and Safe Streets Act of 1968 outlawed wiretapping and bugging in most situations. It does allow an employer to listen in on its own phone lines if (1) the employee consents to the monitoring, (2) the employer is listening on a phone extension during the "ordinary course of business," or (3) the employer is a communications company checking the quality of the transmission. Some states have laws that outlaw even employers listening on an extension unless both parties to the conversation are aware that this is happening. On several occasions, organized labor has placed bills before Congress that would require anyone, including employers, to put an audible beep on any line that was being monitored to warn both the employee and the other person on the line. So far these have never gotten out of committee.

States with Electronic Surveillance Statutes

California	Illinois	New Jersey	Washington
Connecticut	Louisiana	Pennsylvania	West Virginia
Georgia	Maryland	Virginia	Wisconsin

Bugging is a different matter. Under federal law, one party to the conversation must consent to the bugging for it to be legal. Again, some states require both parties to consent before a conversation may be transmitted or recorded by electronic means. The advantage of having a clear policy is illustrated by a case from Illinois (*Cebula*). A supervisor secretly taped an exit interview without the employee's consent, which is a violation of the Illinois Eavesdropping Act. The employee sued the supervisor and the company. The judge ruled that because it was not company policy to engage in bugging, the company was not liable, but the employee could sue the supervisor personally for this invasion of privacy. Generally, the best way to make it clear that bugging is a violation of company policy is to place a statement to that effect in the employee handbook.

Video cameras are becoming more and more common as a way to keep an eye on a large facility. We are all familiar with the security guard station with half a dozen television monitors displayed on a console. At the same time, the fact that some areas of the workplace are under video surveillance should be disclosed to the employees. Also, such cameras should be kept out of private areas, such as restrooms and locker rooms.

Another area of concern to employees is the ever more common use of computers to check employee performance. Again, this is more of a morale problem than a legal problem at present, but legislation is pending in several state legislatures and in Congress that might change that. Most morale and legal problems can be avoided if employees are told how computers are being used to monitor them. If that is not being done, employers should dispel rumors and say that it is not being done. Companies with electronic mail facilities should explain to employees if their electronic mail is being monitored or relieve their fears if it is not.

SAMPLE EMPLOYEE HANDBOOK PROVISION

In an effort to maintain quality in relationships with both suppliers and customers, the MNO Company routinely monitors all phone conversations on company phone lines. An employee who wishes to be sure that a personal conversation is private should make use of one of the pay phones located in

---

several areas. The MNO Company also uses video surveillance cameras to enhance the effectiveness of our security personnel. The cameras are in plain sight for everyone to see. There are no hidden cameras, and there are no cameras in restrooms. The MNO Company does not routinely monitor the electronic mail network but reserves the right to do so. The MNO Company does not use bugs or hidden microphones. If any employee believes he or she has been electronically bugged or finds what he or she believes might be a hidden microphone, the employee should report this immediately to security.

CONCLUSION

The area of privacy invasion is difficult and sensitive. In no other area is it as important to have up-to-date information about the relevant federal and state laws. This is particularly true when electronic surveillance or undercover agents will be used. However, in no other area are employers in as good a position to protect themselves than through the use of well written and legally reviewed employee handbook provisions. Employee morale will be improved by telling employees exactly what their privacy rights are at work, and legal problems will usually be avoided at the same time.

Chapter 16

Free Speech and Whistle-Blowers

The right of free speech is generally considered to be the most important and fundamental right in the U.S. Bill of Rights. It guarantees both that citizens may discuss political issues without fear of reprisal and that people may say what they like about their thoughts and beliefs without government interference. The extent to which it protects the right of employees to say what they wish without being fired is a very different matter.

FREE SPEECH RIGHTS FOR PUBLIC EMPLOYEES

The story of protecting the right of employees to speak out has to begin with the free speech rights of public employees. The First Amendment to the U.S. Constitution protects the right of free speech. In a series of decisions beginning in 1968 the U.S. Supreme Court ruled that this provision protects all government employees from being discharged or disciplined because they exercised their right of free speech under the Constitution. The first case to come to this conclusion was *Pickering*. This case involved a teacher who sent a letter to the local newspaper that was critical of the school board that ran her school district. She was dismissed. The Supreme Court ruled that the purpose of the right of free speech is to protect the right of citizens to make informed judgments when they vote and the right of government officials to act in an informed way. The Court ruled that this teacher must be reinstated to protect these rights. By protecting the teacher's right to speak, the Court was protecting the right of other citizens to hear what she had to say about important issues of public concern.

Following this decision, some public administrators felt that public employees were using this right in an attempt to keep their jobs. The scenario goes like this: A public employee feels that he or she is about to be fired. In anticipation of this action, the employee goes to the local newspaper and criticizes the way his or her bosses, usually elected officials, are running their operation. Then if the employee is fired, it looks like retaliation for this exercise of the right of free speech. In 1977 the Supreme Court dealt with this problem in the *Mt. Healthy* case. In this case, a teacher called the local radio station to criticize the school district's dress code and found herself out on the street soon afterward. The school district argued that it had good reasons to fire her, including fighting with other teachers and using obscene gestures with students. The Supreme Court ruled that in these free speech cases, the government employee first had the burden of proving that the discharge was motivated by a desire to retaliate against him or her for exercising the right of free speech. Then the employer may demonstrate that it had good reason to fire the employee absent the exercise of free speech rights. Then the employee may come back and try to demonstrate to the satisfaction of the jury that these so-called good reasons are just a pretext, a trumped-up excuse for wrongfully firing the employee. Ultimately, it will be up to the jury to decide who they believe, the boss or the employee.

However, over the years, the Supreme Court has made it clear that this right to speak out does not protect all kinds of speech. The Constitution was not intended to prevent government employers from discharging public employees whenever the employees speak. Rather, it was intended to protect government employees only when they speak out on what the Court has come to call "matters of public concern." For example, in one 1983 decision, *Connick*, an assistant district attorney circulated a questionnaire around the office asking his coworkers' opinions on various office policies, such as the transfer policy and the lack of an employee grievance committee. His boss, the district attorney, fired him for insubordination, and the case went all the way to the U.S. Supreme Court. The Court ruled that these particular actions were simply not protected by the First Amendment. The Court felt that the issues discussed in this questionnaire were relevant to the running of the office, but were not of interest to the general public. In other words, unless the discussion is about matters of public concern, the speech is not protected by the First Amendment.

What if the speech is about a matter of public concern but also causes disruption at work? That was the issue in a 1972 case decided by the federal Seventh Circuit Court of Appeals (*Donahue*). This case involved a chaplain at a government mental hospital who was critical of the hospital's procedures in an interview with a reporter from the local newspaper. The Court said that even if the government employee is speaking out on matters of public concern, a government employer would be free to discharge him or her if the speech caused harm at the workplace. Specifically, the judges said that the discharge would be reasonable if the speech (1) interfered with harmony among coworkers, (2) interfered with the need for confidentiality, (3) interfered with the employee's ability to perform his or her duties, (4) was totally untrue, which would suggest that the employee was incompetent, or (5) interfered with a close working relationship between the employee and his or her supervisor in a situation that called for personal loyalty. None of these applied in this case, so the chaplain got his job back.

FREE SPEECH RIGHTS FOR PRIVATE EMPLOYEES

This concept becomes relevant to private employers because more and more courts are ruling that private employees have a similar right of free speech. More and more state supreme courts have ruled that private employers may not fire their employees for reasons that violate public policy. This is called common-law wrongful discharge. In these cases, the state supreme court is saying that even though the legislature has not gotten around to passing a statute on this subject, it simply cannot stand by and allow employees to be discharged for some outrageous reason. In 1988 a court ruled that it was a violation of New Jersey public policy for a private employer to fire an employee for speaking out on an issue of public concern (*Zamboni*).

In 1983 the Connecticut legislature did get around to passing a statute on this subject. The exact language of this statute is of interest because courts in other states might look to this statute for guidance. The Connecticut law says:

> Any employer including the state and any instrumentality or political subdivision thereof, who subjects any employee to discipline or discharge on account of the exercise of such employee of rights guaranteed by the first amendment of the United States Constitution or section 3, 4, and 14 article first of the constitution of the state, provided such activity does not substantially or materially interfere with the employee's bona fide job performance or the working relationship between the employee and the employer, shall be liable to such employee for damages caused by such discipline or discharge, including the costs of any such action for damages. If the court determines that such action was brought without substantial justification, the court may award costs and reasonable attorney's fees to the employer.

While this statute recognizes that both public and private employees have a right of free speech that should not be infringed, it also provides a significant benefit to employers by allowing the judge to award them money if an employee brings a free speech lawsuit for frivolous reasons. In states that have not passed such a statute, employers are just as potentially liable for damages, but generally will not be allowed to ask for their attorney's fees if a frivolous lawsuit has been filed.

Should employers have anything in the employee handbook about this? That is a difficult question. There are a number of factors to consider, not the least of which is what the courts in your particular state have ruled in this area. In most states in which the courts and the legislature have not spoken on this issue, silence will probably be the best policy. After all, employers should avoid giving employees rights in the employee handbook that they would not otherwise have under statutes and court decisions. On the other hand, if the legislature or the courts have spoken, then a handbook provision can provide some defense by demonstrating that company policy was violated if an employee who exercised his or her right of free speech was in fact retaliated against. Also, the handbook provision would emphasize the legitimate reasons why any employer, public or private, can limit the free speech rights of its employees. This policy can also emphasize that anything an employee says might be construed as an official statement of the company or public entity. Any employer has a right to control what is said to the general public on its behalf.

SAMPLE EMPLOYEE HANDBOOK PROVISION

We at the MNO Company recognize that our employees have the right to speak out on issues of concern to the general public. At the same time, we expect our employees to recognize that some statements may cause disharmony among coworkers or interfere with the employee's ability to perform his or her duties. We ask employees who are planning to make a public statement that might have these negative effects to discuss their statement with the director of human resources before making it. Also, whenever an employee of the MNO Company makes a public statement, it is possible that those hearing it might believe this statement to be a statement of the MNO Company's official position on the topic under discussion. We expect all employees to either clear such statements with the appropriate company official or make it clear that they are not speaking for the company. We also expect that employees making statements concerning the activities or policies of the MNO Company will check their facts with the appropriate company official before making a statement that might turn out to be false and place the company in a bad light. All of us at the MNO Company recognize that our success depends on our maintaining our positive image with the general public, and we hope that our employees will help us to continue to enhance that image whenever possible.

WHISTLE-BLOWERS

Whistle-blowers are employees who are speaking out about a particular subject: the illegal or corrupt activities of their employer. Whistle-blowers are protected by both statutes and court decisions in many situations. First, there are numerous federal statutes that protect whistle-blowers. The federal civil service laws protect federal employees from being discharged for revealing violations of law or mismanagement unless national security is involved. There is a long list of federal statutes protecting public and private employees who blow the whistle on everything from civil rights violations to safety violations to pollution violations. As a general rule, employees who take a complaint to the appropriate federal agency are going to be protected from retaliation by their employer. These laws also protect union members who bring a complaint before the National Labor Relations Board, truck drivers who complain about truck safety, and miners who complain about mine safety.

Some Federal Laws that Protect Whistle-Blowers

Asbestos School Hazard Detection and Control Act. Governments and agencies that receive assistance under the act may not retaliate against an employee who reveals to the public any information concerning asbestos problems in school buildings.

Clean Air Act. Retaliating against employees who commence, testify, assist, or participate in any proceeding under the act is prohibited.

Energy Reorganization Act. Retaliating against employees who commence or assist in a proceeding under this Act or the Atomic Energy Act of 1954 is prohibited.

False Claims Act. Retaliating against employees of federal contractors who reveal fraudulent acts against the federal government is prohibited.

International Safe Containers Act. Retaliating against employees who report unsafe containers to the Secretary of Transportation is prohibited.

Mine Safety and Health Act. Retaliating against employees who report safety violations or refuse to work in a mine they reasonably believe to be unsafe is prohibited.

Occupational Safety and Health Act. Retaliating against employees who report safety violations to the Occupational Safety and Health Administration is prohibited.

Railroad Safety Act. Retaliating against employees who report safety violations or refuse to work on railroads they reasonably believe to be unsafe is prohibited.

Surface Transportation Assistance Act of 1982. Retaliating against employees of interstate trucking companies for refusing to operate an unsafe truck or making complaints about unsafe trucks is prohibited.

On top of these numerous federal laws are a variety of state laws. In many cases these state laws duplicate federal laws and protect workers who bring complaints about such things as civil rights, safety or pollution violations to the appropriate state agency. Also, a large number of state supreme courts have ruled that employees who bring a violation of the law to the attention of the appropriate government official may not be fired for doing so, even if there is nothing about this issue in the particular statute in question. Some courts say that implied in the statute is the desire of the legislature to protect such people. Other courts say that this is a type of common-law wrongful discharge, an area where the courts will protect people simply because it is good public policy to do so.

Also, a majority of states have also passed a general whistle-blower protection statute. It is important for employers to realize that most of these laws were passed to protect employers, not employees, despite all the statements by politicians to the contrary. To see why this is so, we must look at what happens when this issue is dealt with simply by the common-law decisions of judges. As long as that is the case, almost any statement concerning wrongdoing will be covered by the concept of common-law wrongful discharge. The person making the statement will have years after the event that led to the whistle-blowing incident to file a lawsuit. This allows employees who become disgruntled many months or even years after they observe a legal violation to then come forward and blow the whistle. Also, if an employee brings a frivolous suit, there is usually no protection for the employer.

States with Whistle-Blower Protection Statutes

Alaska	Illinois	Missouri	Pennsylvania
Arizona	Indiana	Montana	Rhode Island
California	Iowa	Nebraska	South Carolina
Colorado	Kansas	Nevada	Tennessee
Connecticut	Kentucky	New Hampshire	Texas
Delaware	Louisiana	New Jersey	Utah
District of	Maine	New York	Washington
Columbia	Maryland	North Carolina	West Virginia
Florida	Michigan	Ohio	Wisconsin
Hawaii	Minnesota	Oregon	

To see how a state whistle-blower statute can help, we have only to look at the best whistle-blower statute ever written, as far as employers are concerned, the New York Whistleblower Act (Labor Code Section 740). The New York law protects people who blow the whistle on an activity that presents "a substantial and specific danger to the public health and safety." Therefore, the New York courts have ruled that it does not protect employees who blow the whistle on things that do not involve a substantial and specific danger to the public health and safety, such as defrauding the government through fraudulent billing schemes (*Remba*). Also, the New York statute allows the judge to award attorney's fees to the employer if the employee does not really have a complaint covered by the statute.

Of course, not all state whistle-blower statutes are as kind to employers as New York's law. In New Jersey, employees are protected if they reasonably believe that the employer's policy, practice, or conduct is in violation of a state law, rule, or regulation. This is a very broad definition that would include almost every incident we can reasonably think of. Often, these state statutes also protect people who refuse to violate the law. For example, the New Jersey statute protects people who refuse to participate in any activity, policy, or practice that they reasonably believe is unlawful, fraudulent, criminal, or incompatible with a clear mandate of public policy concerning the public health, safety, or welfare.

Many of these state whistle-blower statutes require the person to blow the whistle in a particular way or to a particular person within a short period of time in order to be covered by their provisions. Many require that the complaint be made to a public agency, the attorney general, or some other specific government official. Some of these laws protect employees only if they blow the whistle in a very short period of time—sixty days in Wisconsin; ninety days in Michigan or Texas.

For employers, all of this can be very embarrassing if it turns out that someone in the company was violating the law without the knowledge or consent of upper management. The company ends up with the worst of all possible worlds:

The company has to pay a fine for violating the law, pay damages to the discharged whistle-blowing employee, and face a storm of negative publicity.

A relatively new area of whistle-blowing activity involves reporting fraud against the government. This is particularly true if an employee or anyone else learns of fraud against the federal government because of laws passed to protect people who report such fraud. The people who find and report fraud are generally protected from retaliation and can receive a reward for reporting the fraud that can run into the millions of dollars.

If a company wishes to avoid some of this, it can try to do so with a good policy statement in the employee handbook. Again, deciding whether or not to include a statement on this issue is difficult, and the decision should be made only after consultation with an attorney familiar with the legal circumstances in the particular state. There are potential negative consequences, such as possibly giving employees rights that they would not otherwise have. On the other hand, anything a company can do to express its intention to obey the law and to separate itself from supervisors or employees who violate the law without the knowledge or consent of upper management can help to minimize or even eliminate some legal liability.

SAMPLE EMPLOYEE HANDBOOK PROVISION

The MNO Company is involved in a number of areas where the company is required to obey complex legal provisions. The MNO Company is a law-abiding citizen, and every employee at every level is instructed to obey the law at all times. Any employee who believes that the MNO Company is not obeying the law should bring that concern to the appropriate manager or, if in doubt, to the director of human resources. While employees have the right to take their concerns to government officials, the MNO Company hopes that these issues can be solved internally before it is necessary to bring in government law enforcement officials. If a legal violation can be dealt with internally, that will save time and money and help prevent negative publicity.

CONCLUSION

More and more both courts and legislatures are taking steps to protect the free speech rights of both public and private employees. In more and more statutes, the rights of whistle-blowers are discussed and protected. Any employer in the United States has to realize that retaliation against a whistle-blowing employee will bring at the least negative publicity and at the most a large damage award. At the same time, every employer should try to take steps to encourage employees to make their complaints to someone inside the company rather than to government officials or the press.

Chapter 17

Wrongful Discharge and Lifestyle Issues

A century ago there was no such thing as wrongful discharge in the United States. Employers could fire employees for any reason, or for no reason at all. Employees were routinely fired because they belonged to a labor union or because they were over fifty years old. It is obvious to everyone that things are very different today. Yet the average American employer still has much more freedom to discharge employees than the average European employer. Also, the average American employer has much more freedom to control the workplace than the average European employer. While in many countries employers must prove that they have "good cause" before employees may be discharged, in the United States the burden of proving that the discharge was motivated by an illegal reason is generally on the employee. Given that the person with the burden of proof usually loses, this is a significant difference. Montana is the one exception to this rule, with a statute that requires employers to declare a probationary period and fire employees only for good cause when the probationary period is over.

COMMON-LAW WRONGFUL DISCHARGE

Employers, both public and private, tend to focus only on federal and state statutes that deal with hiring and firing. In most states, there is another set of rules that have been developed by the courts to deal with situations that are not covered by the statutes. These rules say that in some cases employees may sue for wrongful discharge even though no statute has been violated. How and why courts began to develop the idea of common-law wrongful discharge is best illustrated by looking at the first wrongful discharge decision, handed down in California in 1959. The case involved a suit by Mr. *Petermann*, who was an official of the Teamsters Union in California. His supervisors at the Teamsters Union ordered him to lie to a committee of the state legislature. When he refused to commit perjury, they fired him, and he sued. The California court ruled that it was clearly a violation of public policy to allow an employer to discharge an employee for refusing to commit a crime.

Over the years, more and more state supreme courts agreed with the California courts that some reasons for firing an employee, even a private employee who is working without a contract, are simply so terrible that the employee should be allowed to sue in order to stop this kind of practice. The two major areas of common-law wrongful discharge involve employees who were fired because they refused to commit an illegal act and those who were fired because they reported illegal conduct to government authorities. By the 1990s, most state supreme courts had accepted the doctrine of common-law wrongful discharge, and many state legislatures had reacted by passing whistle-blower protection laws that covered both whistle-blowers and those who refused to commit illegal acts. In most states employers were better off having a statute that spelled out exactly what kinds of actions and statements were covered by the law and what kind of procedure the employee had to follow in order to be protected by the law.

Other kinds of conduct have also come to be protected by this concept. For example, many state supreme courts have ruled that employees may not be discharged because they exercised a legal right or performed a legal duty. By exercising a legal right, the courts mean doing things like filing for workers' compensation or filing a complaint under a state or federal law. While most state and federal laws that deal with the employment relationship already protect employees who file complaints, the courts have essentially ruled that even if this is not specifically spelled out in the statute, it will be assumed that the legislature intended to protect such people. The courts say that it is against public policy to allow someone filing a complaint to be discharged. This also applies to employees who are fulfilling a legal duty, such as performing jury duty or testifying when ordered to do so by a court. Again, while many states have statutes that protect employees from discharge in these circumstances, in those that do not, the courts have moved to provide protection for them.

This idea that employees may not be discharged for reasons that violate public policy may soon be used to extend the protection of various civil rights statutes to employers that are too small to be covered under the statute. Courts may rule that even though the legislature or Congress chose to exempt small employ-

States with Supreme Courts that Have Accepted the Concept of Common-Law Wrongful Discharge

Alaska	Illinois	New Hampshire	Tennessee
Arizona	Indiana	New Jersey	Texas
Arkansas	Iowa	New Mexico	Utah
California	Kansas	North Carolina	Vermont
Colorado	Kentucky	North Dakota	Virginia
Connecticut	Maryland	Ohio	Washington
District of	Massachusetts	Oklahoma	West Virginia
Columbia	Minnesota	Oregon	Wisconsin
Hawaii	Nebraska	Pennsylvania	Wyoming
Idaho	Nevada	South Carolina	

ers, firing someone for his or her race, sex, or other protected characteristic is a clear violation of public policy and therefore extends the idea of common-law wrongful discharge to these small employers using this legal concept. California courts are already moving in this direction (*Rojo*).

So far, these courts have ruled that employers may not discharge employees for a "bad" reason and have found the definition of "bad" in statutes and constitutional provisions that express public policy. The time may be fast approaching when employees will be protected by both court decisions and statutes from being fired for a stupid reason or for a reason unrelated to the job. That brings us to the next issue, discharge for lifestyle.

LIFESTYLE AND OFF-DUTY ISSUES

There was a time in the United States when employers felt perfectly justified in knowing about and interfering in the private lives of their workers. After all, the workers lived in a company house, bought groceries at a company store, and received medical treatment in a company clinic. Many employers expected their employees to attend church and to live what the employer considered to be a normal life. Civil rights statutes began to prevent employers from doing this when they outlawed things such as religious discrimination. Over the years, examples of outrageous conduct on the part of some employers led some state legislatures to pass statutes to protect employees from being discharged for things that had nothing to do with work. For example, by the mid-1990s, a majority of states had statutes that protected the right of people to smoke tobacco and prohibited their being discharged for this reason. Kentucky even amended the state civil rights act to add smokers to the list of people protected by its provisions.

Some states passed more general laws. For example, Nevada law makes it unlawful to discharge an employee because he or she uses any lawful product off the employer's premises. This would, of course, protect smokers, drinkers, and everyone else who uses a legal product away from work. Some states, such as Colorado and North Dakota, have gone further, with statutes that make it illegal to fire an employee because that employee participated in any lawful activity off the employer's premises during nonworking hours.

Sexual activity and dating are one area of off-duty behavior in which some employers have gotten into trouble trying to control the actions of their employees. The most famous case is *Rulon-Miller v. IBM*. Ms. Rulon-Miller began dating a coworker named Blum when they both worked at IBM. Blum then left IBM to go to work for a competitor. Several years later, IBM executives decided that Ms. Rulon-Miller should stop dating Mr. Blum because they felt that this could constitute a conflict of interest. When Ms. Rulon-Miller refused to stop dating Mr. Blum, she was fired. She sued for wrongful discharge and intentional infliction of emotional distress and received $300,000 in damages.

This case is of particular interest to us because the case turned on the court's interpretation of IBM's employee handbook and personnel policies. IBM had a policy prohibiting employees from being involved in conflicts of interest, but this policy did not discuss socializing or entering into personal relationships with the competition's employees. Also, IBM policy specifically stated that the company would not interfere in an employee's private life unless that private life "reduced his ability to perform regular job assignments, interfered with the job performance of other employees, or . . . affected the reputation of the company in a major way." The court also pointed to a memo that had been signed by a former company chairman and distributed to all the employees that said that IBM's "first basic belief is respect for the individual, and the essence of this belief is a strict regard for his right to personal privacy." In other words, IBM was tripped up by its own employee policies.

The court ruled that these IBM policies constituted a contract between IBM and its employees in which IBM promised not to interfere with the private lives of its employees, including their personal relationships. It is not clear how the courts might have ruled in this case if there had been no policies and no memo from the chairman.

More and more courts are using the constitutional right to privacy found in the U.S. and state constitutions to protect the right of public employees to engage in any lawful activity outside of work. For example, when one school district fired an unwed and pregnant schoolteacher, a federal judge ordered her reinstated. The judge felt that the woman's right to have a child outside of marriage was greater than the school district's right to protect schoolchildren from the sight of an unmarried pregnant schoolteacher (*Ponton*). In another case, a federal judge refused to allow a schoolteacher to be fired simply because she allowed a man to stay overnight in her apartment (*Fisher*). The extent to which a more general right to privacy might protect private employees discharged for similar reasons remains to be seen. At the same time, most private employers would not have cared about these kinds of incidents. The school districts cared because of their special role in society.

Court decisions and statutes make it more and more difficult for employers to write policies that both are legal and protect the legitimate interests of the employer. Two standard policies should be reevaluated: policies limiting outside employment and policies attempting to control conflicts of interest.

Outside Employment

Many companies have policies that either forbid or limit outside employment. On the one hand, when hiring a full-time employee, employers feel justified in expecting that when he or she is not at work, he or she will be resting and getting ready to come back to work refreshed the next day. On the other hand, some employees find it necessary to hold down an extra job in order to make ends meet, and employers would not want to deprive themselves of a good employee who could not live on what the company was able to pay. Statutes such as Colorado's make these policies problematic. The Colorado statute says that employers may not discharge employees who engage in lawful activities during nonworking hours, and having a job would usually qualify as a lawful activity.

Instead of outlawing all outside employment, employers should consider a policy that is more flexible and instead makes it clear to employees that the employer expects, and has every right to expect, that employees will come to work rested and refreshed and not drag in after working many hours at another job. Also, employers have a legitimate interest in knowing where their employees are in case they must contact them.

SAMPLE EMPLOYEE HANDBOOK PROVISION

The MNO Company expects that professional and managerial employees are devoting their full time and effort to fulfilling their duties with the company. The MNO Company also expects that all other full-time employees are not engaged in activities outside of work that will prevent them from doing their best when they are working at the MNO Company. Any employee, full-time or part-time, who is employed for wages outside of the time spent at the MNO Company is required to inform the director of human resources about this outside employment and provide the director of human resources with phone numbers and addresses so that we can contact you if necessary while you are at your other place of employment.

Conflict of Interest

Conflict of interest policies are also difficult to write in a way that does not lead to legal problems. IBM lost the *Rulon-Miller* case because of the way it had written its policies, including the conflict of interest policy. Some employers in some states might be better off without a conflict of interest policy of any kind. On the other hand, many employees might not realize that they were doing something that might constitute a conflict of interest if this is not discussed with them and made a part of the employee handbook.

SAMPLE EMPLOYEE HANDBOOK PROVISION

The MNO Company is engaged in a large number of projects and does work for governments around the world. We expect our employees to do everything they can to help us maintain and expand our business and to refrain from doing anything that might interfere with our success. It is often difficult for employees to know if something they are doing might constitute a conflict of interest, and that is why we spend time on this subject as part of our new-employee orientation. Generally, it is a conflict of interest to provide information to a competitor or deal with a competitor in any way without discussing it first with the director of human resources or some other appropriate executive of the MNO Company. We expect employees who see business opportunities that MNO might be interested in to inform the company before taking advantage of them. We also expect employees who have personal financial or other interests that might color their judgment when dealing with either customers or suppliers to inform the appropriate executive at MNO before continuing to engage in conduct that might raise issues of conflict of interest.

OFF-DUTY MISCONDUCT

So far we have been discussing off-duty conduct that is legal but questionable. Outside the realm of civil service and union contracts, which require good cause before employees may be dismissed, the issue for most employers is whether or not they can fire someone who has brought disrepute on the company by off-duty conduct that is either illegal or immoral. Again, this is an area of the law which is changing. For example, presumably the Colorado statute that prohibits discharge for engaging in any lawful activity would prevent discharge for activities that are immoral but not illegal. More and more this is becoming the line companies should draw when dealing with these issues. A company should at least expect employees charged with committing a felony or a misdemeanor punishable by time in jail to inform the company as soon as possible. The company would even be interested in traffic violations to the extent that employees drive company vehicles.

SAMPLE EMPLOYEE HANDBOOK PROVISION

Every employee at the MNO Company is required to inform the director of human resources if he or she is charged with any crime, including traffic violations, and to keep the director informed about the outcome of the case. We expect our employees to obey all laws, both at work and away from work, and to recognize that their actions, even away from work, can reflect on the reputation of the MNO Company.

POLITICAL ACTIVITY

There was a time in America when employers felt free to hire or fire employees based on their political affiliation. Those days are long gone. For government employees, the Supreme Court has ruled that to hire and fire on the basis of political affiliation, with rare exceptions, is a violation of the First Amendment to the U.S. Constitution (*Elrod, Branti*). Several states have statutes that prevent even private employers from attempting to influence the political activities or political opinions of their employees. Other states have statutes that prevent employers from trying to influence the way employees vote in elections. In states without specific statutes on these issues, we can expect courts to rule that discharging an employee because of his or her political opinions or political party affiliation would be considered a kind of wrongful discharge.

The next question is: Do we want to have a provision in the employee handbook on this issue? The only real answer is that such a provision would have both advantages and disadvantages. On the one hand, if an employee was discharged for political reasons, the company could point to the handbook provision and argue that such a discharge was against company policy and that the person who did the firing should be sued, but not the company. A company might get away with that, but it would have to be willing to hire the employee back to show its good faith. On the other hand, a company that puts a provision such as this in the handbook is bound by that provision and should realize that it will certainly have to live up to that promise, regardless of what the courts in a particular state might have ruled absent a handbook provision. It is also important to realize that such a provision would apply to the members of radical parties such as the American Nazi Party as well as Democrats and Republicans.

SAMPLE EMPLOYEE HANDBOOK PROVISION

We at the MNO Company believe that everyone should be allowed to hold and express political opinions without interference from an employer. It is the policy of the MNO Company not to take a person's political affiliation into account when making personnel decisions. At the same time, we recognize that the expression of strong political opinions at work can be disruptive. We expect all our employees to spend their time at work working and to save their political activities and political arguments for after working hours and away from MNO facilities.

CONCLUSION

When it comes to writing handbook provisions and personnel policies in this area, it is important to realize what should not be said. Promises should not be made that the company may not want to live up to. If promises and policies are stated in the handbook, then they should be complied with.

Chapter 18
Wages, Hours, and Immigrants

The federal Fair Labor Standards Act (FLSA) was originally passed in 1938 and has been amended several times in the years since (29 U.S.C. sec. 201, *et seq.*). The Fair Labor Standards Act is primarily concerned with minimum wages, overtime, and child labor. The Equal Pay Act, which guarantees women equal pay with men, is technically an amendment to the Fair Labor Standards Act. Almost every state also has laws controlling minimum wages, overtime pay, and child labor, and employers must be sure to comply with both the state and federal laws and regulations in this area.

The Fair Labor Standards Act has a large number of tests that a business must meet before the business is covered by its provisions. Small retail and service establishments may be exempt from the federal law because they are too small; they should consult an attorney about this possibility. Also, a wide variety of exemptions apply to a wide variety of types of jobs, such as domestic servants, seasonal amusement park employees, farm workers on small farms, babysitters, and fishermen. Employees of small newspapers and switchboard operators of small telephone companies may also be exempt. Any business, particularly a small business, should discuss with an attorney whether it falls within any of the exceptions to the federal law. It may still have to comply with similar provisions of the state wage and hour laws, however.

MINIMUM WAGES
The federal minimum wage is currently $4.25 an hour. Most states also have a minimum wage, but in most states it is either the same as or less than the federal minimum wage. There are a wide variety of exceptions from the federal minimum wage laws besides the general exceptions discussed above. If an employer provides meals or lodging, the reasonable value of these items can count toward minimum wage. Employees that receive merchandise as part of their compensation may have that counted toward the minimum wage. Also, if employees receive tips, employers may have to pay only half the minimum wage, with tips making up the difference.

Generally employees are considered to be working and entitled to payment during rest or meal periods that last twenty minutes or less, during training periods, during fire drills, and while traveling between work sites. They are not required to be paid during rest or meal periods of more than twenty minutes if the employee is really relieved of all work duties and when traveling from home to work and back home after work.

A difficult area is the question of whether or not the employee must be paid when "on call" for the employer or sleeping at the place of employment as part of a long shift. If an employee is home but on call and is so restricted that he or she cannot go anywhere or do anything other than sit at home, he or she may be entitled to payment for this time. An employee who works less than a twenty four-hour shift must usually be paid for time spent sleeping at the work site. If the employee works a true twenty four-hour shift, eight hours may be deducted for sleep if the employee is really able to sleep. Sleep that is constantly interrupted must be paid for.

OVERTIME: EXEMPT AND NONEXEMPT EMPLOYEES

The general rule under federal law is that an employee must be paid time and a half for any hours over forty worked in a week. The employee is entitled to receive one and a half times his or her regular rate of pay for this overtime work. Bonuses; vacation pay; sick leave pay; payments made under profit sharing, trust, or savings plans; and contributions to retirement, life, accident, and health insurance plans are generally not counted as part of the person's regular rate of pay.

The difficult question in most cases is whether the employee is exempt or nonexempt from the overtime provisions. There are a long list of occupations that are not covered by the federal overtime rules, such as some motor carrier, railroad, and airline employees; some loggers; some motion picture employees; some maple sap workers; and some cab drivers. Some commission salespeople at retail or service establishments, seamen, farm workers, employees engaged in the transporting of farm products, substitute parents for institutionalized children, live-in domestic servants, and drivers and helpers paid on a trip basis may also be exempted from the overtime provisions of the federal law.

It is important to remember that an employer can avoid the overtime problem by lowering the wages of employees who are currently being paid above the minimum wage. For example, if an employee is currently receiving $8 an hour for a forty-hour week and the employer would like to receive fifty hours of work for about the same money, it can lower the regular rate of pay to $6 an hour and then pay time and a half for the ten overtime hours each week. At $8 times forty, the employee was being paid $320 a week. At the new rate, including time and a half for overtime, the employee is receiving $6 X 40 plus $9 X 10, or $330 a week. The more unrealistically low the minimum wage becomes, the less of a problem the overtime requirement should be for employers.

As far as federal law is concerned, most employees fall into one of two categories: exempt and nonexempt. Exempt employees are generally (with special exceptions for special occupations) employees that qualify as executives, administrators, professionals, or outside salespeople.

An executive has the primary duty of managing the business or part of it; regularly directs the work of at least two employees; has the authority to hire, fire, and promote; and exercises discretion. Generally executives make at least

$250 a week (but may make between $155 and $250 a week under some circumstances) and spend at least 80 percent of their time being executives, as opposed to performing routine work tasks (60 percent for some retail and service industries).

An administrator is someone who exercises independent judgment and discretion and whose work relates to management policies and general business operations. He or she regularly spends at least 80 percent of the time exercising independent judgment and discretion (60 percent for some retail and service industries) and makes at least $250 a week (but may make between $155 and $250 a week under some circumstances).

A professional employee usually has a college degree or a graduate degree and does work that requires advanced knowledge in a specialized field of learning. Doctors, lawyers, and teachers fall into this category, as do accountants, scientists, and engineers. Computer programmers also fall into this category. Professional employees make at least $250 a week (but may make between $170 and $250 a week under some circumstances).

An outside salesperson is someone who regularly works away from the employer's regular place of business making sales and taking orders. He or she must spend at least 80 percent of his or her time in sales activities, including doing paperwork, making deliveries, and collecting money.

As a general rule, these exempt employees must fit the above definitions and also must be paid on a "salary basis." That means that the employee is not paid on the basis of hours worked, but instead by the pay period. If pay is deducted for an absence from work of less than a day, the person will no longer be considered to be a salaried employee. The federal Family and Medical Leave Act regulations specifically allow an employer to dock a salaried employee for an absence covered by the statute of less than a day. This leaves us with the ridiculous result that if a salaried employee is away from work for a few hours on personal business, the employer cannot dock his or her pay, but if the employee is sick or hurt and is absent part of a day, the employer may dock his or her pay. It is doubtful that many employers will want to get into this distinction.

The federal law admits only two categories of employees: exempt and nonexempt. All employees are assumed to be nonexempt (protected by the wage and hour laws) unless the employer can prove that they deserve to be exempt. An employer does this by showing that the employee fits into one of the categories listed above and receives a salary that is not related to the "quality or quantity" of work performed. In many companies and government agencies there is a third type of employee, which we will call the salaried nonexempt employee. Many white-collar employees are given a salary every pay period and treated just like exempt employees in every way. However, under the definitions contained in the federal law and regulations, they do not really qualify as exempt employees. This becomes a problem only when one of these salaried nonexempt employees becomes disgruntled, or is discharged, and decides to file a complaint with the wage and hour division of the U.S. Labor Department. The employee will allege that he or she worked overtime and was never paid time and a half. Since the employee was nonexempt, the employer was supposed to be keeping records of his or her time worked using a time clock or other device. Since the employer did not do this, the employee will be assumed to be telling the truth. The employee may have personal time records, and there is no way to tell if these were kept in good faith or constructed overnight. If the salaried nonexempt employee was being paid a salary of $400 a week, it will be presumed by the judge that the rate of pay was $10 an hour, and the employee will be owed $15 a hour for overtime. There may also be penalties and potential criminal liability.

One way to avoid this is to recognize that these employees are nonexempt under federal rules and tell them that their rate of pay is minimum wage plus time and a half for overtime. There is no rule that says that an employer cannot guarantee a nonexempt employee that his or her wages (regular pay plus overtime) will always rise to a certain level. In the case of the person making $400 a week, he or she would have to show that he or she worked a lot of hours over forty in order to be entitled to more than $400 a week. Employers should require such employees to punch a time clock if they want to be on the safe side.

THE MYTH OF COMPENSATORY TIME

Many employers believe that they can provide compensatory time to their nonexempt employees. This is illegal in most cases. A nonexempt employee is entitled to time and a half for any hours past forty hours worked in a week. Of course, an employer is free to work the employee less than forty hours in some other week in order to reduce wage costs, but this would have to be a reduction of one and a half hours for every hour of overtime in order to even out the costs. The 1985 amendments to the Fair Labor Standards Act allow state and local governments to provide compensatory time to certain police, fire, emergency, and seasonal personnel. Special rules apply to these employees, and the regulations should be consulted.

If there is no such thing as "comp time" for nonexempt employees, what about exempt employees? There really isn't any such thing as comp time for them either. Remember, exempt employees are paid on the basis of a salary rather than the quality or quantity of work performed during a particular week. It is of course acceptable for any employer to say to any exempt employee, "You've put in a lot of time on the weekends lately; why don't you take a few days off?" but it is not required. A policy that states that exempt employees who work on the weekend are entitled to take comp time during the week suggests that these employees are being treated like nonexempt employees, and that is something to be avoided. In other words, comp time policies should be reexamined to make sure that they are not turning exempt employees into nonexempt employees unintentionally.

EMPLOYEE CLASSIFICATION

It is important to explain the employee classification system in the handbook. Most organizations have three types of employees: salaried exempt, salaried nonexempt, and hourly nonexempt. Many organizations also divide their hourly nonexempt employees into part-time and full-time. In most companies part-time employees are not entitled to receive company benefits such as health insurance. This is confusing because there are many laws that turn on how many employees an organization has, and each law defines *employee* differently in terms of the number of hours the person works in a week. While at present no law requires employers to provide benefits such as health insurance, there is a danger if some full-time employees receive such benefits and other full-time employees do not. There might be violations of discrimination laws or some other problem hidden in this policy. There will certainly be morale problems. Because of this, many companies provide benefits to all full-time employees and not to part-time employees. If that is the case, then what constitutes a full-time employee should be spelled out in the handbook to avoid confusion.

SAMPLE EMPLOYEE HANDBOOK PROVISION

Here at the MNO Company we have full-time and part-time employees. Part-time employees are generally not entitled to any company benefits, such as health insurance and paid vacations. The director of human resources will inform every employee whether he or she is full-time or part-time. Also, we have three basic types of employees based on the federal Fair Labor Standards Act. Our employees are classified as either salaried exempt, salaried nonexempt, or hourly nonexempt. An exempt employee is exempt from the overtime provisions of the Fair Labor Standards Act. A nonexempt employee is entitled to overtime pay regardless of whether he or she receives a paycheck calculated for the hours worked each week or a regular salary. Because of this, salaried nonexempt employees are given a statement showing what their regular rate of pay is and guaranteeing them overtime pay whether they work overtime or not. This practice is to avoid potentially open-ended liability under the law. If you are a salaried nonexempt employee, this practice will be explained to you when you are hired. No hourly nonexempt employee should ever work overtime without express orders to do so from his or her supervisor.

OTHER POLICY CONSIDERATIONS

Section 541.118 of Title 29 of the Code of Federal Regulations is confusing and important. It is confusing because it does not spell out exactly what it means. It is important because any employer that violates it may find itself liable to employees who were thought to be salaried exempt employees for a great deal of back pay for overtime that it had not counted on paying. This regulation states that an exempt employee must be paid on a salary basis in order to qualify for exempt status. The person must receive a definite amount each pay period regardless of the quality or quantity of work performed and without regard to the number of days or hours worked during a particular week. While it is generally assumed that an exempt employee can have his or her pay docked if the employee misses a whole day the regulations are confusing in this regard. They state that an exempt employee's pay may be docked if they miss a whole day or more for "personal reasons" other than sickness or accident. However, the regulations under the federal Family and Medical Leave Act seem to contemplate that an exempt employee may have his or her salary docked if he or she misses work for many days, a single day, or a part of a day for reasons covered under the act. These reasons include the illness of the employee or the employee's children.

Section 541.118 also states that an exempt employee may have his or her pay docked if he or she is sick or hurt if the employer has a sick leave policy that provides compensation for exempt employees who are ill and the employee either has not yet qualified under the policy (presumably because the employee has not been with the employer long enough) or has used up the allowed sick leave days. Again, this would seem to be overridden by the 1993 federal Family and Medical Leave Act.

Section 541.118 also states that exempt employees may not lose salary because of "absences due to jury duty, attendance as a witness, or temporary military leave." The employer is allowed to offset (deduct from the paycheck) any pay the employee receives for engaging in these activities. The regulation also allows employers to impose penalties on exempt employees because they violate "safety rules of major significance." In one case, the employees, police sergeants, were docked three days' pay for violating the conflict of interest policy (taking a free sandwich). The judge ruled that because their pay was docked for a reason other than a violation of safety rules, these employees were not really exempt and were entitled to the full protection of the Fair Labor Standards Act (*Pautlitz*), which meant that they were owed a lot of overtime pay. In the next chapter we will be discussing paid and unpaid leaves, and the requirements of this section of the federal regulations will have to be uppermost in our minds.

CHILD LABOR

Both the federal government and the states have laws and regulations that control child labor. The basic federal rule is that people must be at least sixteen for most jobs and at least eighteen for jobs designated by the Secretary of Labor as hazardous. People under the age of sixteen are allowed to perform some types of work, such as delivering newspapers, acting, working for their parents in nonhazardous jobs, or making evergreen wreaths at home, without regard to their age. People between the ages of fourteen and sixteen may work if the work is outside of school hours, does not exceed three hours on a school day and eight hours on a nonschool day, and does not exceed eighteen hours on a school week and forty hours on a nonschool week. These fourteen- to sixteen-year-olds may do only certain kinds of work and may not engage in hazardous work or be involved in manufacturing, mining, or processing. Of course there are special rules for farm work, and many states have rules that are more restrictive than the federal rules. If there is any doubt about an employee's age, the employer should require a birth certificate or a certificate of age issued by the state or the federal government.

ILLEGAL ALIENS

The Immigration Reform and Control Act of 1986 (8 U.S.C. sec. 1324a) made it illegal for employers to hire illegal aliens or legal aliens who are not authorized to work under the terms of their visa. Every employer with three or more employees is required to fill out an I-9 form for every employee when he or she is hired. The employee must prove that he or she is either a citizen or a legal alien who is entitled to work. Employers are required to verify on the I-9 form that they saw proper documentation, which might be a U.S. passport, a naturalization certificate, or a permanent resident card with employment authorization from the Immigration and Naturalization Service (INS). Most people prove citizenship with a driver's license and a Social Security card or a birth certificate. The employee must provide the proper documentation within three days of being hired unless the job will last less than three days, in which case the employee must present proof at the same time he or she is hired.

Employers are required to keep the I-9 forms as long as the employee is employed and for either three years after the date the employee was hired or one year after the employee was terminated, whichever is longer. Generally, employers are better off to keeping their I-9 forms together in one place in case the federal government ever wants to see them.

The Immigration Reform and Control Act also made it illegal to discriminate against someone because of his or her national origin or, if the person intends to become a U.S. citizen, his or her citizenship status. It is not clear how employers are supposed to know if someone intends to become a U.S. citizen.

SAMPLE EMPLOYEE HANDBOOK PROVISION

The MNO Company intends to comply with all laws, including the child labor and immigration laws. This means that we hire only people who are old enough and eligible to work under both federal and state statutes. Generally, if there is any doubt about age, proof of age should be required. Every employee hired by MNO is required to complete an I-9 form and prove that he or she is either a U.S. citizen or an alien eligible to work under U.S. immigration laws. All employees are expected to comply with these laws and to inform the director of human resources if they have any reason to believe that a coworker is either under age or an alien who is not eligible to work under U.S. immigration laws.

WAGE PAYMENT AND GARNISHMENT

When employees must be paid is controlled by state wage payment laws. Some states have different rules for different occupations, so a call to the state labor commissioner is in order. Some states require a paycheck at least twice a month, but in some states the paycheck must come every two weeks (there is a difference). Of course, an employer is free to pay its employees more often than state law requires. An employer may also pay some employees weekly and others biweekly or twice monthly. In some states it is legal to pay some kinds of employees on a monthly basis. It is often easier to pay employees who are eligible for and receiving overtime pay every week to avoid confusion and violation of the overtime rules. If an employee is absent on payday, employers must be careful not to release the employee's paycheck to someone without the his or her written authorization. This protects the employer from charges that proper wages were not paid on time. Some employees ask for their paycheck early. It is usually best to avoid this practice. If you do it for one employee, you have to do it for all or face discrimination charges.

Some state laws are draconian when it comes to imposing penalties on employers who do not pay on time or who wrongly withhold the final paycheck because of a pay dispute. Also, some state laws require the final paycheck to be paid within hours or days of the final day at work. State laws should be consulted to make sure that these rules are not violated.

In some cases employers are ordered by a court to withhold some of an employee's wages. This process is called *wage garnishment*. The federal Child Support Enforcement Act (42 U.S.C. sec. 666) requires employers to comply with any court order to withhold wages for child support. The act also makes it illegal to fire, discipline, or refuse to hire someone because his or her wages are subject to garnishment for child support. Most states have laws and regulations that allow garnishments for other purposes. Of course an employer is going to comply with a court order to withhold wages. The Internal Revenue Service and state tax authorities may also obtain a court order to withhold wages to pay back taxes. In some states it is legal for creditors to require people who owe money or buy on credit to sign a voluntary wage assignment agreement allowing the creditor to receive payment directly from the employer if payment is not made. Generally, it is illegal to discipline, discharge, or not hire someone because he or she signed a legal wage assignment agreement or because his or her wages are subject to garnishment, either because statutes protect these workers or because this is considered common-law wrongful discharge (against public policy). The federal Bankruptcy Act prevents employers from discharging employees because they have had to file bankruptcy (11 U.S.C. sec. 525).

The federal Consumer Credit Protection Act (15 U.S.C. sec. 1671 *et seq.*) limits the amount of wages that can be garnished and prohibits the discharge of employees who have their wages garnished. Generally garnishment may not take more than 25 percent of the employee's disposable income (or thirty times the federal minimum wage, whichever is less), but special rules apply to garnishments caused by child-support orders or the need to collect back taxes. If there are both federal and state rules, then the rule that allows the least amount to be taken out of the paycheck controls. If there are more creditors asking for money than there is money available, most states have rules that state which debt takes priority. Generally child-support payments take priority.

SAMPLE EMPLOYEE HANDBOOK PROVISION

The MNO Company has a variety of types of employees, and different classifications of employees may receive their pay on different days or at different intervals. To avoid problems, the MNO Company will not make advance payments or release a paycheck to anyone other than the employee or his or her representative (who must have a signed authorization from the employee). In the event that employees have their wages garnished or assign their wages, the MNO Company will comply with the law and make the payments as required by law. We expect all employees to cooperate in this process if it becomes necessary. Any questions concerning pay or wage garnishment should be directed to the director of human resources.

INDEPENDENT CONTRACTORS

It is important to realize that the employee handbook should be given only to employees. While that seems like a truism, it is very important. Generally, the law assumes that if someone pays someone else for labor, the person being paid is an employee. If that person is an employee, in most cases he or she will be protected by the federal Fair Labor Standards Act and similar state laws concerned with wages and hours. The person will also be covered by unemployment and workers' compensation statutes and will be entitled to union representation if he or she wants it. The person's employer will be expected to withhold income taxes and Social Security taxes from the person's paychecks. Independent contractors are obviously not employees and are not covered by unemployment or workers' compensation unless they pay for it themselves.

Any organization that deals with independent contractors should have a written contract to that effect. While that alone is not enough, it will help to prove that the organization acted in good faith. The law on whether or not someone is an independent contractor is changing, mainly because so many employers have abused the law by trying to pretend that people who are employees are really independent contractors. Every agency involved with employers has a different definition of an independent contractor. The Internal Revenue Service has a list of twenty factors that it looks at in making the decision. These include whether the person is given detailed instructions or left to perform the task without supervision, whether or not the person is trained to perform a special task, whether the person works at the employer's place of business, whether the person is paid by the hour or by the job, and whether or not the person brings his or her own tools. Many state courts have begun to use what is called the "relative nature of the work" test, which means that anyone who is hired to do what the employer does on a regular basis is an employee. Anyone hired to do something special that is outside the employer's regular business and who also works for others is an independent contractor.

If you think you are hiring an independent contractor, you should ask for proof that he or she carries workers' compensation insurance coverage. If he or she does not, you may be liable for medical bills if the person is injured on the job.

CONCLUSION

The laws and regulations concerning wages, hours, and immigrants are far more confusing and complex than they need to be, but employers are expected to know and apply the laws and regulations regardless of their complexity. Ignorance of the law is never an excuse. Employers are expected to comply with federal and state laws and to know which applies if there is a conflict (sometimes federal law will override state law; at other times the state law will control). Employers are expected to withhold wages when ordered to do so, but only to the extent required by law.

APPENDIX: 20 Factors to Determine if Someone is an Independent Contractor

1. *Instructions.* Employees usually work under close supervision and are told when, where, and how to do their work. Independent contractors are given an assignment and left to accomplish it.

2. *Training.* Employees are usually given special training by their employer. Independent contractors come to the job fully trained and ready to go.

3. *Integration.* Employees usually do work that is an integral part of their employer's business. Independent contractors provide peripheral services.

4. *Personal service.* Employees usually do the work themselves. Independent contractors may send a substitute.

5. *Hiring assistants.* Employees are usually provided with assistants by their employer. Independent contractors hire assistants themselves.

6. *Continuing relationship.* Employees work for their employer on a regular basis, usually every business day. Independent contractors work at irregular intervals as there is work to do.

7. *Hours of work.* Employees usually have set hours of work. Independent contractors control their own work time.

8. *Full-time work.* Employees usually work forty hours a week for their employer. Independent contractors usually work part-time.

9. *Work done on premises.* Employees usually work at their employer's place of business. Independent contractors may work anywhere, depending on what has to be done.

10. *Order of work.* Employees usually perform their work in the order set by their employer. Independent contractors control the order in which they do things.

11. *Work reports.* Employees usually submit regular reports to their employer. Independent contractors report on work progress as goals are met and when the job is finished.

12. *Payment.* Employees are usually paid by the hour, week, or month. Independent contractors are paid by the job.

13. *Expenses.* Employees usually have their business and travel expenses paid by their employer. Independent contractors pay their own expenses, although they may add them to their final bill for services.

14. *Tools.* Employees usually have tools provided by their employer. Independent contractors provide their own tools.

15. *Investment.* Employees usually do not invest in the business. Independent contractors have invested in their business.

16. *Profit for loss.* Employees usually receive wages whether or not the business is making money. Independent contractors can make a profit or loss depending on income and expenses.

17. *Multiple firms serviced.* Employees usually work for only one company. Independent contractors provide services for several companies.

18. *Available to public.* Employees usually work for their employer rather than the general public. Independent contractors make their services available to the general public.

19. *Right to fire.* Employees can usually be fired at any time by their employer. Independent contractors usually work under a contract for a specific job.

20. *Right to quit.* Employees can usually quit at any time. Independent contractors usually work under a contract for a specific job and must finish that job or face legal liability for the failure to finish.

Chapter 19

Paid and Unpaid Leaves

Most organizations find that they cannot function without some policies on paid and unpaid leave. It is not simply a question of deciding what the policy will be and implementing it. As we saw in Chapter 14, the federal Family and Medical Leave Act requires employers with more than fifty employees to grant unpaid leave for a variety of reasons, including the illness of the employee, and the regulations written by the U.S. Labor Department assume that an employee handbook will deal with this issue. A sample employee handbook provision is contained in Chapter 14. As we saw in Chapter 18, federal regulations require employers who wish to take advantage of the exemption from overtime pay to do so by paying executive, administrative, professional, and outside salespeople a salary and meeting other requirements specified by regulation. For example, salaried employees must be given some kind of paid sick leave, although the regulations do not say how many days of paid sick leave must be allowed. Also, the regulations require that salaried employees be paid for days that they serve on a jury, testify in a court proceeding, or perform temporary military duty (deducting the pay received for these activities). It is an interesting question whether the Fair Labor Standards Act really gives the U.S. Labor Department the authority to write regulations such as these, but they have never been declared to be invalid and are still in force as this is being written. Laws in some states require employers to allow employees some unpaid time off in order to vote, and there may be any number of special provisions in the statutes of most states.

The existence of these and other laws and regulations means that for many policies, a distinction will have to be made between salaried and hourly workers and between full-time and part-time workers. While some of the salaried employees will be exempt employees under the Fair Labor Standards Act, others will not be, but we will assume that the company wishes to treat all salaried employees the same for the purposes of the policies discussed in this chapter.

VOTING LEAVE

In states that require unpaid leave for voting, the state law should be used as the basis for this policy statement. In the absence of a state law, employers should make an effort to be reasonable, while of course realizing that time off to vote could be disruptive to the organization. Many employees will be able to vote before or after working hours, but employees who work a long day shift may not be able to do this. It is impossible for an employer to know whether or not an employee will need time off unless the employee provides this information. In a few states, such as Texas, the polls are open for several days before the official election day, and anyone is allowed to vote during those days regardless of whether or not he or she will be out of the jurisdiction on polling day. In these states, it should not be necessary to grant time off to vote or even discuss it in the employee handbook.

SAMPLE EMPLOYEE HANDBOOK PROVISION

The MNO Company realizes that some employees will not be able to vote before or after work. We ask such employees to inform their supervisor or the director of human resources at least one week before an election in which such an employee wishes to participate during regular working hours. Full-time hourly employees will be given a reasonable amount of time off without pay to vote. Full-time salaried employees will be given a reasonable amount of time off with pay to vote. The MNO Company expects all employees to time their trip to the polls in a way that causes the least disruption to the smooth functioning of the company. In most cases, it is assumed that employees can vote before or after work.

JURY DUTY, TESTIFYING IN COURT, AND TEMPORARY MILITARY SERVICE

As we saw in Chapter 18, the U.S. Labor Department expects exempt employees to be given paid leave to perform jury duty, testify at a trial, or serve temporarily in the military. Employers are allowed to deduct any compensation provided to the employee for providing these services. Federal law and most states require that employers not discharge someone because he or she had to perform jury duty and that the employee be reinstated in his or her old job when the jury duty is over. While there are few specific statutes dealing with employees who must be absent to testify before a court, in most states it would be considered wrongful discharge (a violation of public policy) to discharge someone for this reason.

The U.S. Labor Department regulations assume that exempt employees are being paid for temporary absences for military duty with a deduction for any pay received by the employee while on duty. It is not always clear how long is "temporary." The federal Veteran's Re-employment Rights Act of 1958 requires that employees who are inducted into more than temporary military service be reinstated in their old job when they leave the military, whether they are full-time or part-time employees. Employees must apply for their old job back within ninety days after separating from the military, and of course must still be able to perform the job. If they have become disabled, they may have a right to reasonable accommodation if that will allow them to perform the essential functions of the job they used to hold.

Federal and state laws generally require that employees who must attend summer military reserve duty be given leave without pay and be given the option of taking this either as unpaid leave, leaving any right to paid vacation intact, or as paid vacation. Again, different types of employees may have to be treated differently.

SAMPLE EMPLOYEE HANDBOOK PROVISION

Salaried employees who are summoned to participate in a court proceeding as either a juror or a witness will be given paid leave of up to five days in any one calendar year in order to fulfill this obligation. Any amount received by the salaried employee for these services will be deducted from the employee's pay for this period. Hourly employees will be given unpaid leave in order to fulfill these obligations.

Salaried employees who are called to temporary military duty will be given up to two weeks' paid leave in order to fulfill this obligation. Anything over two weeks will be considered not to be temporary. Any amount received by the salaried employee for this service will be deducted from the employee's pay for this period. Hourly employees will be given unpaid leave in order to fulfill temporary military obligations.

Any employee, salaried or hourly, full or part-time, who is called to active duty with the U.S. military for a period of less than four years will be entitled to reinstatement to his or her old position to the extent required by federal and state laws and regulations.

MATERNITY, MEDICAL, AND SICK LEAVE

We will assume for the purposes of this discussion that the employer has the Family and Medical Leave policy discussed in Chapter 14 and is required to follow the provisions of the federal Family and Medical Leave Act of 1993. While this act applies only to employers with fifty or more employees, employers with fewer employees should consider offering a similar policy for the sake of good employee relations. This act requires up to twelve weeks of unpaid leave during any one year because of the birth or adoption of a child; because of the illness of a spouse, child, or parent; or because of the employee's own serious health condition. Generally most employers will find it advantageous to cover maternity and medical leave under this general Family and Medical Leave provision rather than having a separate maternity leave provision. A few states, such as California, have special maternity leave laws that should be consulted before writing a Family and Medical Leave policy.

Generally, federal and state laws in this area require only unpaid leave and reinstatement in the job when the illness or pregnancy is over. The question for employers is, do they wish to also provide some kind of paid sick leave? As we saw in Chapter 18, some kind of paid sick leave is required for exempt employees under U.S. Labor Department regulations. Often employers provide some kind of paid sick leave for salaried employees (exempt and nonexempt), but not for hourly workers. Some employers provide a combination of paid sick leave and paid personal leave. There are a number of issues to consider, not the least of which is how much paid leave to give and who to give it to. The federal Family and Medical Leave Act applies only to employees who have been employed for at least twelve months and worked at least 1,250 hours during that twelve-month period. Employers may or may not wish to do the same thing with sick leave. Also, the policy should state how much sick leave or sick/personal leave an employee can accumulate. One of the purposes of sick leave or sick/personal leave is to allow employees to recover from illness or prevent illness when they just need a rest. If employees save up this kind of leave and never take it, then it is not serving its purpose.

SAMPLE EMPLOYEE HANDBOOK PROVISION

Full-time salaried employees at the MNO Company receive one day of sick/personal leave for every two months of work completed. Employees may accumulate up to twenty days of sick/personal leave. An accumulation over twenty days will be lost. This is paid leave, paid at the employee's regular salary. Full-time salaried employees who are eligible for Family and Medical Leave under our Family and Medical Leave policy and the federal Family and Medical Leave Act must use up their paid sick/personal leave before taking unpaid leave. Employees who have accumulated sick/personal leave days when they terminate their employment with MNO Company will receive payment for those accumulated days up to the twenty-day limit allowed by this policy.

VACATION LEAVE

In writing policies and employee handbook provisions concerned with any paid leave, whether it is sick leave, personal leave, or vacation leave, it is important to spell out how many days may be accumulated in the course of a career. In most states it is assumed that employees will be paid for any accumulated paid leave when they terminate their employment unless this is specifically dealt with in the handbook. Generally it is best, in terms of employee relations, to allow some accumulation, but to limit the amount that can be accumulated to some reasonable level. After that point, employees are faced with the requirement that they take it or lose it. After all, the purpose of a paid vacation is to allow the employee to rest and come back to work refreshed. That cannot happen if all the vacation time is saved up and then used to cushion eventual termination or retirement.

Many employers provide paid vacations only to their full-time salaried employees. The types of employees who are entitled to receive paid vacation should be spelled out in the handbook to avoid confusion. Often, issues such as vacations and holidays are dealt with in a collectively bargained union contract for hourly employees.

SAMPLE EMPLOYEE HANDBOOK PROVISION

Full-time salaried employees at the MNO Company receive one day of paid vacation for every month worked at the company. Employees may accumulate up to twenty days of paid vacation. An accumulation over twenty days will be lost. Requests for vacation times must be made to the employee's direct supervisor and will be scheduled to take into account the work process at MNO Company. Generally, most vacations will be scheduled during the summer. Vacation must be taken in increments of at least one week at a time. If a company holiday falls during an employee's paid vacation, the employee may add a day or days at the beginning or end of the vacation period to take this into account.

COMPANY HOLIDAYS

During the year, most organizations in the United States take certain days off, on which the organization is simply shut down. While governments may designate certain days as government holidays, private employers are free to decide which holidays to take. This is one area where an employer should consider polling the employees to get their input. The employer can decide that ten holiday days will be taken in a calendar year and ask the employees in a survey to vote for which ten days they would like off. The list would usually include:

New Year's Eve and New Year's Day
Christmas Eve and Christmas Day
Thanksgiving Day and the Friday after Thanksgiving Day
Labor Day, Memorial Day, and Independence Day
Lincoln's Birthday and Presidents Day
Martin Luther King Day
Good Friday
Veterans' Day and Columbus Day

During any given year, some of these days will fall on the weekend, so if the organization generally works Monday through Friday, some adjustment must be made to this list each year.

SAMPLE EMPLOYEE HANDBOOK PROVISION

Each year the MNO Company surveys employees concerning which holidays to take during the coming year. Generally twelve days are taken as holidays and the facilities of MNO Company are shut down. A list of the holidays for the coming year is posted on bulletin boards in December after the employee survey. Full-time salaried employees are paid during these holiday periods as if they were performing regular service.

CONCLUSION

The question of which holidays to take is very important in terms of good employee relations. Employees who find themselves working on holidays when most people are off from work do not appreciate it and may turn their resentment on their employer. While there is little in the way of legal requirements in this area, a consultant should be asked what most similar employers in the area do in this regard. Vacation and sick leave policies can be a major problem if they are not considered to be reasonable by the average employee. This is certainly one area in which some input from employees can be helpful.

Chapter 20

Dealing with Unions

From our perspective at the end of the twentieth century, the idea of labor unions seems perfectly natural. It was not always so. In the nineteenth century, in many states of the United States, labor unions were considered to be criminal conspiracies. Courts routinely issued orders to stop most union activity, from picket lines to strikes. The legal theory was that a strike or picket line was a threat to the value of the business, and anyone who posed a threat to the value of property could be ordered to stop doing whatever it was that he or she was doing. This did not really begin to change until well into the twentieth century.

CREATING FEDERAL LABOR LAW

For the first third of the twentieth century, the battle between organized labor and American business was anything but a fair fight. Legislatures passed special statutes concerned with picketing and rioting that were used mainly against organized labor, while judges in almost every state issued orders restricting union activity. With the election of Franklin D. Roosevelt to the presidency in 1932, things began to change. After significant debate, Congress passed the National Labor Relations Act, commonly called the Wagner Act, in 1935. For the first time the right of workers to organize together into labor unions and bargain collectively with employers over wages and working conditions was guaranteed by law. The National Labor Relations Board was created to enforce the act. The board consists of five members appointed by the president and approved by the Senate to serve a five-year term. As a general rule, the Board acts as a court, deciding cases brought to it on appeal from its own regional offices. The board has a general counsel who enforces the provisions of the law. Generally, an individual cannot bring a complaint to the board without the help and permission of the general counsel. The National Labor Relations Act has been amended several times in the decades since it was first passed.

WORKERS' RIGHTS

The National Labor Relations Act set out to both define the rights of working people and outlaw certain activities that employers had engaged in in the past as part of an effort to limit union membership. Section 7 of the act protects the right of working people to organize, form, join, or assist labor organizations such as labor unions. Section 7 also guarantees that working people may bargain collectively with their employers over issues such as wages and working conditions. It guarantees workers the right to take concerted action for their mutual aid and protection. Section 7 also protects the right of working people to not organize, form, join, or assist labor organizations if they do not wish to do so.

It is important for everyone involved in the work process in the United States to recognize that a group of workers does not have to constitute an official union to be protected by the provisions of the National Labor Relations Act. Any time working people get together for their mutual aid and protection, they are protected in this activity by the act, whether they belong to an official labor union or not. Any time working people meet to discuss their wages and conditions of work, they may be covered by the law. For example, when some workers walked off the job because it was too cold to work and were discharged, the National Labor Relations Board ordered them reinstated, and the U.S. Supreme Court enforced the order (*Washington Aluminum*). It did not matter whether the employees belonged to a formal union or not. Generally, a single worker taking action or speaking out alone will not be protected by the act.

UNFAIR LABOR PRACTICES BY EMPLOYERS

Section 8 of the act defined what are called unfair labor practices by employers. An employer commits an unfair labor practice if it tries to interfere with employees who wish to exercise their rights under Section 7 of the act. This means that employers may not discharge or discipline employees for organizing, joining, or assisting a labor union or labor organization. Employers may not create their own labor organizations for employees to join or dominate or interfere with the formation or administration of a union. This also means that employers may not provide funds to labor organizations. These provisions prevent employers from forming their own company unions. These company unions were used before 1935 to make employees think they were represented by a labor union when the union in fact was only a tool of their employer.

Because of the desire to both allow employees to form unions if they wish to and prevent the formation of unions dominated by employers, the act prevents employers from either discouraging employees from joining a labor union or encouraging them to join. Employers may not discriminate against people who belong to a union the employer dislikes or in favor of people who belong to a union the employer likes. Employers may not discharge or discriminate against employees who belong to unions or who file charges with or testify before the National Labor Relations Board. If a union has been chosen by the majority of employees in a bargaining unit, an employer is required to bargain with the union over wages, benefits, and working conditions.

UNFAIR LABOR PRACTICES BY UNIONS

While the original Wagner Act was primarily concerned with unfair labor practices by employers, it has been amended several times to recognize that labor unions can also commit unfair labor practices. Many of these changes were contained in the Taft-Hartley Act of 1947. Labor unions are prohibited from coercing employees into joining a union or forcing employees to select a particular person or union to represent them in collective bargaining. Unions may not try to cause employers to discriminate against workers who belong to rival unions or who fail to belong to the right union.

Just as employers must bargain collectively with unions that have been chosen by the workers, so unions chosen by the workers have a duty to bargain collectively with the employer. Unions may not try to force employers to discriminate against nonunion companies in their business dealings or try to force workers to stop using, handling, or transporting the products of an employer that has not yet signed a union contract. Unions also must honor existing union contracts and may not try to force an employer to violate an existing contract with another union. Unions may not strike in order to force an employer to assign work only to the members of a particular union. Unions may not charge excessive initiation fees and may not require employers to pay employees for work that was not actually done (commonly called *featherbedding*).

JURISDICTION, PREEMPTION, AND ENFORCEMENT

The National Labor Relations Act applies to all private employers that have anything to do with interstate commerce, which for all practical purposes is all private employers in the United States. The act does not apply to a few groups of employees, such as government employees, agricultural workers, domestic servants, people working for a parent or spouse, employees covered by the Railway Labor Act (primarily railroad and airline workers), independent contractors, and supervisors. To the extent that these workers wish protection, they must look to either special federal laws such as the Railway Labor Act or state law.

For most other private employers, federal judges have ruled that Congress intended to exercise complete control over labor-management relationships covered by the National Labor Relations Act. This means that state laws that are concerned with this area simply do not apply. This area is preempted by federal law. It does not matter whether or not state laws conflict with federal law. This means that a worker covered by the act who files a lawsuit in state court will eventually have his or her case thrown out if the employer raises the preemption issue. Since employees usually must file a complaint with the National Labor Relations Board within six months of the incident, employers usually wait more than six months before bringing this issue up. That may mean that the employee is then out of luck.

While the National Labor Relations Act appears to give the National Labor Relations Board full authority to deal with labor-management relations for all private employers, the board has never felt that it had the resources to deal with small employers. It has issued a set of regulations spelling out which employers it will concern itself with. Generally, before the board will exercise jurisdiction, an employer must either sell or buy goods or services that have been in interstate commerce and are worth more than $50,000 in a year; in the case of a retail concern, it must have a volume of at least $500,000 a year before the board will take jurisdiction. The board tends to use the same standards whether the employer is a profit-making or nonprofit organization, but the board may decline to take jurisdiction over some charitable and religious organizations. The board has special rules concerning how large employers engaged in some businesses must be before the board will exercise jurisdiction over them. These special rules apply to employers such as apartment house owners, automobile dealers, educational institutions, communication companies, gambling casinos, guard services, hospitals, day-care centers, hotels, and shopping centers. An employer should usually assume that the board will take jurisdiction over it unless told otherwise. Any employer who thinks it might be small enough to escape jurisdiction should get legal advice on this issue and contact the regional office of the National Labor Relations Board for information.

The combination of the doctrine of preemption and the fact that the board will not accept jurisdiction over small employers means that the employees of small employers may simply be out of luck where the issues covered by the National Labor Relations Act are concerned. While they have rights under the act, they must go to the board to enforce those rights. If the board refuses to take up the case because the employer is too small, there is really no place else the employee can go.

Generally, anyone who feels that his or her rights have been violated must go to the nearest regional office of the National Labor Relations Board and file a complaint. It will then be up to the general counsel of the board to decide if he or she is willing to take the case. People cannot go directly to a court, and they cannot plead their own case before the board. This means that someone with a complaint must first convince the local representative of the general counsel's office to take the case. Then there is a hearing before an administrative law judge, who will make findings of facts and make a ruling. This decision may then be appealed by either party to the board itself. The board acts as a kind of court of appeals. It may hear the appeal or allow the decision of the administrative law judge to stand without real review.

UNION ELECTIONS

As a general rule, a union that wishes to organize an employer will begin by contacting some of the employees and asking them to sign authorization cards. These cards ask to join the union and authorize the union to act as the employee's representative. An authorization card must be dated, and the date must be recent for it to count. Generally a union must have authorization cards from at least 30 percent of the employees in a bargaining unit before it can ask the National Labor Relations Board to hold an election. The union may first go to the employer and ask the employer to grant it recognition. Generally, employers should avoid doing this because of the danger that they may seem to be favoring a particular union, which is illegal, and because they may well win the election. An employer may conduct its own poll of the employees involved, but this process is also fraught with danger. If the employer appears to be influencing the vote in any way, if the ballot is not secret, or if there is any coercion or anything else goes wrong, the employer may well find itself charged with violations of federal labor law.

Usually it is best to let the National Labor Relations Board conduct an election. The board will decide what the appropriate bargaining unit is. The election will usually be held at the employer's place of business, with a representative from the board there to assure that the election is fair. Employees will vote by secret ballot either for or against union representation. If a majority of the employees in a particular bargaining unit vote for representation, then the board will certify this union to be their exclusive bargaining representative.

Usually there is a period of a month during which both the union and the employer may conduct a campaign on the issue of whether or not it would be good for these employees to be represented by a union. Once the date for the election has been set, the employer must provide a list of the names and addresses of all the employees in the bargaining unit. This list is called an *Excelsior list*.

The regional representative of the board will determine which employees belong to the bargaining unit, following rules laid down by the board. Generally security guards must be in their own unit, and professional employees may not be mixed with other employees. Professional employees are employees who perform intellectual work rather than routine or manual labor. They usually have advanced knowledge in a particular field and have studied in an institution of higher learning as opposed to an apprenticeship program. Of course supervisors may not be in the bargaining unit. The board has laid down regulations concerning how employees in some industries should be divided up rather than relying on a case-by-case analysis. For example, hospital employees are broken up by regulations into nurses, physicians, other professionals, technical employees, skilled maintenance employees, clerical employees, guards, and other nonprofessional employees.

All employees in the relevant bargaining unit are eligible to vote, but both the union and the employer may have observers at the polling place to challenge the eligibility of employees to vote in this election.

RUNNING THE EMPLOYER'S CAMPAIGN

Generally an employer who wishes to resist the union's efforts must plan an election campaign, just as anyone running for public office would plan a campaign. What will be the main theme of the campaign? Who will be in charge of the campaign? How much money and time are you willing to spend on the campaign?

After over half a century of court decisions and rulings by the National Labor Relations Board, we have a pretty good idea of the kinds of campaign activities an employer is allowed to engage in. Employers may hold meetings and explain their position. Employers may pass out campaign literature and campaign buttons ("Just say *no*") to the employees.

Employers are allowed to tell their employees that they are against unionization in this case, and why. Employers can point out the good things about the current work situation, such as the current level of wages and benefits. At the same time, these must be truthful statements. Employers can point out the bad things about unions, such as the need to pay union fees and dues and to be subject to union discipline. Employers can point out that once there is a union contract, employees will have to take their problems to a shop steward rather than directly to their supervisor. Employers may discuss the fact that the major weapon of a union is to call a strike, and that if the union calls a strike, all union members will be expected to comply. Employers can point out that if employees go out on strike for better wages and working conditions (which is called an economic strike), they may be permanently replaced.

On the other hand, there are things employers may not do or say in the course of an election campaign. Employers may not promise higher wages and better working conditions if employees vote against the union. Employers may not use coercion or threaten to shut down or move away if the union wins the election. Employers may not say that there will be a strike if the union wins or spy on union campaign activities. Employers may not question employees concerning their union activities or discriminate against employees who belong to or support the union. Employers may not visit employees at their homes in an effort to influence the way they vote or call them into private meetings with a supervisor. Employers may not increase wages or benefits during the campaign. Employers may not interrogate employees about their own opinions or the actions of the union. Employers may not keep employees from discussing the union or the election during their breaks or lunch periods. Employers may not hold any campaign meetings within twenty-four hours of the election.

What is good campaign strategy in politics is good campaign strategy in a union election. Employers should take the initiative and provide employees with accurate information about the election process. Employers should deal with potential negative factors before the union raises them and try to point out special circumstances that caused those negative factors to come into existence. Employers should not simply wait and respond to what the union says. Generally, an employer that really appears to care about the potential negative effect of union representation has a better chance than an employer who simply yells and screams that unions are creatures of the devil.

The best campaign tool is to both talk and listen. Employers are allowed to hold meetings to discuss the campaign. Employees should be encouraged to ask questions, and their questions should be answered as accurately as possible. Keep in mind that employers win about half of these union organizing elections.

It is important for employers to treat the union just like any other outside group. If the company cafeteria is rented out or lent to outside groups for meetings, then the union must be given the same privilege. If outside solicitors are allowed to come onto company property, then union organizers must be allowed to come onto company property. Security guards should treat every nonemployee that shows up at the gate the same way and not have a special procedure for union representatives. That is why most work facilities are closed to nonemployees. If that is the case, this should be posted at the gate, and a provision should be placed in the employee handbook.

SAMPLE EMPLOYEE HANDBOOK PROVISION

All MNO facilities are closed except to employees and authorized guests of the company. We expect all employees to follow security procedures, including informing their friends and relatives that as a general rule they will not be allowed past the security gate. No solicitation is allowed on company property, including the parking lots.

BARGAINING WITH THE UNION

If the union wins the election, then the National Labor Relations Board will certify that it is the exclusive representative of the employees in the bargaining unit. The employer will not be able to bargain with individual employees over wages and benefits in most cases. Both the union and the employer are required to bargain in good faith in an attempt to reach an agreement. While these negotiations are going on, the wages and benefits of the affected employees should not be changed. Both sides must meet and attempt to reach an agreement. Both sides must sign a written contract if an oral agreement is reached on an issue. Employers may not require that the union end a strike before beginning negotiations.

While it is common for both sides to begin the bargaining process by presenting the other side with a written proposal, this process is not required and may not be a good idea in all situations. While employers are required to bargain in good faith, they are not required to come to an agreement.

In the 1969 *General Electric* case, the company made an offer and announced to the world and to the employees that this was its best offer and that it had no intention of changing its mind. The federal Second Circuit Court ruled that this strategy was a violation of the National Labor Relations Act because it amounted to a refusal to bargain. General Electric also refused to provide the union with information it had requested concerning costs and benefits. This was also found to be a violation of the law. Employers must provide information that is reasonable when it is requested by the union and must actually bargain rather than making the union a take-it-or-leave-it offer.

Federal law divides the subjects that can be discussed into three groups: illegal, mandatory, and voluntary. It is illegal under federal law for a union to ask for a closed shop or for racial discrimination. On the other hand, federal law requires both sides to bargain over wages, hours, and the terms and conditions of employment. Terms and conditions of employment include such issues as vacation pay, company housing, drug testing, seniority rules, and the existence of an agency shop. Everything else can be considered to be voluntary. This means that either side may bring it up, but the other side does not have to agree to discuss it or put provisions concerning it into the contract.

There are three types of shops: the closed shop, the union shop, and the agency shop. A closed shop is an agreement to hire only union members. A closed shop is illegal under federal law. A union shop is an agreement that all employees hired into the bargaining unit will join the union within a set period of time, usually thirty days. An agency shop is an agreement that everyone who is hired into the bargaining unit will pay union dues, even if he or she does not join the union. In twenty-one states, right-to-work laws prevent employers and employees from agreeing to impose either a union or an agency shop on the employees. This means that in these states, even if a union contract has been signed, employees in the bargaining unit may refuse to either join the union or pay union dues. Even if a contract appears to require employees to join the union, the U.S. Supreme Court has ruled that people cannot be forced to join a union against their will (*General Motors*). That means that even if a contract appears to call for a union shop, it really calls for an agency shop. Employees have a right to become what are called "financial core members," meaning that they pay dues and fees but are not real union members. If they are not real union members, they cannot vote in union elections and they cannot be disciplined or fined by the union for doing things the union does not like, such as crossing a picket line during a strike.

Right-to-Work States

Alabama	Iowa	North Carolina	Utah
Arizona	Kansas	North Dakota	Virginia
Arkansas	Louisiana	South Carolina	Wyoming
Florida	Mississippi	South Dakota	
Georgia	Nebraska	Tennessee	
Idaho	Nevada	Texas	

Federal law prevents employers from changing wages, hours, and working conditions until an impasse in the negotiations has been reached. An impasse is not reached just because one of the two sides is tired of talking or because no progress has been made. An impasse has been reached only if both sides have discussed an issue and tried to reach an agreement. There must be no real possibility of any further progress before it can be said that an impasse has been reached. Once an impasse has been reached, the employer is free to make changes without the agreement of the union. Just because an impasse has been reached concerning one issue does not mean that discussion of the other issues must end. On the contrary, negotiations on other issues should continue in good faith. However, once an impasse has been reached, a strike or picket line becomes an acceptable union tactic. If employees strike over economic issues, the employer is allowed to hire permanent replacements.

This issue of hiring permanent replacements is complex, and legislation is before Congress to make hiring permanent replacements illegal. Until that legislation becomes law (if it ever does), the current rules have been worked out by federal courts and the National Labor Relations Board. As a general rule, employees who go out on strike because the employer has engaged in an unfair labor practice have the right to get their jobs back when the strike is over. If the employees go on strike for economic reasons (they want higher wages, for example), then the employer is allowed to hire permanent replacements. That means that strikers are not entitled to get their jobs back after the strike. However, they may not be fired. This is often difficult for employers to understand. These employees occupy a special position. They have not been fired, but they are not working. After the strike, as jobs come open, these employees must be offered any jobs that are substantially equivalent to those they had before the strike. However, if the employees take jobs with other companies that are substantially equivalent, they are viewed as having quit. Also, if the employees engaged in misconduct during the strike, they may be fired and no longer have to be treated in this special way. Some strikes, such as sitdown strikes, are illegal, and the strikers are not entitled to any protection under the law from discharge by their employer.

While the right to strike is protected by federal law, there are also provisions that try to make this step unnecessary. If a party to an agreement wishes to modify or terminate the agreement, it must give sixty days' notice to the other side. If a strike might harm the national health or safety, the president may order an eighty-day cooling-off period.

Union members have a right to resign from the union during a strike, and once they do so, they are beyond the reach of any union discipline or fines. If there is a union shop or agency shop agreement, the resigning union members must still pay dues. Generally, employees must resign from the union before they cross a picket line or go back to work during a strike if they want to avoid being subject to union discipline and fines. The U.S. Supreme Court has ruled that union members have the right to resign during a strike (*Pattern Makers*).

Employers are often surprised at the kinds of things they must bargain with the union about. For example, if the employer plans to subcontract work out, and that will affect employees in the bargaining unit, this must be discussed with the union. The U.S. Supreme Court has ruled that employers must bargain over contracting out work even if all the jobs in the bargaining unit will be eliminated (*Fiberboard*). Employers may have to bargain over this issue and may have to wait until the current contract expires before contracting out this work.

The same applies to employers who wish to close down a plant. Just as contracting out work affects the workers, they are certainly affected when a plant is closed down. Whether or not the employer must bargain over this depends in part on why the plant is being closed down. If it is being closed down because wages and benefits make it unprofitable, then this must be discussed with the union. On the other hand, if the plant is being closed down because of factors that do not involve labor costs, such as the desire to be closer to a supplier or customer, this may not be a mandatory subject for discussion. Also, if the plant is being closed rather than moved and this work will no longer be done by the company, then bargaining would not be required. Of course, if the work will simply be contracted out, that would have to be bargained over.

ARBITRATION AND MEDIATION

The hope is that most disputes between employers and unions can be settled without a strike. To further that goal, the federal government provides a federal Mediation and Conciliation Service. This service will help unions and employers come to a mutually agreeable contract if both sides are willing to accept its help. In some cases the two sides may agree to accept the decision of an arbitrator.

Generally, most union contracts require that disputes under the union contract concerning issues such as whether or not a particular employee should be discharged be handled ultimately by an arbitrator. It is up to the union to decide whether or not to take a case all the way to arbitration. In most cases, the employee is stuck with the union's decision. However, the union has a duty to provide fair representation to all employees covered by the contract, whether they are union members or not. An employee can sue the union for breach of this duty. The employee must prove two things: that the employer violated the union contract, and that the union violated its duty to provide fair representation in the grievance and arbitration process (*Vaca*).

UNIONS AND COMPANY POLICY

Should an employer have a general statement in the employee handbook concerning unions? There are pros and cons. On the one hand, if an employer later wishes to argue that a manager was acting without authorization when he or she violated the labor laws, this might be easier if there was a statement in the handbook. On the other hand, any promises made in the handbook will have to be lived up to. Of course, what is said will depend on whether or not the company currently has to deal with a union for a group of employees.

SAMPLE EMPLOYEE HANDBOOK PROVISION

The MNO Company does not currently have any contracts with any unions. It is against company policy to discriminate against anyone because he or she belongs to a union. It is also against company policy to discriminate against anyone because he or she does not belong to a union.

CONCLUSION

Whether or not a company can prevent a union from winning an organizing election depends much more on the way employees are treated in general than on anything said during a union organizing campaign. Just as politicians usually win or lose elections based on their performance in office, so employers win or lose union organizing elections based on their past actions toward their employees. Employees who feel that they are treated fairly, paid fairly, and allowed to express their opinions freely will usually not vote to have union representation. On the other hand, employees who feel that they have not been treated fairly, paid fairly, or listened to will vote to have union representation.

APPENDIX: Do's and Don'ts of Union Election Campaigns

1. *Facts about the election process.* Do tell employees how the election will be conducted and that they are free to vote for or against the union even if they have already joined the union or signed an authorization card. Don't try to use threats or promises in an effort to force employees to vote against the union.

2. *Current wages and benefits.* Do tell employees about the current level of wages and benefits. Don't threaten to reduce wages or benefits if the union wins the election, and don't change wages and benefits during the campaign.

3. *Facts about unions in general.* Do tell employees that unions require the payment of initiation fees and dues and that communication will be handled by union officials if the union wins. Don't lie about unions.

4. *Facts about this union.* Do tell employees facts about this union and its leaders if they are true. Don't lie about the union or its leaders.

5. *Discrimination.* Do tell employees about the company's record of treatment toward them in the past. Don't discriminate against union members or union supporters.

6. *Strikes and picket lines.* Do tell employees that unions may ask their members to go out on strike and to walk a picket line. Members who refuse may be fined. Also, employees can be told that if they go out on strike for better wages and benefits, the employer is allowed to hire permanent replacements. Don't tell employees that a strike is inevitable or that the company will close down or move away if the union wins or goes on strike.

7. *Counter the union's campaign.* Do listen to what the union is saying and correct any misinformation or false promises. Don't lie about the union's position or make false promises of your own.

8. *Communication will change.* Do point out that after the contract is signed, communication will be between union and management, not between individual employees and management. Don't suggest that the union will not represent employees fairly.

9. *Union finances.* Do point out how much union officials make and that union dues will probably be automatically deducted from employees' paychecks. In states that do not have a right-to-work law, employers should point out that the union will ask for a union or agency shop, which means that everyone will have to pay dues whether he or she belongs to the union or not. Don't lie about the union or its past practices.

10. *Surveillance.* Do supervise the workplace and watch everything that goes on at work. Don't spy on the union or union meetings outside of the workplace.

11. *Unions at work*. Do prohibit union organizers from coming on the premises if other solicitors are also kept away. Don't prohibit union organizers from coming onto the premises if other solicitors are not kept away, and don't prohibit discussions concerning the election during breaks and lunch hours.

12. *Speeches and meetings*. Do hold meetings and make speeches telling employees why they should not vote for the union. Don't make any speeches or hold any meetings within twenty-four hours of the election.

Chapter 21

Employee Communications

The most important commodity in any organization is accurate and timely information. Only companies that know what the customer wants and react quickly survive in today's competitive marketplace. Also, only companies that are able to deal with problems while they are small and manageable come out on top. Innovation and creativity are important to any organization, regardless of its structure. Much of that information, innovation, and creativity must come from the employees.

Before discussing ways to encourage employees to communicate with management, it is important to realize that communication is a two-way street. Companies that want to hear from their employees should also make a significant effort to talk to them. We are constantly hearing about employees who read about major changes in the company they work for in the newspaper instead of hearing about them from management.

There are a variety of ways to communicate with employees. For smaller companies, a short information piece placed in every pay envelope is an excellent and inexpensive way to keep the lines of communication open. Bulletin boards are another inexpensive way to communicate. For large organizations, everything from a company newspaper to closed-circuit television is a possibility.

Should this desire to provide information to employees be discussed in the employee handbook? Probably not. While communication is always a good idea, an organization should be careful not to make promises that it cannot keep, and that is not just possible but probable when it comes to promises to keep employees informed. Remember, a promise made in the employee handbook is a promise that may be enforced in court—or, at the very least, a promise that may be the cause of low morale when it is not kept.

On the other hand, the desire to encourage and receive communication from the employees should be discussed in the employee handbook. Employees should be informed about the kind of communication that is expected from them and what is being done to encourage it. Also, all employees should be on notice that they may be asked to participate in a variety of communication schemes, and they will be better able to do so if they have been told about the possibility in advance.

Of course, one of the best tools of communication is the employee handbook itself. If it is given to every employee and discussed in a new-employee orientation meeting, a great deal of confusion can be avoided and a great many questions can be answered before they are even asked.

BULLETIN BOARDS

Bulletin boards placed in strategic areas around the facility are an excellent way to communicate with employees. It is important to realize that several federal and state laws require that notices be posted for the employees to see. The federal Fair Labor Standards Act requires employers to post a notice about the minimum wage. A similar state law may require that a similar notice concerning stage wage laws be posted. The federal Employee Polygraph Protection Act requires that a notice explaining the act be posted. There are federal and state safety laws, including the federal Occupational Safety and Health Act, that require that certain safety notices be posted. The federal and state civil rights laws require that basic information about them be posted. The federal Family and Medical Leave Act of 1993 requires that employers who are subject to its provisions post a notice explaining the law to employees. State law may require notices about unemployment, workers' compensation, and disability insurance. Employers should contact the U.S. Labor Department and their state labor commissioner for information and copies of acceptable notices.

Too many employers never put anything on the bulletin boards except these official notices. You can tell a lot about the amount and quality of information that is going out to employees from management by looking at the bulletin boards. If the last notice from management concerning something of interest to employees is dated 1924, you know that this is not a very communicative company. Just as a notice can be put in every pay envelope every payday, a copy of that notice can be placed on the bulletin boards and be replaced every payday.

COMMITTEES AND SURVEYS

Employee committees are a great way to get information in a usable form from employees. As we saw in the last chapter, however, employers are not allowed to form labor organizations, and in some cases the National Labor Relations Board has decided that a standing employee committee that was formed to discuss such things as wages and working conditions constitutes an internal labor organization and is a violation of the National Labor Relations Act. This problem can certainly be avoided. First of all, a labor organization exists for a significant period of time. A short-lived committee formed to advise management on wages and working conditions would usually not be considered to be a labor organization. An employee survey is of course not a labor organization and can often provide the same information and make everyone feel as if his or her opinion counts for something.

A labor organization is concerned with wages and working conditions. Employee committees that are not concerned with wages and working conditions would not qualify. In most cases, employers will be forming committees to provide information on other issues.

It is important to realize that it is very much to an employer's advantage if these communication efforts, including surveys and employee committees, are a part of the company's routine management process before a union comes knocking at the door. If a committee is formed all of a sudden when a union shows up, it is much more likely to be seen by the employees and the National Labor Relations Board as part of an effort to undermine the union. Also, the kinds of communication that an employer must engage in when fighting a union representation election will seem much more natural and believable if similar communication has been forthcoming before the election issue ever arose.

There is another issue that should be considered when discussing the need for employee communication policies. Many states now have whistle-blower protection laws. These laws protect people who report violations of law by their employers to the appropriate government official. It is much cheaper for employers if they provide their employees with a way to make a similar report inside the company without fear of retribution. Also, if employees are told that they should report any violations of law to a particular person and do not obey that instruction, this can be raised in any trial that may result. It can certainly be asked why the employee did not follow the internal communication policy. Of course, if the answer is that there was no such policy the employer is going to look even worse.

SAMPLE EMPLOYEE HANDBOOK PROVISION

The MNO Company got where it is today, in part, because of a willingness to listen to employees. It is the policy of the MNO Company to encourage employees to express their ideas and concerns to their supervisors. The MNO Company tries to keep employees informed about changes in the company and the world that might affect them, and the company expects the employees to do the same thing. Employees are instructed to report any violations of law or company policy to the director of human resources as quickly as possible. It is the policy of the MNO Company to obey all laws, and if an employee believes that a law is being violated by either the MNO Company or someone with whom the MNO Company interacts, this should be communicated as quickly as possible.

EMPLOYEE SUGGESTION PLANS

It is not an exaggeration to say that behind the success of most successful organizations there is a history of employee suggestions that were listened to and implemented. Often it is a story of an employee's getting a suggestion listened to and implemented against great odds and after fighting the company bureaucracy. In their book *In Search of Excellence*, Tom Peters and Robert Waterman talk at length about the need for employees to take their ideas and push them through to success, and how this is more possible in excellent companies than in companies that fail.

When Americans read about Japanese companies operating in the United States, one of the things they find most astounding is the number of suggestions that are made by employees and then implemented by the company. While many American companies cannot provide accurate information on this subject, most

Japanese companies can tell you how many suggestions were made at a facility in a year and how many were implemented. The numbers run into the thousands at many Japanese companies, and the results are impressive.

It is easier to see how a suggestion plan should be handled by first looking at a failure. The most famous failed suggestion plan in American legal history is the case of *Lone Star Steel*. Lone Star Steel began its suggestion plan program in 1962 by offering to pay for suggestions that led to either increased production or cost savings. When John Scott was hired as a brick mason in 1966, he began to get ideas about how his work could be improved. Steel is soaked in large brick pits where the steel cools to the right temperature. These pits fill up with slag that falls off the steel and have to be constantly rebuilt. John Scott suggested that the pits could be redesigned to allow the slag to slide to one side of the pit, making the pit much easier to rebuild and allowing it to be put back into production much faster. John Scott submitted his written suggestion in 1975 and was told to forget it. The reason given for rejecting his suggestion was that it had been considered before and rejected. John Scott did not give up. He kept arguing that his idea was a good one. Finally he was allowed to come in on his own time and rebuild one pit to his specifications. He began the work at Christmas 1979. When he was finished, the new design proved to be a success. Ultimately sixteen pits were rebuilt using John Scott's new design.

John Scott then asked for a reward under the company suggestion plan. At some point, John Scott had been told that the person making any suggestion that saved money would receive at least 5 percent of the first year's savings. By one estimate, John Scott's new design saved the company $60 million in the first year of full operation. A company committee formed to decide how much employees should be compensated for their suggestions voted to give John Scott nothing for his idea.

John Scott then sued Lone Star Steel in a Texas court, and the jury awarded him $3 million to compensate him under the company suggestion plan. They concluded that the suggestion plan was a contract and that the company had breached the contract by failing to pay John Scott for his suggestion. The jury also awarded another $3 million as punitive damages because they felt that the company had acted in bad faith and with malice and had also committed fraud against John Scott.

While the company had never given out a copy of the actual suggestion plan, with all the legalese, it had mentioned the plan in the employee handbook. Because the actual plan was never given out, the judge felt that only the statement in the handbook could constitute a contract. The judge also felt that all the special limiting language in the detailed plan that was intended to protect the company from this kind of liability was not part of the contract because the employees never got to see it. While the detailed written suggestion plan stated that the awards committee could decide to give nothing for a suggestion, the company magazine had said that "cash awards will be paid for all suggestions adopted." Again, because the company magazine had been given to the employees, this also became a part of the contract between the company and its employees.

The company argued that the plan could not be enforced as a contract because everything was too indefinite. The Texas judge did not agree. Ultimately a Texas appeals court overturned the award of punitive damages but upheld the award of $3 million for breach of contract.

The *Lone Star Steel* case raises a number of key points that every company should consider. Lone Star Steel had a suggestion plan, but employees were not given a copy. That was a mistake because the plan would have limited the company's liability. The plan had no top limit on the award. A top limit of any kind, even $1 million, would have saved the company a lot of money. The plan was discussed in the company magazine and the handbook, but not in enough detail to protect the company. Some employers talk about having a suggestion plan, but they have total discretion over how employees will be rewarded. That is not a plan, it is just the way business works. It should not be presented as a suggestion plan.

While some companies have an ongoing suggestion plan system, others prefer to have a suggestion plan contest from time to time. The idea of such a contest is to bring together employees who usually would not interact with one another and get employees involved and working in groups. In instituting such programs, it is important to have a written brochure that explains the rules and what the winners will win. There should be an end to the contest, but enough time should be allowed for real concrete suggestions to be developed. At least two months should be allowed for the contest. Whether or not employees participating in the contest will be paid for the time involved should be discussed in the brochure to avoid hard feelings and potential legal liability.

It is important to realize that not all suggestions make money or save money. They may simply improve the product or service. This can have as important an impact on the company in the long run as suggestions that have an immediate monetary result.

SAMPLE EMPLOYEE HANDBOOK PROVISION

We have two kinds of suggestion plans at the MNO Company. The first is our ongoing suggestion plan. Any employee may submit a suggestion in writing to the director of human resources at any time. The director will forward these suggestions to the appropriate company officials for consideration and possible implementation. Every year, in March, the director will appoint a committee made up of three managers and three employees to review the last year's suggestions. The three employees will be chosen at random from among all employees. The director shall act as chair of this committee. This committee will decide what awards will given for suggestions. The top award will be an all-expenses-paid trip to Europe for three weeks for the winner and his or her immediate family. At least one top award will be given out every year. The committee may decide to give out more than one top award. The committee may also decide to make cash awards of $5,000 or less. The decision of the committee is final, and both the company and the employees will be bound by its decision.

Second, here at the MNO Company, we do have a special employee suggestion contest from time to time. These contests are separate and apart from the usual suggestion plan process. These contests involve group entries, and only groups of at least five employees may participate in the contest. Prizes will be announced for each contest as the contest is announced.

Participation in the ongoing suggestion plan process and the special suggestion contests is strictly voluntary. We at MNO hope that all employees will want to take part. Many important improvements have been the result of employee suggestions.

CONCLUSION

Some companies like to say that they realize that every employee "comes complete with a brain." Other companies like to say to their employees things like "You are not paid to think" or "Don't think, just do." It is important for everyone involved in deciding on personnel policies and writing the employee handbook to know which kind of company this is. It would be better not to have a communication or suggestion section in the employee handbook than to have such a section be a cruel joke. There is also a potential for legal liability if promises made in the employee handbook are not kept. At the same time, you can tell a lot about a company by reading the employee handbook, and most good employees are not going to want to work for a company that does not encourage communication and suggestions.

APPENDIX: Do's and Don'ts of Suggestion Plans

1. *Information.* Do provide employees with written information about the suggestion plan. Don't write about the plan in company newsletters unless you are willing to live up to what is said there about the plan.

2. *Reward limits.* Do set out what the upper limit to any suggestion reward is. Don't make promises you cannot keep.

3. *Final decision.* Do make sure that whoever is given the authority to make the decision concerning suggestion rewards is given final authority. Don't lead employees to think that the decision can be appealed to a higher authority. That higher authority may turn out to be a court.

4. *Good faith.* Do administer the plan in good faith, giving everyone a fair chance to win a prize. Don't put people in charge of the plan who do not understand its legal and management implications.

5. *Idea guidelines.* Do set out guidelines concerning the kinds of suggestions you are looking for. Don't make the guidelines too limited.

6. *Publicity.* Do publicize the winners of the suggestion plan programs. This should improve both employee morale and the image of the company in the local community. Don't lie about the plan to anyone, even the local newspaper reporter.

Chapter 22

Workplace Safety

In chapter 20, we discussed the desire of most employers to avoid having to deal with unions. If low wages is the most common reason why employees turn to a union, unsafe working conditions is the second most common reason. For most employers, workplace safety is not a major concern until an employee is seriously injured or killed. Then it is too late. As a result of that injury or death, there may be fines, penalties, and even jail, not to mention higher workers' compensation payments and a terrible guilt. Workplace safety is one place where an ounce of prevention is worth a pound of cure. It is important that one person be in charge of all aspects of safety. In an organization that is too small to have a full-time safety director, this should usually be the director of human resources.

There are two main sources of unsafe working conditions: supervisors who do not have enough appreciation of the need for safety, and employees who do not want to be bothered with wearing the necessary safety equipment. It is very important to make it clear to both these groups that the organization is very serious about safety, which means accident and illness prevention. Employees should be trained in safety and the use of safety equipment before they begin work in any job that might in any way result in injury (which is every job).

SAMPLE EMPLOYEE HANDBOOK PROVISION

The MNO Company has a very good record in the area of safety, and we intend to keep it that way. Every employee is expected to ask for and receive safety training before beginning any new job. Supervisors are expected to make sure that every job is performed safely and that all employees are wearing proper safety equipment. Anyone in the MNO Company who believes that a task could be performed more safely should discuss that idea with the director of human resources. The director of human resources is responsible for all aspects of safety at the MNO Company, and anyone who has any questions, comments, or complaints about safety should contact the director.

FEDERAL AND STATE OSHAs

In the 1960s, everyone agreed that too many employees were being killed or injured needlessly in American industry. In 1970, Congress passed a law creating the Occupational Safety and Health Administration (OSHA) to write and enforce safety regulations and the National Institute for Occupational Safety and Health

(NIOSH) to conduct research into ways to make the workplace safer. The Occupational Safety and Health Act was passed with overwhelming support from both Republicans and Democrats (29 U.S.C. sec. 651 *et seq.*). Everyone believed that sensible regulations sensibly enforced could reduce deaths and injuries on the job and that both employers and employees would benefit.

States and Territories that Have Their Own OSHAs

Alaska	Kentucky	North Carolina	Vermont
Arizona	Maryland	Oregon	Virginia
California	Michigan	Puerto Rico	The Virgin
Hawaii	Minnesota	South Carolina	Islands
Indiana	Nevada	Tennessee	Washington
Iowa	New Mexico	Utah	Wyoming

While the act allowed states to set up their own OSHAs and thereby be relieved of having to comply with federal OSHA standards, during the 1970s both employers and employees argued against this. Large companies argued that it would be easier for them to comply with one set of regulations instead of fifty, while labor unions felt that most state OSHAs would not be as stringent as the federal OSHA. During the 1980s about half the states passed the necessary legislation and created the necessary agency to become exempt from the federal OSHA regulations. Half of these states created their own state agency because they believed that the federal agency was not doing an effective job, and the other half created their own agency because they felt that the federal agency was being too stringent. Connecticut and New York set up state OSHAs, but only to deal with safety in state and local government agencies. In theory, the state OSHAs must have regulations and enforcement procedures that are at least as stringent as those of the federal OSHA before the federal OSHA will relinquish jurisdiction to the state agency. Of course, some well-publicized disasters in states such as North Carolina raise serious doubts that that is really the case. In the rest of this chapter we will discuss the rules and procedures of the federal OSHA, with the understanding that in some states similar rules and procedures will be enforced by a state OSHA instead.

The federal law (and state laws that supersede the federal law) applies to almost all employers, regardless of size. While some recordkeeping regulations apply only to employers with more than ten employees, the requirement to have a safe workplace applies to all employers, private and public. Special rules apply to miners (they are covered by the federal Mine Safety and Health Administration) and seamen (they are covered by U.S. Coast Guard regulations). Also, homeowners who hire domestic servants to clean house or take care of children are usually not covered by OSHA.

The federal OSHA states that all employers have a general duty to furnish to each employee a place of employment that is free of recognized hazards that are "causing or likely to cause death or serious physical injury." A hazard may be considered recognized if the employer knew that it was a hazard or if it is generally known in the industry to be a hazard. One federal circuit court has ruled that a hazard shall be considered to be recognized even if its presence can be detected only with the use of special sensing equipment (*American Smelting*). A hazard can be anything from the presence of a dangerous chemical to the absence of handles on a valve (*Champlin Petroleum*).

Congress assumed that the Secretary of Labor would write a great many safety regulations and that those would form the basis of the enforcement effort. That has proven to be more difficult than anticipated, in part because technology is always changing and in part because the regulation-writing process is difficult. The Secretary of Labor publishes proposed standards in the *Federal Register*, and a thirty-day comment period follows. If anyone asks for a hearing, the secretary is required to hold one. Then the regulations are published as final in the Federal Register, and for the next sixty days they may be challenged in a federal circuit court. After that, individual employers may ask for a variance in their case because of their special circumstances.

ENFORCEMENT

The federal OSHA requires employers to provide a safe workplace, train employees about potential hazards, post warnings and notices, keep records of work-related injuries and illnesses, and notify OSHA of any major accidents. Employers have both a general duty to provide a workplace that is free of recognized hazards and a specific duty to obey federal (or state) safety regulations. OSHA enforces the rules with fines. The usual fine is less than $1,000, but that can add up if several violations are found. The fine for willful or repeated violations is up to $10,000. In most cases, when a violation is first cited, the employer is asked to pay a small fine and given a specific period of time to correct the violation. If the violation is not corrected on time, a fine of $1,000 per day until the violation is finally corrected may result.

There are also criminal penalties. An employer who willfully violates a safety standard and causes the death of an employee can be fined up to $10,000 and sent to prison for up to six months. Employers who cause a second death can be fined up to $20,000 and sent to prison for up to one year. Anyone who warns someone about an upcoming OSHA inspection can be fined up to $1,000 and sent to prison for up to six months. Anyone who lies to OSHA can be fined up to $10,000 and sent to prison for up to six months. There are also special penalties for anyone who assaults or kills an OSHA inspector.

As a general rule, if an OSHA inspector finds a violation, he or she will issue a citation. The employer or an employee (or the employee's representative) has up to fifteen days to contest all or part of the citation. If the fifteen days pass without notice of contest, the citation becomes final and not appealable. Any citations and notices of appeal of a citation must be posted on the employer's bulletin board. This gives employees a chance to become involved in the process. Usually employees become involved because they believe that the time allowed to correct the problem is too long. Appeal is made to the Occupational Safety and Health Review Commission, although the actual hearing is usually in front of an administrative law judge. Anyone who is involved in the hearing—the employer, the employee, or OSHA—can appeal the judge's decision to the commission if this is done within twenty days of the day the decision is mailed out to these parties, but the commission usually does not grant an appeal. Then either side may appeal to a federal circuit court.

STATE CRIMINAL CHARGES

In some cases, the actions of employers have been so outrageous that a small fine or a few months in prison did not seem like enough to some district attorneys, who instead charged employers with crimes such as manslaughter and battery under the state penal code. For example, managers in Michigan were charged with manslaughter when a worker left in a van died of carbon monoxide poisoning (*Hegedus*). Executives of an Illinois company were charged with aggravated battery when forty-two workers were poisoned after working around hazardous chemicals without any ventilation (*Chicago Magnet*). In New York, managers of a thermometer manufacturing company were charged with assault after their employees were exposed to mercury vapors (*Pymm*). In each of these cases, the executives charged argued that federal safety law had preempted this area of law and that they could not be made to face charges under the state penal code. In 1989 and 1990, the supreme courts of Michigan, Illinois, and New York all ruled that Congress did not intend to preempt this area of law by passing the Occupational Safety and Health Act.

EMPLOYEE RIGHTS

As a general rule, workers who file complaints with OSHA (or the state OSHA) or do anything they are allowed to do under the act are protected from discharge or mistreatment by their employer. Things employees are allowed to do under the act include testifying at a hearing, participating in an inspection tour, contesting a citation, going to court to challenge a decision, or asking the employer to meet the posting obligations.

An employee also has a right to refuse to work if the employee has a reasonable, good faith belief that performing a task poses a real danger of death or serious injury, the employee is unable to get the employer to correct the problem, and there is no time to try to eliminate the problem through the usual method of filing a complaint with OSHA. Employees who as a group refuse to work because of unsafe working conditions are also protected by the National Labor Relations Act.

INSPECTIONS AND SEARCH WARRANTS

The whole idea behind the Occupational Safety and Health Act was that the Secretary of Labor would promulgate safety regulations, and then OSHA inspectors would go out and conduct inspections to prevent serious illness or injury. OSHA has a list of priorities: (1) Situations involving imminent danger have first priority, (2) areas where major injuries or death have occurred are next, (3) complaints by employees are next, and (4) routine inspections to find violations are last on the list.

The U.S. Supreme Court has ruled that OSHA may not conduct an inspection without a search warrant if the employer refuses to allow the inspection (*Marshall*). OSHA inspectors do not need a warrant to come into areas that are not kept private. This means that they can come into open fields and into buildings that are generally open to the public. Another reason to maintain a closed workplace, besides a desire to keep out union organizers, is to keep out OSHA inspectors. If any area is generally open to the general public, then police and OSHA inspectors cannot be kept out. Also, OSHA inspectors can fly over in a helicopter without a warrant. Inspectors do not need a warrant if they reasonably believe that they have an emergency situation involving possible imminent death or serious injury.

The one thing inspectors cannot do without the employer's consent is come into a private building that is closed to the general public absent a real emergency. Should employers insist on a search warrant? It depends. Generally, it makes the inspectors angry if they are forced to get a search warrant. In most cases they will be able to get a search warrant and return within twenty-four hours. That means that in most cases employers should not insist on a search warrant unless they have a serious violation that can be corrected in less than twenty-four hours. Employees, or their representative, have a right to come along on an inspection tour, although if there is no union, it is not easy to figure out which employee should come along.

RECORDKEEPING REQUIREMENTS

From time to time we hear that OSHA has levied a very large fine against a large employer. In most cases these large fines are the result of a failure to keep the correct records. Two groups of employers are exempt from the recordkeeping requirements: employers in low-hazard industries, such as retail, banking, insurance, real estate, and law; and employers with less than eleven employees. All other employers are required to "maintain a log and summary of all recordable occupational injuries and illnesses." This log is kept on OSHA Form 200, which requires employers to list the name of each injured employee and details of any occupational illness or any injury that results in medical treatment beyond first aid, results in a loss of consciousness, results in restriction of work or motion, or results in a transfer to another job or death. Obviously, when in doubt, keep a record. As a general rule, this log must be kept for at least five years, and a summary of each year's record showing numerical totals must be posted for employees to see during the month of February. Employers must also post a "Job Safety & Health Protection" notice in every language spoken by at least 10 percent of the workforce. Copies of this notice and the log can be obtained from the U.S. Department of Labor.

Employers who use hazardous materials must keep records for thirty years concerning employee exposure and employee medical examinations if they were conducted. This allows OSHA and employees to be able to look back to see if an illness was caused by exposure to a hazardous substance. These exposure records must be given to employees within fifteen days of a request. Employees can see only their own medical records unless they have a court order. OSHA does not require that employees be given medical exams, but if they are given medical exams, the records must be kept for thirty years (longer under the rules of some states).

Also, employers must notify OSHA if there is a major accident. A major accident is an accident in which one or more employees die or five or more employees are sent to the hospital. Every employer, even small employers and others that are not required to keep a log, are required to provide this notice to the nearest OSHA office within forty-eight hours of the accident.

Every employer should consider conducting its own accident investigation to help if any charges are filed because of the accident and to aid in preventing similar accidents in the future. The investigation should look to see if procedures should be changed, different protective clothing should be required, training should be altered, or the job should be redesigned. It is important that all employees be made aware of the need to report any occupational illness or accident to their employer as quickly as possible.

SAMPLE EMPLOYEE HANDBOOK PROVISION

If anyone sees an accident, he or she should report this immediately to a supervisor or the director of human resources and to the emergency office. Every employee is also expected to report any illness that might in any way be related to work to the director of human resources as quickly as possible. Employees are given emergency training from time to time in order to keep minor injuries from turning into major injuries.

HAZARDOUS MATERIALS AND THE EMPLOYEE'S RIGHT TO KNOW

OSHA requires that employers who use hazardous materials train employees about the materials they may use on the job, even small employers that might not be subject to the usual recordkeeping requirements. Hazardous materials include any substance that might damage skin, eyes, or lungs, including combustibles, gases, explosives, corrosives, and sensitizers. Every manufacturer of a hazardous material is required to send a Material Safety Data Sheet (MSDS) to its customers. Employers are required to keep these MSDS forms where employees can see them. Employers are also required to train workers in how to use hazardous materials and what to do in case of an accident.

Hazardous materials must be labeled clearly, and employees should be trained in their proper use and disposal, including the use of any safety equipment that might be required. The MSDS will contain recommended safety precautions and emergency procedures that should be used in case of an accident. The MSDS should also provide symptoms of exposure, exposure limits, whether

Material Safety Data Sheets Should Contain

1. Identity of the chemical
2. Characteristics of the chemical
3. Known health effects of the chemical
4. Time limits for safe exposure
5. Precautions that should be taken when handling
6. Protective equipment that should be used when handling
7. Emergency first aid procedures that should be used
8. Name of manufacturer, importer, or distributor

or not the material is a known carcinogen, and what protective clothing should be used when the material is handled. Every employer who uses hazardous materials must have a written hazardous material communication program. This must include a list of all hazardous materials in the facility. OSHA inspectors will want to see this list and compare it with materials found in the workplace. All containers and pipes containing hazardous materials must be clearly labeled.

The hazardous material communication program should include training employees about the materials. Employees should be trained to read the labels and Material Safety Data Sheets. Employees should be trained in the use of proper protective clothing and the proper precautions to take when using these hazardous materials on the job. They should also be taught what to do in case of an emergency.

Over half the states have right-to-know laws that must also be followed. These give employees the right to know about any hazardous materials they

States with Hazardous Material Right-to-Know Laws

Alabama	Kentucky	New Jersey	Tennessee
Alaska	Louisiana	New Mexico	Texas
Arizona	Maine	New York	Utah
California	Maryland	North Carolina	Vermont
Delaware	Massachusetts	North Dakota	Virginia
Florida	Michigan	Oklahoma	Washington
Hawaii	Minnesota	Oregon	West Virginia
Illinois	Missouri	Pennsylvania	Wisconsin
Indiana	Montana	Rhode Island	Wyoming
Iowa	New Hampshire	South Carolina	

may come into contact with in the workplace. Different state laws require the keeping of different forms and records and require that copies of these records be given to particular state agencies. In New York, for example, the definition of "toxic substance" is even broader than the federal definition of hazardous material, and the law requires that some records be kept for forty years.

SAMPLE EMPLOYEE HANDBOOK PROVISION

Hazardous materials are used in some facilities of the MNO Company. A file of Material Safety Data Sheets is kept in all facilities in which hazardous materials are used. Employees who come into contact with hazardous materials will be trained in their safe use and should consult the Material Safety Data Sheets if they are in doubt about the proper safety precautions that should be taken with a particular substance. Employees who do come into contact with hazardous materials are expected to participate in the Hazardous Materials Communication Training Program. Any employee who wishes to may see the Hazardous Materials Communication Plan for the facility where he or she works. Employees are expected to handle all hazardous materials with caution and to be sure that they are trained in the proper safety and use guidelines before using any hazardous material.

WHITE COLLAR INJURIES AND ILLNESSES

During the 1970s and 1980s, the emphasis in workplace safety was on blue-collar workers, particularly workers exposed to hazardous materials. In the 1990s, the emphasis has shifted to white-collar workers and the many dangers they face on the job. The four major areas of concern for white-collar workers involve repetitive motion injuries, video display terminals, bad air, and job stress.

Repetitive Motion Injuries

Repetitive motion injuries come about because of months or even years of performing the same motion over and over again. This most often affects backs that have been used to lift and bend or wrists that must make the same motion over and over again in the course of a day. Repetitive motion injuries accounted for almost half of all workplace injuries in 1990. In California alone, the number of reported repetitive motion injuries surged from 3,000 in 1982 to 18,100 in 1991. There were 281,800 cases reported in 1992, according to the U.S. Labor Department. People who use computer keyboards for long periods of time may find that their wrists can no longer move in certain directions without pain. Most of these injuries can be prevented by using a back or wrist brace, taking periodic breaks from the motion, doing special exercises to stretch tendons before work or to relieve pressure, and re-designing the job. Costs of workers' compensation, disability insurance, and health insurance will go up for any employer who does not take the repetitive motion problem seriously.

SAMPLE EMPLOYEE HANDBOOK PROVISION

One of the major health problems in the American workplace today is repetitive motion injuries, sometimes called repeated trauma injuries. These injuries are caused by performing the same tasks over and over again in the same way for long periods of time. Backs, wrists, elbows, and shoulders are the most vulnerable. These injuries can be prevented by the use of braces or supports, changing the way some tasks are performed, taking breaks, or performing a variety of tasks to avoid long periods of repeated motion. Early warning signs include numbness or tingling in an arm, leg, or finger or persistent and recurring pain from movement or pressure. Any employee who experiences any early warning sign should report that fact immediately to a supervisor or the director of human resources.

Video Display Terminals

Video display terminals are another potential source of health problems for today's workers. With more and more workers using their own personal computers, more and more people are sitting in front of a video display terminal for very long periods. As yet there are no national guidelines for terminals, but Sweden does have a safety standard, and American employers should consider buying equipment that meets the Swedish standard. Also, there are many workers who could make good use of liquid crystal displays instead of video display terminals. Liquid crystal displays do not emit the radiation that video display terminals emit. However, both types of displays may cause eyestrain if not used correctly, with proper lighting and proper seating. Many of the eye and muscle strain problems that result from using computer terminals for long periods of time can be prevented by requiring periodic breaks in which exercises are performed to get the body and eyes back to normal. These breaks and exercise sessions should be considered essential for these kinds of workers.

Sick Office Buildings

More and more office workers are finding that they suffer upper respiratory diseases because of the air they breathe in their office building. The Environmental Protection Agency calls this "sick building syndrome." Closed office buildings that recirculate air through the heating and air conditioning system can simply spread disease throughout the building. These systems can also circulate pollution caused by paint, pesticides, or other chemicals found in the average American office building. Employers can prevent much of this by building office buildings with windows that can be opened and by having heating and air conditioning systems that use heat exchangers to vent inside air out and bring outside air in. Filters can help with some hazards. Proper ventilation is a must for areas that contain hazardous materials.

Job Stress

Job stress is another major cause of illness on the job, although it often is not recognized as such. In about half the states, job stress can be used to file a workers' compensation claim. In the other half, it may result in a lawsuit for employer negligence. In other words, it is something every employer must begin to recognize and get serious about dealing with. People with stress may be considered disabled under the Americans with Disabilities Act, which means that their jobs may have to be restructured to accommodate the problem. This may mean transferring some employees, allowing them to work part time, or even firing a supervisor who stresses everyone out. A lot of job stress could be avoided if employers made a real effort to make the job just a little more *fun*!

SAMPLE EMPLOYEE HANDBOOK PROVISION

The MNO Company is aware that workers are likely to suffer from repetitive motion injuries, eyestrain from video display terminals, and job stress without proper breaks and exercise periods. That is why we have an extensive program of breaks and exercise periods for people subject to these kinds of injuries. There is a tendency to get busy and forget to take these breaks and do these exercises, but it is very important for everyone that these precautions be taken. Job stress can often be avoided by simply taking a break when needed. Employees who feel that they are suffering from high levels of stress should contact the director of human resources about the problem.

SMOKING AND SMOKERS

There are two issues involved with smoking and smokers. The first issue is whether or not employers may refuse to hire people or fire them simply because they are smokers. There are many reasons why an employer would like to do this. Smokers have absenteeism rates that are 50 percent higher than those of non-smokers, have twice as many job-related accidents as nonsmokers, and are 50 percent more likely to be hospitalized than nonsmokers, according to the American Cancer Society. Employers who pay for health insurance would be able to negotiate a much lower rate if all their employees were nonsmokers.

In more than a dozen states, specific laws have been passed to protect smokers from this kind of discrimination. In a few states, laws that prohibit discharging an employee because the employee uses a "legal product" or "engages in a legal activity" away from work will also protect smokers. In most cases they were passed primarily to do just that. Also, the Americans with Disabilities Act will probably be found to protect smokers. This is because the act specifically states that people addicted to illegal drugs are not protected. Generally, if a statute says that one subclass of people is not protected by the law, it is assumed that the rest of that class is protected. In this case, people addicted to legal drugs, such as nicotine, would probably be protected by the act.

On the other hand, none of these laws require an employer to allow smokers to smoke inside a building. In most cases this should not be allowed because secondhand smoke has been shown to be a major health hazard. It makes the other workers sick and can therefore increase disability and illness and cause health insurance premiums to go up. Also, more and more cities and states are passing statutes and ordinances to control smoking inside buildings. The no smoking policy should be dealt with in the employee handbook.

SAMPLE EMPLOYEE HANDBOOK PROVISION

Smoking is not allowed inside any MNO facility or building. This is a strict policy, and it is strictly enforced. Employees who must smoke may do so outside the building during a break from work. Smoking is hazardous both to the person smoking and to those who breath the smoke secondhand. The MNO Company will pay half the cost of programs designed to help our employees stop smoking. Employees who wish to quit should contact the director of human resources for information about approved programs.

ALCOHOL

The Americans with Disabilities Act specifically protects alcoholics, while at the same time saying that they may be held to the same standard of performance as every other employee. It is assumed that this also means that alcoholics do not have to be provided with any special accommodation at work. Alcohol given at work or by employers—at a picnic or company party, for example—can result in legal liability if a drunk worker injures himself or herself or someone else. In 1991 the Idaho Supreme Court ruled that a company was liable for the death of a person killed by a drunk employee driving home from a company party (*Slade*). Drunk employees who injure themselves will usually be covered by workers' compensation. The only way to avoid liability is to keep alcohol out of the workplace. Picnics can be just as much fun without alcohol.

SAMPLE EMPLOYEE HANDBOOK PROVISION

No alcoholic beverage of any kind is allowed in any MNO building or facility. Alcoholic beverages are not to be served at any MNO company function, including a picnic, dance, or party. While employees are of course free to consume alcoholic beverages on their own time away from work, employees who come to work unable to perform their job because of alcohol will not be provided with any accommodation. The MNO Company will pay half the cost of some alcohol treatment programs. Interested employees should contact the director of human resources for information about approved programs.

AIDS AND COMMUNICABLE DISEASES

One of the stated purposes of the Americans with Disabilities Act was to protect people with AIDS. People with other chronic diseases, such as tuberculosis, will also be protected by both the federal act and most state laws barring discrimination against the handicapped. This means that they must not be fired if they can do the job with reasonable accommodation. Accommodation may mean giving the infected person protective clothing. OSHA has issued guidelines for workers in health care, funeral work, linen services, food preparation, and other occupations that would either expose the worker to disease or allow the worker to expose others to disease. All employees should be warned to use gloves and other protective gear when dealing with any body fluid, including blood, from someone else. In some fields, every new employee should have a medical examination (remember, disabled employees may not be discriminated against in this regard; if any employees are examined, they must all be examined). However, with protective gear, people with AIDS and many other communicable diseases can be accommodated in most cases. Employers who wish to fire or not hire someone because he or she has a communicable disease should consult an attorney expert in this area.

SAMPLE EMPLOYEE HANDBOOK PROVISION

Employees with AIDS and other diseases are protected by the Americans with Disabilities Act. This means that they will be allowed to work if they can do so with reasonable accommodation. All employees should realize that diseases such as AIDS and hepatitis are carried by blood or in other body fluids. When helping an injured coworker, gloves and other protective gear should be worn if the person is bleeding. Any employee who becomes ill with a contagious disease should report this to the director of human resources so that proper precautions can be taken and emergency personnel can be warned. All medical information is kept confidential and revealed only to company officials who need to know.

CONCLUSION

Workplace safety is important. High worker's compensation premiums and other expenses make it irrational not to attempt to prevent illness and accident to the fullest extent possible. The added cost of failing to comply with OSHA regulations can and should be avoided. Any employer, even the smallest, should work to protect the health of its workers. This will pay large dividends, as well workers work better for a lower cost.

APPENDIX: OSHA Hazard Communication Standard

1. *Hazardous materials lists and MSDS file.* Companies that manufacture, import, or distribute hazardous materials are required to prepare a Material Safety Data Sheet (MSDS) for each hazardous substance and distribute it to anyone who buys the substance. Employers may rely on the MSDS but must keep a list of all hazardous substances used in a workplace. OSHA inspectors will compare the list against materials observed in the workplace and the Material Safety Data Sheets on file at the workplace.

2. *Hazardous materials communication plan.* All employers who use hazardous materials are required to have a written hazardous materials communication plan. The plan must include instructions on labeling and on how to use the Material Safety Data Sheets, instructions for employee training in hazardous materials, and a statement concerning who is responsible for carrying out the plan. Employees and their representatives have a right to see this written hazardous materials communication plan.

3. *Hazardous materials labels and warnings.* The makers and distributors of hazardous materials are required to place labels on all hazardous materials. Employers are required to make sure that the labels remain intact and that proper warnings are placed near hazardous materials.

4. *Hazardous material safety data sheets.* Employers are responsible for keeping Material Safety Data Sheets in the workplace in a place where employees may easily consult them. These MSD sheets should be kept up-to-date.

5. *Hazardous material employee training.* Employees who use or might be exposed to hazardous materials must be trained in their use and the proper safety precautions that should be taken with each type of material. Employees should be taught how to read and understand labels, warnings, and Material Safety Data Sheets that they might encounter on the job. Employees should be taught when to use protective equipment and what precautions to take to avoid injury to themselves and others.

6. *Hazardous material trade secrets.* Employers must provide information about hazardous materials when requested by a health professional treating an injured or ill employee who may have been exposed to the material, even if the material is a trade secret or is related to a trade secret.

Chapter 23
Workers' Compensation

At the end of the twentieth century in the United States, it is hard to imagine a time before workers' compensation. It was the first of dozens of laws that would be passed in the category of social legislation. The reason for the passage of these laws in both the United States and Great Britain in the early twentieth century was the great cost to society in general of injured workers. The basic idea of workers' compensation was, and still is, that the cost of injury or death caused by the manufacture of a product should be borne by the consumer of that product. Workers' compensation insurance premiums make sure that these costs are borne by the employer rather than society in general. This original purpose is sometimes lost sight of at the end of the twentieth century, when the focus seems to be more on holding the line on costs than on taking care of injured workers. To understand why the system is the way it is requires a trip into history.

ANCIENT DUTIES AND DEFENSES

Two centuries ago, in both Great Britain and the United States, courts decided that employers had a series of duties that they owed to their workers. Specifically, employers had a duty to (1) provide a safe workplace, (2) provide safe tools and machines, (3) provide competent and trained fellow workers, (4) write and enforce safety rules, and (5) warn of known dangers. The enforcement of these duties by the courts meant that many injured workers could sue and receive compensation. To correct what some courts felt was an imbalance in this situation, employers were allowed to use three defenses against suits by injured employees.

The first defense was called the fellow servant doctrine. This doctrine says that if a fellow employee was at all at fault, the injured employee could not sue the employer. The second defense was called the assumption of the risk doctrine. This doctrine says that any employee coming to work in a dangerous work environment has assumed the risk of being injured in ways that one would reasonably expect given that dangerous environment. For example, we would expect mine shafts to collapse, so a miner killed by such a collapse could not sue. Third, and last, was the doctrine of contributory negligence. This doctrine said that if the employee was at any way at fault, he or she could not sue the employer even if the employer was much more at fault than the employee. As a result of these three defenses, very few employees actually recovered for their injuries, which led to many disabled former workers going to the government for assistance, if any was available.

WORKERS' COMPENSATION INSURANCE

This led Great Britain and most American states to pass laws requiring most employers to buy workers' compensation insurance. The basic idea behind workers' compensation insurance was that the cost of a product should reflect the cost of helping injured workers rather than having that cost borne by the entire society. In some states, workers' compensation is optional for employers. However, no employer in its right mind would neglect to get workers' compensation insurance. That is because in those states that allow employers to opt out of the workers' compensation system, the statute also says that if an injured worker sues for violation of the ancient duties, the employer without workers' compensation insurance may not use any of the three classic defenses: fellow servant, assumption of the risk, or contributory negligence. This means that in most cases, injured employees who sue will win, and there will be no limit to the possible damage award.

Workers' Compensation Systems

1. Are no-fault systems that pay for injuries or illnesses that are work-related.
2. Do not care if either the employer or the employee was at fault unless either party engaged in willful conduct to injure itself or someone else.
3. Limit payments to a specific amount set by the statute.
4. Cover the cost of medical expenses for the injured worker.
5. Require employees to give up their common-law right to sue.
6. Remove from employers their defenses if they do not get workers' compensation insurance.
7. Provide a method for quickly determining if the employee is covered by the system through administrative hearings instead of a trial before a judge.
8. Require employees to provide notice to both their employer and the state commission if they think their injury or illness is work-related.
9. Allow both parties to sue third parties who may have caused the injury or illness.

Workers' compensation systems replaced a system in which most workers could not sue at all, while a few workers did sue and received large damage awards, with a system in which injured workers receive a lower, but guaranteed, benefit. The old system was based on fault. An injured worker had to prove that the employer was at fault (and that the employee was not at fault) before collecting any money in court. The new workers' compensation system was, and still is, a no-fault system. The question is not whether or not the worker or the employer was at fault. The question, rather, is whether or not the injury is job-related.

IS THE INJURY JOB-RELATED?

The whole point of workers' compensation is to provide injured or disabled workers with payments to replace lost income and to pay for medical expenses caused by work-related injuries. It is not always easy to tell if an injury is work-related. Most workers' compensation statutes state that an injury (or occupational illness) will be covered if it "arose out of and in the course of employment." Deciding whether or not something "arose out of" the work has not always been easy. What if someone is struck by lightning or a falling tree branch while doing his or her job? Years ago, courts ruled that these were simply acts of God that could happen to anyone at any time and therefore were not job-related. Today most courts would rule that if the workers would not have been where they were when they were struck by lightning, they can recover from worker's compensation. What if someone is injured by exposure to heat or cold? Again, courts decades ago might have said that the weather is another act of God, and employers should not have to pay. Today, most courts would rule that if the employee was working in the heat or the cold and would not have been exposed to the elements had it not been for the job, her or she can recover. The same applies to the dangers of the street. A worker who is sent on a errand or who must travel as part of the job would not have been exposed to the dangers of the street were it not for the job and is going to be covered in most states today. Generally, if workers would not have been exposed to a hazard had they not had to come to work or obey orders, they are going to recover. This will even be the case with workers who are the victims of assaults at work unless the person doing the assaulting is a personal enemy who just happened to catch up with the employee at work.

The second major requirement is that the injury must occur "during the course of employment." The issue here is where the employee happens to be when he or she is injured. Generally employees are not covered while they commute to and from work. On the other hand, once they park in the employer's parking lot, they will be considered to be at work and covered in most states. If the employee is making a trip for the employer or picking up something for the employer on the way to work, he or she will be covered. If the worker is engaged in horseplay, some courts say that this is covered, while others say that it is not. If the employee makes a personal side trip while on a business trip or while running an errand for the boss, he or she will usually be considered to be on personal, not work-related, business and will not be covered. However, once the employee is back on the path required by the work-related errand, he or she is again covered by workers' compensation.

WHO IS COVERED

In most states, all but a very small fraction of workers are covered by the workers' compensation statute. In some states domestic servants and farm workers are not covered. Special federal programs and statutes apply to longshoremen and harbor workers, railroad workers, and sailors. In most states, even very small businesses with very few employees are expected to get workers' compensation insurance or face the consequences.

There are a number of injuries and illnesses that have been difficult for the workers' compensation system to deal with. Heart attacks are particularly problematic because it is still not clear what causes them. How much are they the result of poor diet and lack of exercise? How much does overwork and stress at work really increase the possibility of having a heart attack? Many states have amended their workers' compensation statutes to deal with this issue. In some states a worker who has a heart attack is not covered by workers' compensation unless the attack was the result of unusual exertion at work. Some ask if the job caused more "wear and tear" on the heart than would have been the case if the employee had not had this particular job. The Nevada statute simply says that heart attacks are not covered by workers' compensation, period.

Mental disorders and stress are another area in which different states take different approaches. In California, mental disorders caused by stress are covered, but under recent changes in the law, the job must account for at least half the mental stress. Other states do not include stress-related illness caused by the normal occurrences of the workday under the workers' compensation system. That is not necessarily good news for employers in those states. Employees may still be able to sue (generally, if something is not covered by workers' compensation, they can sue) and receive very high damage awards if they can prove that the employer was negligent and that this caused their mental injury.

Decades ago only injuries were covered. Today most statutes also cover occupational illnesses. It is not always clear what will qualify as an occupational illness. This depends in part on how the statute is written and what evidence there is to support the idea that the employee would not be suffering from this particular problem were it not for exposure to chemicals or other hazards at the workplace.

Workers can be disqualified from coverage for a number of reasons, depending on the state. In some states, workers who are injured through "willful misconduct" may not recover from workers' compensation. In other states, workers who "willfully disobey safety rules" may not receive benefits. Some states will not allow an injured worker to collect if he or she was intoxicated during the injury. In other states the question is whether or not the intoxication caused or increased the likelihood of the accident. Generally, suicide is not covered, but there are many exceptions, such as the suicide of a worker who has been driven crazy by work.

CLASSIFICATION OF DISABILITY

In most states workers are classified as either temporarily or permanently disabled and as having either a partial or total disability. Of course, workers are also classified as either dead or alive. For workers who have died on the job, workers' compensation acts as a kind of life insurance, providing benefits for the worker's spouse and children for a period of time.

For a temporarily disabled worker, compensation is supposed to make up for lost income until the worker can go back to work. For a permanently disabled worker, workers' compensation provides some compensation for the loss the worker has suffered. Unlike other kinds of disability insurance, workers' compensation is paid if the worker can no longer do the kind of work he or she was doing before the accident or illness, even if there are still many jobs that the worker is capable of doing. Also, workers' compensation pays for the medical expenses caused by the accident or illness.

Many states have a schedule that provides definite payments for particular injuries. For example, a finger will be worth a set number of weeks of wages, regardless of the impact the loss of a finger has on the particular worker. If an injury is primarily to one part of the body, but has an effect on some other part of the body, the employee will usually not be stuck with the schedule payment.

Discharging Employees

In most states, either under statute or by court decisions, employers who discharge employees because they filed a workers' compensation claim may be sued for wrongful discharge. At the same time, an employer may discharge an employee who can no longer do the job. However, for employers with more than fifty employees, the federal Family and Medical Leave Act will require that the employee be given a period of time off, without pay, to recover. Also, the federal Americans with Disabilities Act and state laws barring discrimination against the handicapped require employers to accommodate the disabled. The majority of complaints filed in 1993 under the Americans with Disabilities Act involved injured workers who felt that they could come back to work if the employer provided them with reasonable accommodation. Given these laws and the desire of most employers to keep their workers' compensation premiums down, every effort should be made to help an injured worker get back to work.

An employer will usually be justified in firing a worker who files a workers' compensation claim if the worker violated safety procedures at the time of the injury. In most states, workers may also be discharged if they lied about past workers' compensation claims or past illness or disability if that past illness or disability made this injury more likely.

Claims Procedure

In most states, employers must get (or would be crazy not to get) workers' compensation insurance. Injured or ill employees are required to notify their employers within a short period of time if they think their injury or illness is work-related. We have already seen an employee handbook provision that asks employees to report any work-related injury or illness as quickly as possible. This provision protects employers, who can point to it if an employee fails to provide the necessary notification. After investigation, if the employer does not intend to challenge the claim, workers' compensation works just like a combination of health and disability insurance. The insurance company pays the worker for lost income based on a schedule and pays the medical bills.

In some cases the employer will wish to contest the claim. Generally, in most states, the employer notifies the insurance company that it does not believe that the worker is entitled to benefits, and the insurance company then refuses to pay benefits. Then employees must file a claim through the state review process. This is different in every state. In some states, the worker gets to hire an attorney; in other states, attorneys are not allowed to help injured workers with their workers' compensation problems. In most states a special administrative system handles workers' compensation claims. In contested cases a hearing will be set, and an administrative law judge will hear the evidence and make a ruling.

There may be a settlement, but in workers' compensation there are many ways in which an injured employee or the employer can reopen the case. If the employer now has evidence that the employee was faking, the case may be reopened. On the other hand, if the injury has gotten worse over time, the injured worker may reopen the case.

Once the administrative law judge has made a decision, either the worker or the employer may usually appeal to a special commission. Once the commission has made a decision, this decision may be appealed to a court, but in most states the courts will overturn the commission only if there was "no substantial evidence" to support its decision. That is seldom the case.

SUING SOMEONE ELSE

All too often in the United States, employers view injuries and occupational illnesses at work as a conflict between the injured worker and the company. That does not have to be the case. In most cases, the worker is injured, and the employer should be glad it is not going to be sued but will be covered by workers' compensation insurance instead. It will be to the advantage of both the employer and the injured employee if they can work together to sue someone else for the injured employee's damages. The employee will receive far more than he or she would have under simple workers' compensation insurance, and the employer may be off the hook for all or part of the money that would have been paid by workers' compensation. In other words, this can be a win-win situation for both parties. It is also good for worker morale to see the employer working with an injured worker to help him or her get more money than would otherwise have been the case.

Who can be sued? There are a wide variety of potential third-party defendants. A third-party defendant is someone who contributed to the injury in some way. If the injury involved a product, it may be that the product can be shown to be defective. In this case, the people who made, distributed, or sold the product may be sued under product liability laws, which in many cases will allow for a large recovery. If the injury involved a hazardous material, the maker, importer, or distributor of that hazardous material may be at fault if it did not label the material correctly or failed to provide the correct Material Safety Data Sheet. If the injury happened on someone else's property, it may be that that person's negligence was at least partly the cause of the injury, and so that person can be sued. Most property owners have insurance that covers liability. If the injury involved an automobile accident, there may be another party at fault, and that party's automobile insurance may provide a remedy.

ENCOURAGING EMPLOYEE COOPERATION

Employers need to make a fundamental decision early on. Are they going to fight every workers' compensation claim and get a reputation as a tough but unfeeling boss, or are they going to try to turn every injury into a chance to demonstrate how humane and caring they are? There are few employers in between these two extremes. For employers who plan to be tough and damn the consequences, the following employee handbook provision might be in order.

SAMPLE EMPLOYEE HANDBOOK PROVISION

Here at the XYZ Company we know that most people who file a workers' compensation claim are faking it. We intend to vigorously investigate any workers' compensation claim and make any injured worker fight for every dollar. We have a private detective firm on retainer to investigate fakers, and we intend to prosecute people who try to fake an injury to the full extent of the law. Anyone who files a false workers' compensation claim can be sent to prison, and that is where we want to see them.

An Alternative Approach

The alternative is to express real concern for any injured workers and at the same time attempt to provide all workers with an incentive to work safely and help with accident investigations. Many employees simply do not know how workers' compensation works and should be told by their employer if good employee relations are to be maintained.

SAMPLE EMPLOYEE HANDBOOK PROVISION

At the MNO Company we have workers' compensation insurance for all our employees. It is important that every employee report any accident or illness that might be in any way job-related to the director of human resources as quickly as possible. It is important for all employees to realize that the more we have to spend on premium payments for workers' compensation insurance, the less money we have to pay our employees. As an incentive for everyone to work more safely, we budget a certain amount every year to cover workers' compensation premiums and the cost of temporary workers who are needed to replace injured workers. If we spend less than the budgeted amount in a year, that money will be used to fund a safety appreciation party at the end of the year.

HELPING WORKERS RECOVER

Studies show that workers recover faster and their medical costs and workers' compensation costs are lower if someone at work takes an interest in their health and well-being. It would be good for any company to develop a policy that encourages employees to visit injured workers and cheer them up. Also, someone in the Human Resources Department should be assigned to keep up with any seriously injured or ill worker, visit the worker, and see how his or her return to work can be speeded up. This is good business, and it is good for the morale of the other employees.

The Americans with Disabilities Act will be used to force employers to accommodate injured workers who are capable of returning to work with some accommodation. Why fight it? Why not make a big deal about providing this accommodation instead? Employees who see that their employer really does want to help them get back on their feet are likely to recover more quickly at less cost to everyone.

CONCLUSION

The focus at the end of the twentieth century is on helping employers keep workers' compensation costs down in order to keep American companies competitive on the world market. Many states have reformed their workers' compensation laws to further this goal, or soon will. At the same time, employers must work to keep costs low by preventing illness and accidents whenever possible.

Chapter 24

Employee Duties

It often comes as a surprise to both employers and employees to learn that under American (and English) law, employees have certain fairly specific duties that they are expected to perform, or live up to. Because of this lack of general knowledge concerning this area of the law, it is probably a good idea to have a fairly long section of the employee handbook that explains these duties and tries to make concrete and specific what is abstract and general under the law. It is also true that, while the focus of this book has been on avoiding lawsuits by employees, there are times when employers are justified in suing their employees or former employees. Also, employers may be able to use the fact that an employee violated one of these classic employee duties as a defense against a lawsuit by an employee. This defense will be even stronger if the employees were told about their duties in the employee handbook.

THE DUTY TO WORK TO THE BEST OF ONE'S ABILITIES

The first duty an employee has is to show up for work. This may seem obvious, but if someone has agreed to come to work, then he or she should come to work. In many ways, the passage of the federal Family and Medical Leave Act helps employers as well as employees. Many employers have wondered when it was fair, or reasonable, to terminate an employee who has taken temporary leave because of an illness or accident, or for one of the other reasons covered by the act. Now we have a federal law that says that it is reasonable to expect that no more than twelve weeks will be used for this purpose in any one year. An employee who cannot manage to come back to work after this 12-week period can be terminated and usually should be terminated to avoid charges of discrimination (have a policy on this and stick to it).

Employees are expected to perform to the best of their abilities. If an employee has demonstrated an ability to perform at one level, or should be able to do so given his or her experience and education, then not doing so is a violation of this duty. Employees who do not perform to the best of their abilities can certainly be fired, and should be fired in most cases.

THE DUTY OF CARE

Employees also have a duty to care for, and about, everything that belongs to the employer. Employees are considered to be fiduciaries under the law. Just as a trustee given someone else's property to take care of is expected not to harm it or waste it, the same duty applies to employees. Employees are not supposed to take their employer's property home for their own use without permission, even if it is just a paper clip or a pen. Employees are not supposed to abuse their employer's property, and in fact they are supposed to take care of it as if it were their own. Employees who have information that would be useful to their employer are supposed to tell it to the employer (if the employer has made that possible through open communication policies). An employee who fails to use reasonable care and injures the employer's property may be sued for damages.

The Duty of Loyalty

Employees have a duty to be loyal to their employer. This can mean many different things, depending on the circumstances. If an employee learns of a possible business opportunity, he or she has a duty to inform the employer of this. Of course, if the employer is not interested in taking advantage of the opportunity, then in most cases it would be correct for the employee to do so; however, the offer must be made to the employer first.

There is more to this duty than just the duty to inform the employer about business opportunities. Employees are generally not supposed to perform as suppliers or customers to their employer without letting their employer know that they are doing so. In one case the judge ruled that forming a company to supply the employer with generators violated this duty of loyalty (*Odeco*).

Many cases involve the duty not to compete with the employer without the employer's permission or to provide aid and comfort to competitors. In one case the court allowed an employer to sue an employee who had diverted his employer's business to a major competitor (*SHV*). Often this duty of loyalty is violated when an employee is getting ready to compete with an employer. While employees can quit and form a competing business, absent an agreement not to do so, they must wait until they leave to start the competition. Many cases involve just how much an employee may do while he or she is getting ready to form a competing business. In one case the employee discussed the new company he was planning to create with his current employer's customers while he was still working for that employer. He also discussed with his current employer's employees the possibility of them coming to work for him once he opened his competing operation (*Mulei*). The Colorado Supreme Court said that both of these actions violated the duty of loyalty and allowed the employer to sue for damages. In another case, an employee's wife incorporated a company to compete with her husband's employer, and the husband tried to convince his customers to move their business to his wife's company. The judge not only ruled that the employer was justified in firing this worker but issued a court order barring this employee from ever selling to his now former employer's customers (*Carlson*).

Employees who violate their duty of loyalty may be sued for damages. They may also be sued for the money they received in wages and benefits while they were being disloyal. The law says that employers do not have to pay for disloyalty.

DUTY OF GOOD CONDUCT

As a general rule, employees are expected not to bring disrepute on their employer because of their actions away from the job. This can be tricky because, for many reasons, employers should not spend time prying into the private lives of their employees. At the same time, if those private lives become public and bring disrepute on the employer, the employer has every right to act in self-protection.

This is especially difficult for public employers because their employees have a constitutional right to privacy. In one case, for example, a teacher was fired for alleged immoral conduct committed in his home with the two young daughters of the woman he was living with (*Lile*). The judge felt that this clearly had a negative impact on his job performance and upheld the discharge. On the other hand, a different judge ruled that a female schoolteacher had a right under the constitution to bear a child out of wedlock (*Ponton*). This judge felt that the teacher's right to bear children was greater than her employer's right to protect students from the sight of a pregnant unwed teacher. For private employers, the constitutional right of privacy does not apply, and therefore private employers would have the power to discharge employees in these kinds of situations. Still, if the conduct does not bring discredit on the employer, it should not be used as an excuse for discharge.

DUTY OF CONFIDENCE

Employees have a duty not to disclose information given to them in confidence by their employer. As long as the information is not generally known outside the business and would injure the employer if it were generally known, the employee has a duty not to reveal it. The difficult problem is knowing what is and what is not confidential. Employers have a duty to make it clear to employees that something is confidential if most employees would not know that from the very nature of the information.

Employees have a more specific duty not to reveal trade secrets. Again, most employees don't know that trade secrets may include product specifications, customer lists, vendor lists, software, sales and marketing plans, and pricing information. Trade secrets may also include formulas, recipes, blueprints, research test results, and business plans. This is why a statement in the handbook can be both informative for the employees and helpful for the employer. Also, employers should direct employees to let someone (someone specific, such as the director of human resources) know if anyone tries to get confidential or trade secret information out of them.

Most employees have no more desire to help the competition than their employer does. If they have been made to understand that "we are all in this together, and if a competitor wins, we lose," that should not be a problem. Nevertheless, it does not hurt to remind workers about this in an employee handbook provision.

The Five Major Employee Duties

1. The duty to work to the best of one's abilities
2. The duty to take good care of the employer's property
3. The duty to be loyal to the employer
4. The duty to behave away from work in a way that brings credit to the employer
5. The duty to keep all confidences and to not reveal confidential information to anyone outside the company

SAMPLE EMPLOYEE HANDBOOK PROVISION

Under American law, employees are considered to have a series of duties that they owe their employers. We at the MNO Company expect our employees to live up to those duties.

The first duty is the *duty to work to the best of your abilities*. Employees expect us to pay them. In return, we expect employees not only to come to work on time but to do their very best. We hope that employees who do not feel that they can do their very best because of some factor that can be corrected will discuss that with their supervisor or the director of human resources. We spend a lot of money on training and equipment, and we hope that our employees will help us to make the most of that investment.

The second duty is the *duty of care*. At MNO Company, employees are entrusted with machines worth a great deal of money. We expect employees to treat these machines, and all MNO property, with the utmost care. The more we have to spend on maintenance and repair, the less we have to pay employees.

The third duty is the *duty of loyalty*. If employees see a business opportunity that they think the MNO Company might take advantage of, they are duty bound to inform the company about it. Also, employees are not allowed to compete with MNO Company in any way. Employees who act as suppliers or customers or who own or work for suppliers, customers, or competitors are expected to inform the director of human resources of this as quickly as possible.

The fourth duty is the *duty of good conduct*. We have a right to expect our employees to conduct themselves away from work in a way that brings credit on the MNO Company and to avoid acting in a way that might bring ridicule or disrepute on the company. Employees who feel that they might have done something that violated this duty are expected to discuss this with the director of human resources as quickly as possible.

The fifth duty is the *duty of confidence*. Employees are expected not to reveal confidential information to anyone outside the company. This includes information about trade secrets, pay, product specifications, software, customers, vendors, marketing or business plans, price information, product formulas, recipes, blueprints, production processes, or our employees. This duty extends to employees who no longer work for MNO Company. Also, all books, reports, files, and records kept or developed by an employee belong to the MNO Company, not to the employee.

NONCOMPETITION AGREEMENTS

Some employees occupy special positions with an employer or have received special training from an employer. Employers would like to protect their investment by making such employees sign an agreement not to compete with the employer for a reasonable time after leaving the company. These agreements are very difficult to enforce in today's legal climate. Many judges do not like these agreements because they keep someone from making a living in the town he or she has come to call home. Forcing someone to choose between leaving town and giving up his or her occupation is not something judges like to do. In almost every state, special rules apply concerning which employees can be made to sign noncompetition agreements. Also, in different states, judges are willing to enforce agreements of this kind for different lengths of time. An employer who wishes to have an enforceable noncompetition agreement should have an attorney draw up the agreement to make sure that it meets the state's current requirements. Also, some judges will not enforce such an agreement unless the employer gave something extra to the employee when the employee signed the agreement. This something extra can be anything from a one time bonus to a small raise. This should also be discussed with an attorney at the time the agreement is drawn up.

Employers must keep in mind that in some states agreements not to compete will not be enforced at all against employees while in other states only certain kinds of employees can be asked to sign such agreements. Employers must also remember that these agreements must be reasonable with regard to the time, geographic area, and work activity covered. Employers cannot expect to keep a former employee from competing for more than one or two years, and only in the geographic area where the employee worked for that employer. Employers must also be specific concerning what it is the employee will not be allowed to do in that area, and if this has been written too expansively, the courts will not enforce it.

NONSOLICITATION

Nonsolicitation is very different from noncompetition. A noncompetition agreement means the employee cannot earn a living. A nonsolicitation agreement simply means that the employee agrees not to solicit the customers he or she worked with at the current employer. Judges hate noncompetition agreements but generally like nonsolicitation agreements. Judges do not think it is unfair that employees who build up a relationship with a group of customers while working for employer A should have to wait a reasonable time before going to those customers on behalf of employer B. Employers should have salespeople and other employees who work with customers on a regular basis sign a nonsolicitation agreement. There should also be a provision in the general employee handbook to cover everyone else.

SAMPLE EMPLOYEE HANDBOOK PROVISION

Employees who work directly with customers are prohibited from soliciting those customers for another company for a period of two years after leaving the MNO Company. Anyone coming to work for the MNO Company agrees to abide by this provision and to not, directly or indirectly, seek to do business with any person or company that he or she worked with or serviced while working at the MNO Company.

INVENTIONS AND CREATIONS

Many employers mistakenly believe that if one of their employees invents something on company time at a company facility, the employer owns the invention and may get a patent. That is not necessarily true. For this reason, every employee who is working in a capacity that might result in an invention should be asked to sign a specific agreement on this subject. At the same time, some kind of provision on this subject should also be in the employee handbook to cover everyone else.

The law does assume that if someone writes something or creates something while at work (other than patentable inventions), these creations do belong to the employer rather than the employee. As a general rule, if something is created, it is covered by the copyright act. If an employee writes or creates something that is within the scope of his or her employment, the employer is considered to be the author and holds the copyright (17 U.S.C. sec. 101). Of course, it is not always clear what is and what is not within the scope of someone's employment. Again, this should be dealt with in a special contract if an employee is hired to write or create things at work. A provision in the employee handbook could also help in some situations.

SAMPLE EMPLOYEE HANDBOOK PROVISION

Employees who invent, write, or create things while at work agree that these inventions and creations belong to the MNO Company. Employees agree to help the MNO Company patent and copyright inventions and creations made while they are employed at the MNO Company and to assign patents or copyrights to the company if that is necessary. Employees also agree to cooperate with the MNO Company in obtaining patent and copyright protection for their inventions and creations. If the MNO Company decides not to seek a patent but to keep the invention a secret, employees agree not to divulge any information to anyone else about any inventions they created or worked with while at the MNO Company.

CONCLUSION

In the world in which we live, the focus is more and more on employee rights. But employers have rights too. They have the right to expect their employees to live up to the ancient duties of employees and to expect employees to work for the best interest of their employer, not a competitor. In most cases, the average employee is not going to know anything about these ancient duties unless he or she is told about them in the employee handbook. Issues such as whether or not an employee should be asked to sign a noncompetition agreement should be dealt with when the employee is first hired, if at all possible. Employees who invent or create things at work should also be asked to sign a specific contract that deals with those issues. Employers should do everything possible to protect themselves and avoid confusion and conflict by using well-written agreements and employee handbook provisions.

Chapter 25

Firing Employees

Firing an employee is the hardest thing any employer has to do. It is hard for many reasons. Most employers try to hire the best person for the job. If someone has to be fired, that means that a mistake was made, and it is hard to admit a mistake. Given the structure of American society and the sorry state of the American unemployment compensation system, being fired is a much more tragic thing than it needs to be. However, most employers simply have to take this messed-up system as it is and make the best of it. Being fired is just about the worst thing that can happen to some people, and some employees are going to take it very hard. For employers, this creates a lot of uncertainty because they do not know how any particular person is going to react when he or she is discharged.

CONSTRUCTIVE DISCHARGE AND INTENTIONAL INFLICTION OF EMOTIONAL DISTRESS

Some employers would rather do anything to avoid firing someone, but this has its own problems. Take the *Monarch Paper* case. An executive, Mr. Wilson, had thirty years of experience with the company when the new forty-two-year-old CEO decided that he was going to get rid of the old guys. The new CEO began by writing a memorandum stating that he wanted to get some "new blood" into the company. When Wilson did not get the hint, the CEO called Wilson into his office and gave him three choices: (1) accept a sales job at his current salary, (2) be fired with three months' severance pay, or (3) accept a job as a warehouse supervisor at the same salary but with reduced benefits. As Wilson did not wish to leave a company he had spent thirty years of his life building up, and as he had no real sales experience and felt that he would simply be fired from a sales position in a few months for lack of sales, he took the third option. In an effort to further humiliate him, Wilson was given no real help in running the warehouse, which meant that he spent time at the end of each day pushing a broom and cleaning up the cafeteria. Mr. Wilson became more and more depressed as he saw his life's work going down the drain and finally ended up in the hospital as a manic-depressive. A Texas jury awarded him $300,000 for age discrimination and $3.1 million for damages caused by intentional infliction of emotional distress.

How might this story have turned out differently? Imagine that we have a similar employee (we will call him Bill) and a similar CEO bent on new blood. The CEO could have called Bill into his office and been almost honest with him.

Of course, no manager should say things like "we want some new blood around here," but some things can be said. The CEO could have called Bill into his office, presumably after some conflict concerning how things were going to be done, and had a frank discussion.

> *"Look, Bill, I know you've been here a long time, and you know that you and I don't see eye to eye on a lot of things."*
>
> *"Yes, I know. I think you will see that the way we have done things in the past is still a good way once you've been here awhile."*
>
> *"No, that's just not acceptable. I think it would be best for both you and the company if we had a parting of the ways."*
>
> *"I don't know. I've been here for 30 years. I'm too old to start over again."*
>
> *"I agree. Look, what I'd like to propose is that you become a part-time consultant. I think we can work out a contract that allows you to be secure financially and allows me to get on with reorganizing this company. Here is the name and phone number of the company attorney. Have your attorney get in touch with her and let them negotiate something that will be good for both of us."*
>
> *"I see. Well, I don't know."*
>
> *"Look, Bill, I don't want to fire you for a lot of reasons, not the least of which is that you have been with this company for a long time. At the same time, I have to move the company forward. I think making you a consultant for a couple of years as part of your leaving the company is a good idea. You think about it. I think you and I should leave this up to the lawyers."*
>
> *"I'll think it over."*

In this conversation, Bill still has his dignity and some financial security until retirement, and the CEO has what he wants. The cost of all this would certainly have been much less than $3.4 million.

The *Monarch Paper* case is a classic example of trying to get the old guy out by using some trick. If the jury figures out what you are doing, you are usually worse off than you would have been if you had simply worked out some kind of severance agreement. In the *Lakeway* case, the supervisor decided to reorganize the work in an attempt to hide what he was really doing. First, he took the older worker's job and divided it into two parts. Then he gave one part to a younger worker. Then he reorganized the work again and decided that, since there were now two people for one job, the older worker would have to go. No one was fooled, least of all the jury, which found this to be a case of willful age discrimination and awarded double damages as allowed by the federal Age Discrimination in Employment Act.

Not firing a supervisor who has clearly done the wrong thing can often be much worse than firing him or her ever could have been. Take the *Ford* case. Leta Fay Ford had worked her way up at Revlon over many years when a new boss told her that she would be expected to sleep with him as part of her job description. When she refused, he told her he would make her life miserable. She then filed a sexual harassment complaint with the company. Revlon took six months to investigate her charges, and the situation got worse and worse. Finally, at a company picnic, the boss tried to sexually assault Ford in front of witnesses. The company reacted by putting a letter of reprimand in the boss's file. Only after Leta Fay Ford tried to kill herself did Revlon finally fire her offensive boss. She sued, and the jury awarded her $100,000 in punitive damages against Revlon for conduct the jury considered to be outrageous. The Arizona Supreme Court agreed with the jury.

This is a clear example of the kinds of problems that can result when people who need to be fired are not fired. Presumably the executives at Revlon hoped that everything would simply blow over. That was not a very good decision in this situation. Once her boss attacked her, he should have been fired immediately. Can you imagine the employee morale problems this ultimately caused Revlon? Can you imagine the impression this incident made on the people of Arizona who read about it in their newspapers? We have to wonder how much of the Arizona cosmetics market Revlon retained after this story hit the press.

If people who have been harassed until they quit can still sue for illegal discharge (it is called constructive discharge), and if waiting to fire someone or trying to fire someone in a tricky way leads only to higher damage awards, the lesson seems to be: go ahead, fire them.

NEGLIGENT SUPERVISION AND RETENTION

In the cases we have discussed so far, the employer has simply raised the amount of damages the employee will eventually receive when he or she sues for illegal discharge or intentional infliction of emotional distress. There is another problem with keeping bad employees: They may injure someone else. Any time an employee injures a third party while performing his or her job, the employer risks being held liable. In some cases the employer can defend itself by arguing that while what the employee did was reprehensible, the employee was acting outside the scope of his or her job. The employer should not be blamed if this is indeed the case. Employers have been able to successfully argue this in cases where employees assault people. After all, assaulting people was not part of the job description. This works in some cases, but then the injured person may make another argument. He or she may argue that although the employer should not be considered to be automatically at fault, the employer is still liable because it failed to supervise this particular employee or, worse, failed to fire him after finding out that he or she was a danger to the employer's customers. Boy, that really makes an employer look good in the eyes of its other customers!

In one case a divorced man sued the Roman Catholic church for negligent supervision and negligent retention of a priest. The man argued that the priest, who had provided marriage counseling for him and his now former wife, had only made things worse by having sexual intercourse with the wife during the counseling. The Colorado Supreme Court ruled that the man could sue the Roman Catholic church for negligent supervision and negligent retention. However, he would have to prove either that the church knew or should have known that this kind of thing was going on and failed to remove the priest from his job (negligent retention) or that a reasonable provider of this kind of service would have exercised more care in supervising this kind of counselor (negligent supervision). The case was sent back for a trial (*Destafano*).

In another case, a patient sued her therapist and the clinic he worked for. The therapist had engaged in sexual intercourse with her because he viewed it as part of her therapy. The New Jersey judge ruled that sexual intercourse was outside the scope of this individual's job description and that therefore the patient would not be allowed to sue the clinic for injury caused by an employee performing his job. However, the judge did allow the patient to sue for negligent supervision and negligent retention (*Cosgrove*).

These cases suggest that most employers would be better off firing employees such as these if they in fact know that this kind of thing is going on. Also, if they are not in a position to find out if this kind of thing is going on, they should change the way they do business.

So far, employees who are injured by their coworkers have not had a lot of luck suing for negligent supervision and negligent retention. As a general rule, these employees are stuck with workers' compensation payments when they are injured by the negligence of their employer or fellow employees. Of course, in some states, employees are allowed to sue if the employer engages in gross negligence or willful misconduct, and the failure to fire an employee who was a known danger might just be considered to be gross or willful in some cases.

DEFAMATION OF CHARACTER AND FALSE LIGHT PRIVACY INVASION

Another problem that comes up most often when an employee is fired is the problem of defamation of character and what is called false light invasion of privacy. First of all, employers do not have a right to tell lies about their employees. While the law does give employers what is called a conditional privilege to defame their employees, this privilege can be lost for several reasons. For example, the privilege allows an employer to tell a lie, but only if the employer believed that what it was saying was the truth. In one case a school superintendent was asked by another school district to give his opinion about a former teacher. The superintendent said that the teacher who was being inquired about had been a terrible teacher. It turned out that this was a lie and that the superintendent had no reason to believe that what he was saying was true. The employee won a suit for defamation of character (*True*).

The privilege can be lost if the employer tells the lie to someone he or she has no business talking to. The purpose of the privilege is to allow employers to talk to their employees and other employers. In one case, an official from Exxon tracked down an employee to accuse him of theft. The official found the employee in a crowded restaurant, where he made a scene, calling the employee a thief in front of everyone in the restaurant. It turned out that the official had made two mistakes. The employee was not a thief after all, and the Exxon official had said defamatory things in front of people who had no business knowing them. Exxon lost the case (*Exxon*).

As a general rule, employers have a right to tell the truth about why they fired someone, but they should think twice before doing so if the person listening to their story might get the wrong impression. When Mr. Martinez was fired, his employer told everyone that he had been fired for stealing company property (*Diamond Shamrock*). That was technically true, in that Mr. Martinez had cleaned up the shop floor and taken home a handful of nails that would otherwise have been thrown away. However, you can see that anyone hearing that Mr. Martinez was a thief might get the wrong idea. In the law this is called placing someone in a false light, it is part of the law on invasion of privacy. The Texas court ruled that Mr. Martinez was within his rights to sue his employer under these circumstances.

How to Fire People the Right Way

The cases discussed above provide two major lessons. If an employee is a problem, employers are better off firing that employee. On the other hand, there is a right way and a wrong way to fire people, and firing someone the wrong way can be just as bad as not firing the person at all. So, what is the right way?

First, if you want someone to go, you are usually better off talking about this frankly with the person. This discussion should be held away from the usual workplace, and the director of human resources should be present if possible. It may turn out that the person was already thinking about leaving and was just waiting until he or she found something else before telling the employer. Or, it may turn out that the person does not want to go and will kill anyone who tries to fire him or her. This second possibility suggests that a security guard should be nearby when the topic of leaving the company is discussed.

Second, it will be best for the employer if the employee resigns, and in most cases it will also be better for the employee. An employee who resigns can at least keep up the appearance of having made the decision to leave in front of family and friends. While employees who resign may, in a few cases, be able to sue for wrongful or illegal discharge (constructive discharge), it is usually difficult for someone to sue for being illegally fired when he or she was not fired. In the real world, such employees almost never win and attorneys almost never take their case. That means that most employers are going to have a receptive ear when they discuss the possibility of resignation. At the same time, the employer has to realize that employees who resign give up the chance to sue (particularly if they also sign a release) and in most cases, the chance to get unemployment compensation. They deserve to get something in return. That something may be money, a period of time during which they can come to work and spend their time looking for another job, or other things. These can often be negotiated quickly. Other times both sides may need a lawyer. The higher paid the employee and the longer he or she has been with the company, the more money it will cost to get the employee to resign and sign a release.

Third, these conversations should be held early in the week, not on Friday, and they should be in an atmosphere that will be conducive to compromise. The employee's supervisor is usually not the person to take the lead in this discussion, but should be present.

Fourth, whether or not the person resigns, the best thing that can happen to this now former employee is for him or her to find a new job as quickly as possible, hopefully one that pays as much as or more than the old job. I once had a conversation with an employee who had been fired from a job where he had been making $40,000 a year and quickly found a similar job that paid $50,000 a year. I asked him what he wanted to sue for. It seemed to me that, if anything, the employee should have paid his former employer a little something as a thank you for forcing him to finally earn what he had been capable of earning all along. Employers can do a lot to help their former, or soon to be former, employees find another job. This may mean paying the cost of a job search course at the local community college or even paying for outplacement help from a consultant that specializes in helping people find a job. In most cases, this is money well spent.

Fifth, it should be company policy that if anyone, including fellow employees, asks why this person is no longer employed, a standard answer be given: "It is the policy of the MNO Company not to give out that kind of information." Everyone in the company should then live up to that company policy. If anyone asks, including someone from a company at which the person has applied for a job, this should be the answer. The people in the human resources department should confirm that the former employee worked from this date to that date and had this or that job title. Nothing else should be said. If they tell the truth, and the person does not get another job, then the former employee might sue for some kind of wrongful discharge. If they tell a lie, and the person does not get another job, then the former employee might sue for defamation of character. If they lie by telling someone that the employee was good when the employee was in fact bad, then the new employer might sue for causing it to hire a bad employee. If they tell the truth but the new employer does not like this person as an employee, the new employer may decide that what was the truth was in fact a lie designed to trick it into taking a bad apple. In other words, when a recommendation, good or bad, is given, a lot of bad things can happen.

Sixth, don't fight unemployment compensation unless the case is outrageous. Many times discharged employees will simply go on unemployment compensation for a few weeks, then find another job. All too often employers fight this, trying to save a few dollars in unemployment compensation taxes. It usually costs more to fight than it would to give in, in more ways than one. Once the employer resists paying unemployment compensation, the employee has a very good reason to consult an attorney right away. This attorney will urge the employee to file complaints with the EEOC for sex, race, or age discrimination just to get the ball rolling. The attorney will also ask for a real unemployment compensation hearing, at which he or she will be able to size up the other side. Oh, and in a majority of cases, if the employee has an attorney, he or she gets unemployment compensation. Word goes out that the company would not even let a poor old former employee get unemployment compensation without a fight. That does a lot for the morale of the remaining employees. The good ones often start looking for another job at that point.

Seventh, remember Norman. On one episode of the television show *Cheers*, Norman was given the job of firing people by his employer. Norman got the job because he really hated to fire people and usually ended up crying in the process. The fired employees spent their time trying to calm Norman down, rather than thinking about the shaft they had just been given. While that is an exaggeration, it is not far from the ideal. If the employee has done something terrible, then he or she should be fired right away, and there should be no tears. But in most cases the employee has not been caught with his hand in the cash register or assaulting a fellow employee. It is not such a clear-cut case, and the employee has some right to feel injured. Injury must not be turned into insult. People don't sue for wrongful discharge because they feel that some public policy, like the policy that women and minorities should be treated equally, has been violated. That is just the legal peg their lawyer will hang their hat on. No, the reason they sue is because they feel mistreated, hurt, put upon, and abandoned.

REMEMBER THE BIG PICTURE

In one episode of *Star Trek* (the original), the doctor is sent back in time to the beginning of the twentieth century. He sees someone who has been hurt and he reaches for his futuristic equipment, but it is not there. He begins to cry, remembering that back in those days they "sewed up people like rag dolls." I can only hope at some point in the twenty-first century, people in the United States will have the same feeling when they look back on how people were chosen for different jobs and how they chose a career for themselves in the twentieth century. There is no more important decision in life, yet most people make it with very little information. Imagine ten thousand employment centers linked by satellite. Imagine interviews done by closed-circuit television. Imagine people taking a battery of tests to measure both aptitude and interest and spending a few weeks in a dozen different work environments in order to see what they like and don't like about particular jobs and particular work environments. Some day that may be a reality.

We often forget that the whole purpose of an employment system is to find the best person for the job and the best job for the person. It is just that simple. The tragic thing is that for most people who are fired or encouraged to resign, their next job is both better for them and better for their employer. Leaving was the right thing to do, but the person just couldn't see it. The unknown is a frightening thing. The social stigma doesn't help either, or the financial uncertainty when jobs are not plentiful. An unemployment system created for a society still coming out of the horse and buggy era doesn't help either.

So how do you fire someone? With dignity, with respect, and with all deliberate speed. Oh, and sometimes with the advice of a good employment attorney and the help of an outplacement expert!

Chapter 26

Closing Facilities or Laying Off Workers

There are four situations in which special consideration should be given to proper procedure: closing a facility, relocating a facility, laying off a group of workers, and offering early retirement to a group of workers. Issues concerned with early retirement were discussed in Chapter 13. Closing or relocating a facility and laying off a group of workers raise two basic legal issues: Have the federal and state WARN statutes been complied with, and has the union been dealt with in a legal way?

THE WORKER ADJUSTMENT AND RETRAINING NOTIFICATION ACT

Congress passed the Worker Adjustment and Retraining Notification (WARN) Act in an effort to make it easier for employees and local communities to deal with plant closings and large layoffs (20 U.S.C. sec. 2101). The law applies to all employers with 100 full-time employees or a combination of full- and part-time employees who perform at least 4,000 hours of work in a typical week (not including overtime).

The main requirement of the act is a sixty-day notice period if a facility (or a large part of a facility) is going to be closed or if a large number of workers are going to be laid off. A plant closing comes under the act if a facility, or part of a facility, is going to close and cause fifty or more full-time employees to lose their jobs for at least six months or have their hours of work cut by more than 50 percent for more than six months. Even if the workers have an expectation of being recalled, they are still considered to have lost their jobs if these criteria are met. The act also applies to a "mass layoff," which is defined as a reduction in force that, during any thirty-day period, causes a drop in employment of 33 percent if that percentage comes to at least fifty workers, or that affects 500 or more workers, regardless of the percentage of the workforce that this amounts to.

The act does not apply to closings or layoffs that are caused by labor disputes or natural disasters. Also, the act does not apply if the workers being laid off were told when they began work that the project they were working on was temporary. It also does not apply if the company is trying to prevent the closing or layoff and has a realistic chance of raising the money needed to avoid the layoff or closing.

This is called the faltering company exception. It applies only to companies that have a good faith belief that more financing can be obtained and that giving the WARN notice would interfere with raising the capital needed to stay open. This faltering company exception does not apply to a company that is trying to sell itself to avoid the shutdown or layoff (*Local 397*).

The act also does not apply if the shutdown or layoff is caused by an unforeseeable business circumstance. This exception applies only if the circumstance was really not foreseen. For example, in one case, the employer knew that it had lost a customer that accounted for 40 percent of the firm's business and that there was little chance of finding a replacement customer in the near future. The employer did not provide the required notice in hopes that another large customer would appear. The judge ruled that this violated the WARN act (*Kayser-Roth*).

What if the layoff was supposed to last less than six months, and so would not require a notice under the WARN act, but circumstances that could not have been foreseen at the time of the layoff cause the layoff to be extended? The act will not have been violated if management in good faith believed that the layoff would last less than six months and if the new information or circumstances really were unforeseen and unforeseeable at the time of the layoff.

What if two small groups of employees are laid off at one job site several weeks apart and the total comes to more than fifty workers? This may or may not fall under the provisions of the act, depending on the circumstances of the facility, the company, and the employees. As a general rule, to be on the safe side, if fifty or more employees at a single facility are going to be laid off during a ninety-day period, the WARN notice should be given. That assumes, of course, that the employer knew about the layoffs and knew that they would add up to over fifty workers.

THE WARN NOTICE

The federal WARN act requires that sixty days' notice be given of a plant closing or mass layoff. The notice must be given to the employees' union representative, or to the employees individually if they are not represented by a union. Notice must be given to the state's "dislocated worker" director or agency if there is one. The chief executive officer of the government of the locality where the closing or layoff is to take place should also be notified. This will usually be the mayor of the town in which the facility is located. The act assumes that these government officials may be able to do something to stop the closing or layoff, although that has not turned out to be the case in the vast majority of actual events that have occurred since the passage of the act.

Failure to Provide the Notice

What happens if the employer fails to provide the necessary notice? The act allows employees to sue and receive the wages and benefits that they would have received during the sixty-day notice period. Their attorney's fees will also be paid by the employer, and the judge may even award punitive damages in some circumstances (*Finnan*). The required payment of back wages and benefits is limited to the length of the violation. For example, if thirty days' notice was given instead of sixty, then only thirty days' back wages and benefits would be called for. Employers may not subtract money owed for vacation and severance from the required payment. Also, if an employee has worked for this employer for only a short time, the employee is entitled only to back wages and benefits equal to one-half the number of days the employee has actually worked. For example, an employee who had only worked for this employer for forty days before the layoff would be entitled to only twenty days back wages and benefits.

If the employer has already paid wages beyond those required by hours worked or by contracts or other legal obligations, these will be subtracted from the amount owed. When Sears decided to close down its large store in downtown Oakland, California in 1992, it provided notice to everyone and closed the facility on the same day. At the same time, it recognized its obligation to pay for the sixty-day WARN period and did so without the need for litigation. Sears decided that it was simpler and cheaper to handle the closing this way than to provide the sixty-day notice. The employees received the wages they would have received if the notice had been given and were able to spend that time looking for another job, so they were presumably better off than they would have been if the letter of the WARN act had been followed.

The act allows for a civil penalty of not more than $500 a day for each day of violation, but the penalty does not apply if the employer has paid the employees what they would be owed within three weeks of the order to lay off the workers or shut down the facility. Courts are not given the power to stop a layoff or shutdown with a court order.

Employers who violate the act because they believed in good faith that their actions were legal may use that good faith as a defense. Judges may reduce the liability or penalty based on this good-faith belief. The WARN act does not supersede any other legal or contractual obligation. For example, some other laws, both state and federal, may allow judges to stop a plant closing or layoff under some circumstances, and this would still be the case even after the passage of the WARN act.

STATE WARN LAWS

A dozen states have WARN laws that must also be complied with. New York has voluntary guidelines that are not worth the paper they are written on. Some state laws apply to smaller employers than the federal law. Also, some state laws have significantly different provisions and provide for very different penalties. The state laws also provide different exceptions. In other words, the particular state law should be consulted if possible. In most cases, compliance with the federal law will also amount to compliance with the state law, but not always. In Maine, for example, the state law requires the payment of severance pay, which is certainly not required by the federal law.

States with WARN Laws

Connecticut	Maryland	Montana	Virgin Islands
Hawaii	Massachusetts	Oregon	Wisconsin
Kansas	Michigan	South Carolina	
Maine	Minnesota	Tennessee	

REQUIRED LABOR UNION NEGOTIATIONS

It often comes as a surprise to many employers that they are required to negotiate in good faith over closing or relocating a facility. This should not seem so strange, given that the closing of a facility will certainly affect the conditions of work for some workers. If the closing or relocation is not accompanied by a basic change in the nature of the employer's operations, then it is a mandatory subject for bargaining. The employer can avoid this mandatory bargaining if it is able to prove that the work performed at the new facility is significantly different from the work done at the now closed facility or that the work done at the old, now closed, facility is not being done at all at the new facility. The employer may also avoid bargaining if the move is related to a decision to change the basic scope and direction of the company. The employer may also be able to avoid bargaining or being penalized for not bargaining if it can show that labor costs were not a factor in the decision to shut down or relocate the work or that, even if labor costs were a factor, the union would not have been able to grant cost concessions that would have resulted in a decision not to shut down or move the facility.

The whole point of all this is that if the employer is shutting down or moving the facility because of labor costs and will still be doing similar work somewhere else, it should bargain with the union over this in good faith. If the reason for the move has nothing to do with labor costs, then such bargaining is not required. The move may be caused by a desire to be near customers or raw materials or because of a major shift into a new product. These are all situations in which bargaining with the union would not be required because nothing the union could do would change the circumstances.

In some cases the shutdown or layoff is caused by a decision to subcontract the work to someone else. If this is the case, the employer is almost always required to negotiate over this with the union. In other words, subcontracting work out is a mandatory subject of bargaining. The U.S. Supreme Court has ruled that the employer must bargain in good faith over this even if all the members of the bargaining unit will be discharged as a result of the subcontracting (*Fiberboard*).

An employer that has failed to bargain in good faith over subcontracting out work or closing or relocating a facility may find that the National Labor Relations Board has ordered it to hire back the discharged workers and resume operations until bargaining can be completed.

LAYOFF AND REDUCTION-IN-FORCE POLICIES

What happens to laid-off workers may be covered in a union contract. If it is not, then it becomes a matter of company policy and may be covered in the employee handbook. Some companies use the term *layoff* to cover discharged employees who have some kind of right to reinstatement when jobs open up, while a *reduction in force* means that the jobs are gone forever and the discharged employees have no right to reinstatement.

The major issue for any company is whether or not it wishes to give laid-off workers (as opposed to workers who have been fired for good cause) some kind of right to reinstatement when new jobs open up. If such a promise is made, then it must be lived up to. Why would any employer ever make such a promise? Because many union contracts have such provisions and the employer is trying to convince its employees that they do not need a union. Also, if the employer has spent a lot of time and money training workers, it might be to the employer's advantage to bring back those trained workers rather than hiring and training new workers. The legal problem is that once this promise is made, workers will alter their lives in reliance upon it. This may mean not moving away or taking another job for a period of months or even years in hopes of getting back with the employer. If the employer then fails to live up to the promise, the employee can sue for the wages lost during that period of waiting.

There is also the problem that the layoff or reduction in force may simply be a cover for race, sex, or age discrimination. Generally, age discrimination is the most likely. While companies without a union contract are not required to follow seniority when laying off employees, if some objective standard is not followed and most of the laid-off workers are over forty, alarm bells are going to ring. Companies that notice that many of the employees who will be laid off are over forty should consult an attorney before going any further.

Even if the company does not wish to make a promise to rehire laid-off employees, it may wish to promise to notify them of any job openings that come up for some period of time, perhaps the next two years, and to give them an interview if their qualifications match the company's needs. This should not cost much, and it should save money if experienced and well-trained workers can be hired back. At the same time, a promise to give a notice is not the same as a promise to hire back someone who has been laid off.

SAMPLE EMPLOYEE HANDBOOK PROVISION

Any employee who is laid off for any reason should leave his or her address with the director of human resources. During the next two years, the laid-off employee will be notified if any jobs come open that he or she might be qualified for. We have a large investment in our employees, and, when possible, we try to hire them back. However, the MNO Company does not promise to hire back laid-off employees. The laid-off employee will be given an interview and will be hired if he and she is judged to be the best candidate for the job.

CONCLUSION

Closing or relocating a facility or laying off a group of workers raises two basic legal issues: have the federal and state WARN statutes been complied with, and has the union been dealt with in a legal way. In most cases it will be much less expensive in the long run to comply with both laws—provide the WARN notice and bargain with the union—than to ignore these provisions. The reasons for the layoff should be stated as soon as possible to help everyone involved understand what is going on. Good relations with employees, unions, and the community can be maintained if information is provided that allows everyone involved to understand what is happening and why.

Chapter 27

Unemployment Compensation

Unemployment compensation began with the passage of the federal Social Security Act in 1935. While it was originally a federal system, states were allowed to set up their own systems if those systems met federal requirements, and that is what every state has done. While there is still some interaction between the federal government and state unemployment compensation agencies, most employers deal mainly with the state agency.

TAXES

The basis of the system is unemployment taxes paid by employers. It is illegal for an employer to deduct the cost of these taxes from the wages of any employee. (Of course, the more employers have to pay in unemployment taxes, the less they have to pay out in wages.) The tax is essentially a payroll tax on wages up to a specified level. The tax may go up if a particular employer has a large number of former employees filing for unemployment compensation. This gives employers an incentive to try to prevent their former employees from collecting unemployment compensation.

As a general rule, unemployment taxes must be paid on all employees (not on independent contractors). In every state there is a long list of groups of people who are not covered by the system and whose employers do not have to pay unemployment taxes. In most states this list includes domestic servants (if they are not paid much), agricultural workers (for small farmers), work-study students, golf caddies, teenage babysitters, children who work for their parents' business, spouses who work for their spouse's business, people who work for themselves or their partnership, inmates who work for their jailers, and elected officials. While there are some basic federal rules, every state has its own set of regulations on this subject. Every employer must contact the state unemployment compensation agency when hiring an employee to see if unemployment compensation taxes are due. In most cases the employee will be covered and the employer will have to pay, even if the employer has only one employee.

BENEFITS

Most employees who are laid off will be entitled to receive unemployment benefits. As a general rule, the state will look back over the last year and a quarter to determine whether or not the employee meets the basic eligibility requirements and how much his or her benefits should be. Generally, the employee receives the wages he or she received during the best three months of employment, spread out over a maximum of six months. Of course, there is a maximum weekly benefit in every state.

To meet the basic eligibility requirements, first, the worker must have worked a minimum amount over the preceding year or more. Second, the employee must not be an employee whose employer was not required to pay into the unemployment compensation system. A teenage babysitter, for example, does not get unemployment compensation in most states. Third, the employee must be "ready, willing, and able" to work. Unemployment compensation is not the same as workers' compensation or disability. Workers who are not mentally or physically able to work may qualify under another program, but they will not qualify for unemployment compensation. Fourth, the employee must sign up at the unemployment compensation office and begin to look for work. The employee is not required to take the first job that comes along, regardless of pay or skills required. The employee is expected to look for and accept similar work that pays reasonable wages.

In most states, an unemployed worker is not required to take a job that is vacant only because of a labor dispute. An unemployed worker is not required to take a job that would force him or her to join a company union or refrain from joining a real labor union. While people going to school are not usually allowed to collect unemployment compensation, exceptions are made if the person is involved in a job training program approved by the unemployment agency.

CLAIMS PROCEDURE

An unemployed worker is required to file a claim with the unemployment office. That office will then contact all of the employers that that employee worked for during the last year or more. The office will want to know two things: How much did the person make, and why did the person leave? Different states have different ways of calculating what must be included as wages. For example, in some states the value of meals and lodging provided to the employee will count as wages. The employer has to be familiar with the rules and provide the necessary information. Payroll information should include all wages and benefits so that this request for information will be easy to answer.

The second question, why did the person leave, is more important. The law says that anyone providing what he or she honestly believes to be truthful answers to a request for information from a government agency has some extra protection from a libel suit. The law says that such a person has a conditional privilege to defame the employee. That means that, as long as the information is provided in good faith with a belief that it is accurate, it cannot be used as the basis for a libel suit. Employers must still be careful not to reveal the information to others who have no reason to know. Also, employers who intentionally lie in order to avoid paying higher unemployment taxes may lose this privilege.

DISQUALIFICATION

There are six basic reasons why people who otherwise meet the eligibility requirements are denied unemployment compensation. First, as a general rule, people who quit are not entitled to unemployment compensation. The whole point of unemployment compensation is to provide funds to people who are unemployed through no fault of their own. If a person quits, the law views his or her unemployment as being his or her own fault, not that of the employer. Second, people who are fired for misconduct are not entitled to unemployment compensation, again because the system views them as being unemployed through their own fault. Third, people will not receive benefits if they were offered a suitable job and turned it down. Fourth, people who are not working because of a labor dispute may or may not qualify, depending on complex rules that differ from state to state. Fifth, people who are already receiving money from pensions, Social Security, workers' compensation, or other sources may not qualify for unemployment compensation. Sixth, people who have engaged in various kinds of fraud against the government may have lost the right to receive unemployment compensation.

It is important for anyone called upon to answer a request for information about a former employee to realize that to most unemployment compensation agencies, the words *laid off* and *fired* have special meanings. If an employer says that someone has been laid off, that means that that person was let go through no fault of his or her own. The employer simply did not have enough work for the workforce, and someone had to go. That is the person the unemployment compensation system was designed to serve, and that person will automatically get unemployment compensation. To most unemployment compensation agencies, if an employer says that it fired an employee, that means that the employee was discharged because her or she engaged in misconduct. As an employer, if you intend to challenge the grant of unemployment compensation, you want to say that the employee was fired or quit. If you do not plan to challenge the grant, then you can say the employee was laid off.

QUITTING

As a general rule, someone who quits does not get unemployment compensation. There is an exception to that rule. If the person has good reason to quit, he or she may still qualify. Decades ago, the reason had to be very good and very work-related. By the 1990s, more reasons will qualify in most states, and even reasons unrelated to work may qualify in many states.

Remember, all employment relationships are contractual. If an employer has made promises when hiring someone that it is not willing to live up to, then the employee may be entitled to quit and receive unemployment compensation. As a general rule of thumb, an employee should not quit for this reason unless he or she finds the broken promise so important that he or she is no longer willing to work for this employer, regardless of whether or not he or she gets unemployment compensation. In such a case, if the employee does quit, he or she will probably get unemployment compensation. Having one's duties expanded or changed or having one's pay significantly reduced qualifies as a good reason to quit.

Self-protection is another good reason to quit. If the employee can protect his or her health or safety only by quitting, then the employee will usually qualify for unemployment compensation. The threat to safety may be having to be around smokers, which is another reason to keep smoking out of the workplace. The threat must be real, not imagined, and must be significant. Someone who finds something about the job unpleasant is not justified in quitting. Again, if the situation is so dangerous that the employee feels he or she would quit whether or not he or she will get unemployment compensation, then the employee probably will get unemployment compensation. Women who have quit rather than endure sexual harassment have received compensation, as have the victims of racial harassment.

Years ago, most states required employees to quit for a work-related reason before they could collect unemployment compensation. That is no longer the case in many states. If the person has to quit because of a significant personal reason, he or she may still qualify. For example, in some states, having to quit to care for an ill child or parent may qualify. The U.S. Supreme Court has ruled on several occasions that people who quit because their religious beliefs no longer allow them to work must be granted unemployment compensation. In one case, the employee became a member of the Seventh-Day Adventist Church and could no longer work on Saturday, her new Sabbath. While the Florida unemployment compensation agency considered a refusal to work on Saturday to be misconduct, and therefore a disqualification, the Supreme Court disagreed. It ruled that Paula Hobbie was entitled to receive unemployment compensation and that to deny it to her interfered with her right to freely exercise her religion as guaranteed by the First Amendment to the U.S. Constitution (*Hobbie*).

FIRED FOR MISCONDUCT

The main reason most employees are denied unemployment compensation benefits is because they were fired from their last job for misconduct. There is much confusion about this in the minds of many employers. Misconduct means violating reasonable work rules or doing something generally considered to be a violation of the employee's duties. Simply being incompetent is not misconduct. If someone simply cannot do the job, through no fault of his or her own, then that person is generally entitled to unemployment compensation. On the other hand, if the person lied about his or her competence when applying for the job, that would be different. Also, if the employee has demonstrated in the past that he or she can do the job but is no longer "able" to do it, presumably because he or she is no longer willing to try, that employee would not qualify for compensation.

Types of Misconduct

1. Failure to perform up to abilities
2. Deliberate damage to property
3. Excessive unjustified absences or tardiness

---

4. Stealing of property
5. Lying
6. Insubordination
7. Failure to obey reasonable work rules
8. Failure to work
9. Causing sexual or other harassment

Having accidents is not the same thing as misconduct. If someone is accident-prone, that person should not be working around heavy machinery and perhaps therefore should be fired, but the person will generally be eligible for unemployment compensation. While no employer likes to see its machinery or automobiles smashed up, unless the accident was deliberate, this will not justify withholding unemployment compensation.

The main reasons people are denied compensation involve behavior such as insubordination, excessive absences or tardiness, stealing, lying, spending time not working, and failing to obey reasonable work rules. An employer has a right to expect that employees will listen to instructions and then do what they are told. If an employee refuses, uses vulgar language toward the supervisor, or otherwise exhibits an insubordinate attitude, that will disqualify him or her from unemployment compensation. An employer has a right to expect employees to show up on time and to put in a full day's work. If they are late or don't come, or don't work when they do show up, then they should be disqualified. Of course, employees who steal the employer's property or who lie to the employer will generally not receive compensation. Employers have a right to expect employees to obey reasonable work rules. That is one reason to have a well-written employee handbook with reasonable rules spelled out in a readable way. Some employers think that they can get rid of employees by having such complex work rules that no employee can follow them or live up to their requirements. Generally, judges are not fooled by this. If the rules are so complex that no reasonable employee can understand them or live up to them, an employee who violates them will not be considered to have committed misconduct.

At the same time, the handbook can be a problem if it is written in such a way as to suggest that employees will be fired only for the reasons listed in the handbook and only following the procedures spelled out in the handbook. In one case, the employer failed to follow the discipline procedures laid out in the employee handbook, so the judge awarded the employee unemployment compensation (*Brady*). In another case, the handbook had a list of reasons for discharge. The particular activity engaged in by this employee was not on the list, so the court awarded unemployment compensation (*Cablevision*). These cases suggest that policies that seem to guarantee that employees will be discharged only in particular ways for particular reasons should not be placed in the employee handbook.

Sample Employee Handbook Provision

The only person authorized to deal with state and federal unemployment compensation agencies is the director of human resources. If anyone in the MNO Company receives a request for information about a former employee, from an unemployment compensation agency or anyone else, he or she should refer the person making the inquiry to the director of human resources. Anyone who receives any kind of written request for information about a former employee should forward that request to the director of human resources also. From time to time employees may be requested to testify at an unemployment compensation hearing. We expect them to tell the truth. The decision whether or not to challenge a request for unemployment compensation by a former employee will be made by the director of human resources after appropriate fact finding and consultation.

Conclusion

Too many employers take the position that every request for unemployment compensation should be fought, regardless of the circumstances. That is a mistake. Employees who have to fight for their unemployment compensation are much more likely to contact an attorney and sue for civil rights violations or wrongful discharge. If the unemployment compensation system had been allowed to work, they might have found other jobs and gone on with their life. At the same time, employees who do not deserve to receive unemployment compensation should not be allowed to receive it, and employers should help to make sure that they do not. The best approach is to review each case and determine whether or not the employee should be receiving unemployment compensation.

Chapter 28

Employee Discipline and Grievances

Before writing a handbook provision on employee discipline, it is important to come to some decision concerning the basic philosophy of discipline the company wishes to follow. There are two basic approaches. The first approach is to try to develop a discipline system and procedure similar to that which might result from a union contract. Union contracts often call for progressive discipline, which means that the punishment must fit the crime. A small violation results in a written or oral reprimand and perhaps a small punishment, such as a few days off without pay. A larger violation results in a suspension from work or dismissal. Someone who has a series of small violations may be discharged under this kind of policy if he or she has enough violations within a short enough period of time.

A true progressive discipline policy would be very long. It would include a list of violations that would justify immediate dismissal and a list of other violations that might result in a reprimand or suspension for a short time without pay. There might be a third category, minor violations that would result in a letter of reprimand for the first offense and something worse, such as suspension or discharge, if more than one or two letters of reprimand have to be placed in a personnel file within a specific period, such as a year.

SAMPLE EMPLOYEE HANDBOOK PROVISION

Here at the ABC Company we follow a progressive discipline system. If an offense is serious enough, it will result in immediate discharge. Offenses of this nature include (but are not limited to) the following:

1. Theft or intentional destruction of company property
2. Violation of any of the employee duties listed in that section of the Employee Handbook
3. Any violation of a safety regulation that might have resulted, or did result, in serious injury to anyone
4. Possession of a weapon or illegal drugs on company property
5. Excessive absences or lateness without a reasonable excuse or without reporting in
6. Lying to anyone in the company or falsifying any company documents

7. Harassing, fighting with, or threatening any employee or customer

8. Refusing to work or to follow orders or any other insubordination

Minor offenses may result in a letter of reprimand or a short suspension without pay. If they are repeated, or if more than one minor offense is reported within any twelve-month period, it may result in discharge. Minor offenses include (but are not limited to) the following:

1. Being late to work or returning late from a break

2. Not following work procedures concerning recordkeeping

3. Smoking inside any building

4. Minor violations of proper safety procedures

5. Wasting time, money, or supplies

6. Abuse of company property, tools, or machines

7. Failure to wear appropriate clothing

8. Using vulgar or abusive language

THE TWO SIDES OF PROGRESSIVE DISCIPLINE PROCEDURES

There are many arguments that can be made in favor of having a discipline policy like this one. One reason employees turn to a union for help is because they feel that they are subject to arbitrary discipline and discharge. A provision such as this in the employee handbook gives both employees and management some guidance concerning both discipline and discharge. Employees know what to expect. They know that if they commit major violations, they will probably be fired. If they commit minor violations, they will be "written up" or suspended for a few days. Because a general standard concerning the two types of offenses (firing and nonfiring) is written out, everyone has a better idea of what leads to what. Employees feel they are less likely to be subjected to the unbridled discretion of an unfair supervisor. Also, these kinds of procedures can be helpful if someone has filed for unemployment compensation. If the employer has this kind of policy and has lived up to it, the unemployment compensation agency is more likely to go along with the employer's dismissal decision.

There are also disadvantages. Listing offenses in this way may lead employees to feel that they are being treated like children rather than like adults. That can certainly set the wrong tone for employee-management relations. By listing the major and minor reasons, management has tied its hands. It must now live up to the policy. It cannot fire people for a minor first offense, and it must, in most cases, fire someone for a major offense or risk being seen as engaging in discrimination. It would be reasonable for employees reading this provision to believe that as long as they do not violate this policy and do a good job and the company has business, they have a job. In other words, once a provision such as this is placed in the handbook, the employer has to some extent limited its ability to fire employees at will.

Everyone involved in the personnel management business has an opinion on this. Attorneys tend to dislike policies of this kind because they limit the right to fire at will and provide too much of a chance that some supervisor will violate the policy and that that action will lead to a lawsuit. Human resources experts tend to like policies of this kind because they provide a standard for a company, particularly a large company. Since very few employees are really fired for no reason at all, the experts would rather reap the advantages of helping to keep the unions away and making unemployment compensation hearings easier. Both attorneys and human resources experts would agree that employers should avoid going much beyond this sample provision. Avoid saying that two or three minor reprimands are needed before discharge. Avoid saying that the items listed are the total list. Always say "include but are not limited to" when listing offenses. At the same time, recognize that a judge will hold you to that statement. Once a set of offenses that will result in immediate discharge has been listed, any other offenses must be of the same kind. You have made an implied promise that only actions "that are like these listed" will result in immediate discharge. You can no longer fire for minor violations.

NONPROGRESSIVE DISCIPLINE POLICIES

The other option is either not to have any discipline statement in the employee handbook at all or to have something that is much more general and that reserves to management the right to fire or discipline employees for any reason or for no reason at all. The advantages and disadvantages of this approach, of course, are the mirror image of those for progressive discipline. Attorneys like this approach and human resources consultants don't. Employees may or may not feel that they are being treated like children, depending on how the policy is written and what supervisors really do. Unions may use the lack of a specific policy as a reason to vote for union representation, and the unemployment compensation agency is not going to give the employer the benefit of the doubt if there is no specific list of reasons for discharge in the handbook. There is more chance that supervisors will treat people in a discriminatory way and that employees will feel that they are subject to arbitrary treatment at the hands of their supervisors.

SAMPLE EMPLOYEE HANDBOOK PROVISION

At the MNO Company we recognize that in some cases employees will violate rules or engage in actions that do not justify dismissal but do justify some other disciplinary action. In those situations, supervisors are required to write a report and place a copy of that report in the personnel file of the employee involved. Any employee who feels that he or she has been unfairly treated by this process may file a grievance.

A GRIEVANCE PROCEDURE

The lack of a real, functioning grievance procedure is another reason why some employees turn to a union. While everyone hopes that employees in a well-managed organization will not need to resort to a formal grievance procedure, the existence of such a procedure can help in many ways. It provides a backup for normal lines of communication. It allows employees to feel they have somewhere else to go if they cannot get anywhere, and it provides upper management with a way to find out about things that those in lower management positions may not wish them to find out about.

In the nineteenth century, Robert Owen became famous for introducing new kinds of employee-friendly policies at the New Lanark Mill in Scotland. One of his greatest innovations was the introduction of a real grievance procedure whereby rank-and-file employees could get his attention and appeal decisions that they felt were unfair. However, Robert Owen was viewed by all the employees as a fair person. It is probably worse to have a grievance procedure than not to have one if the person who will make the final decision is not someone the employees believe will actually listen to their side of the story. A grievance procedure that results in employees losing the vast majority of grievances is worse than no grievance procedure at all. At least with no grievance procedure, employees know where they stand. Employees are going to view a grievance procedure that never works as another broken promise and a special kind of injustice.

One major issue is the extent to which the topics employees may put through the grievance procedure are limited. First, dismissal should not be subject to grievance. Presumably, no employee is dismissed until that decision has been reviewed by the director of human resources and others, so a grievance would simply be a waste of time. How much further to limit the grievance procedure is a difficult question. Some organizations limit it to the conditions of employment, while others feel that almost any problem should be subject to the grievance procedure.

One thing a grievance procedure should do is bring disputes to an end within a short period of time. An employee should have a fixed amount of time in which to file a grievance or to file an appeal from a grievance decision. This places the burden on employees to either push their complaint or forget about it.

Another thing a grievance procedure should do is require everyone involved to put things in writing. While some grievance procedures call for an initial oral discussion between the employee and the person causing the grievance, usually the employee's immediate supervisor, that sort of thing happens every day. There needs to be a point at which the grievance procedure actually begins, and that is usually when the employee files a written complaint about something. At the same time, the first person to see this written complaint should be the person who has caused the employee to be unhappy. If the employee, using a form supplied by the human resources office, files a written grievance with his or her supervisor, then the supervisor should file a written response. This response may resolve the problem. If it does not, then the position of both sides is on paper and the process can proceed. How many levels the grievance procedure should have depends on the size and complexity of the organization, but for most organizations the next step should be the director of human resources. It is the director's job to know about employee complaints, and the director may be in a unique position to solve the problem by looking at it from an organizational perspective.

There should be a final place to appeal, and it should be the president of the company if that is at all possible. If the organization is too large to allow this, then a particular vice president should be given this responsibility. The person chosen to be the final place to appeal should be someone that the average employee feels will be fair. If that is not the case, then the whole grievance procedure is a waste of time.

SAMPLE EMPLOYEE HANDBOOK PROVISION

At MNO Company we realize that there will be times when a complaint cannot be resolved without some formal grievance procedure. An employee who cannot resolve a problem informally should file a written grievance (on a grievance form obtained from the Human Resources Office) with his or her immediate supervisor. The supervisor will investigate the matter and attempt to resolve the problem. If that is not possible, the supervisor will file a written response, and both the complaint and the written response will be sent to the director of human resources. The director will investigate the matter and attempt to solve the problem. If the employee is not happy about the director's resolution of the problem, the employee may appeal the director's decision to the president of the MNO Company. The president's decision will be final. While it is our hope that most problems can be solved informally, we also recognize that some issues are complex and can be resolved only if problems and responses are put in writing and submitted to someone who is not directly involved. Employees who use the formal grievance procedure will not suffer in any way as long as they have filed their grievance with a good-faith belief that something is wrong that could be corrected by the actions of someone higher up in the company hierarchy. The only decision that is not subject to the grievance procedure is the dismissal of an employee.

CONCLUSION

A well-written grievance policy that is fairly implemented has many advantages for any organization. A badly written grievance policy that is not fairly implemented has many disadvantages. For many organizations, no grievance policy may be the best solution. At the same time, a well-written and fairly administered grievance policy can bring many dividends.

Chapter 29
Evaluations and Records

As a general rule, human resources experts believe that a well-run company will have at least annual written performance evaluations of every employee. However, attorneys are not so sure. Why not? Because the worst thing an attorney can find when looking into a personnel file is a large group of positive evaluations. This is bad enough if the employee really deserved all those positive evaluations. If he or she did not, it is even worse.

What's the problem? Whenever an employee is discharged, the employee is going to consider suing for some kind of illegal discharge. To do so, the employee must find an attorney willing to take the case. Only a small percentage of possible wrongful discharge cases actually get filed in court because it is not worth an attorney's time to pursue a case unless there is a reasonable probability of success. If the employee can show the attorney a series of positive evaluations going back several years, the attorney is more likely to believe the employee's explanation of his or her discharge. The same is true of any judge or jury that might become involved in the case. If the employee was so good, then why did the employer fire him or her? If the employee was not really so good, then why did the employer give him or her such good evaluations?

Most businesses and government agencies have experienced something similar to the grade inflation found in most colleges. Supervisors like to be liked by their employees, and one way to be liked is to give out good evaluations at the end of the year. The employee feels good, the supervisor feels good, and who cares what the lawyers feel? It is only down the road, probably with a different supervisor, that problems arise. The new supervisor has a different style and this employee does not fit into that style, or, worse, this employee was never very good and the former supervisor was simply unwilling to rock the boat and tell the truth. Either way, the new supervisor is faced with a problem. Discharging this employee for poor performance will raise a number of issues because of the many years of positive performance evaluations. Jurors will identify with the employee and use the past evaluations to justify a verdict in the employee's favor. The judge will not have much sympathy with a company that can't even control its own internal evaluation system—a system that it is not legally required to maintain in the first place.

The bottom line is no evaluations are much better than badly done or overly positive evaluations, and more organizations should recognize this and give up trying to do written evaluations of their employees.

If we suppose that, for whatever reason, the organization does wish to have written evaluations, then several rules are in order. First, the average employee should get an average rating. If a person is doing reasonably well, then he or she should receive that rating and should not be rated "good" or "excellent." Second, the evaluation should be more than a few check marks on an evaluation form. The person doing the evaluation should write out, in some detail, what the person has done right and what needs improvement. It is important that supervisors who will be called upon to prepare written evaluations be trained in how to evaluate people.

People writing evaluations must avoid rating their friends high and people they do not particularly like low. Again, this is difficult for people. The problem is, suppose that a few years down the road, the former friend, who never did a very good job, is now doing a terrible job, and we have years of highly positive evaluations to deal with. It will look suspicious if this employee receives a very negative evaluation all of a sudden.

Evaluation forms should not be so long that no one wants to complete them. If they are, then the supervisor is tempted to simply rate everyone high and get the form filled out. A good form will have a half dozen to a dozen major categories, with space to write comments. Two pages should be enough. The form should focus on both objective attributes (gets to work on time) and subjective attributes (works well with coworkers). Concrete accomplishments should be discussed, and every evaluation should point out at least one weakness that needs work and at least one project that was less than perfect. Goals for improvement should be listed so that they can be reviewed at the next evaluation session.

EMPLOYEE SELF-EVALUATION

Should employees play an active part in the evaluation process? Again, there are positive and negative aspects to this. On the one hand, most employees will simply praise themselves if they are allowed to, and this accomplishes nothing. On the other hand, if the employee self-evaluation form forces them to state both strengths and weaknesses and to list both accomplishments and failures, it can be useful. If nothing else, it allows a supervisor to see what the employee believes to be the most praiseworthy thing about his or her performance, and the supervisor may find that the employee's view of the job or the company is totally different from the supervisor's view. This can be very useful information.

The employee evaluation is also a chance to find out what the employee believes should be his or her major focus for the coming year. If the employee is in a position that can grow, then how the employee will be expanding the job in the future should be a topic for discussion during the annual evaluation. Another topic should be the kinds of specialized education or training the employee should be getting in order to become more productive.

THE BEST EVALUATIONS

The best evaluations accomplish a lot, and people need to be trained in order for this to be possible. First of all, the evaluation should actually provide an objective assessment of the employee that both the supervisor and the employee feel is fair. Second, the evaluation should provide a road map for future action. The employee should have an idea of what training to seek and what projects to concentrate on in the coming months. The employee should also have an idea of what his or her future with this company might be. Third, the employee should have received concrete suggestions for improvement. If the employee is late to work too often, then the supervisor and the employee should have discussed ways to help the employee be on time. If the employee is not able to use the new software effectively, then the employee should be signed up for a training program. If the employee is not getting along with a coworker, then strategies for solving this interpersonal problem should have been discussed. If there is not much chance that this employee will be moving up the ladder any time soon, then it is only fair that he or she be told this. If advancement is a real possibility, then this should also be discussed.

Potential legal problems are of two types: promises and defamation. Supervisors must avoid making promises that they cannot keep. An employee who is told orally by a supervisor that he or she will be promoted in the near future may have a case if that promise is not kept. This is particularly true if the employee stops looking for a better job because of this promise. Also, employees can certainly sue for defamation of character based on what is said in a performance evaluation. The supervisor has a conditional privilege to tell what he or she believes in good faith to be the truth. However, supervisors who lie in evaluations in order to serve their own personal goals, such as helping their friends and hurting their personal enemies, may find themselves in court. Again, fear of lawsuits is another reason why most evaluations are not really accurate appraisals of employee performance.

SAMPLE EMPLOYEE HANDBOOK PROVISION

The MNO Company believes that everyone in the organization needs, and deserves, feedback concerning his or her performance. That is why periodic performance evaluations are conducted for everyone. The evaluations will look at everything from quantity and quality of work done to attendance and relations with coworkers. The purpose of these evaluations is to help employees improve and to guide personnel decisions. Every employee is expected to participate in the evaluation process with an eye toward improving his or her own performance and the performance of the entire organization.

PERSONNEL RECORDS

Personnel records are becoming a major problem for many organizations. How many different files should an organization have on one person? First of all, many experts suggest that all I-9 forms be in one place so that they will be easy for a government official testing compliance with the immigration laws to review. There should then probably be three files for every employee. The medical file should have any medical information about the employee. This file would contain information about disabilities and the need for accommodation. It is important that this information be kept separate and that only people who need to know have access to it.

There should probably be a second file with payroll and other financial information. This file would contain information concerning such things as who will be the beneficiary of the employee's group life insurance policy and how much stock the employee has in a stock ownership plan. The names of children and spouses would be in this file for benefit purposes. Again, only people who need access should see the private information in this file.

The third file should contain everything else. All the basic forms, from the job application to job descriptions and performance evaluations, should be in this file. Letters of praise or reprimand should also be in this file.

PRIVACY

Employers need to realize that allowing people inside or outside the organization to see confidential information contained in personnel files can result in a lawsuit for invasion of privacy. In one case, the company doctor told people inside IBM that an employee was paranoid and needed psychiatric treatment. The judge allowed that case to go to the jury on the issue of whether the people the doctor discussed this with really had a need to know (*Bratt*).

The point is that employers should keep confidential information confidential not just because it is the fair and nice thing to do, but because they can be sued if they fail to do so. At the same time, supervisors who do need to know can be told. In one case, a court ruled that supervisors did need to know that an employee was suicidal and a possible safety threat to himself and other employees (*Monsanto*). Everyone who works with employee records should be aware of this potential problem.

EMPLOYEE ACCESS TO RECORDS

The other major problem with employee records is the issue of whether or not employees should be allowed to see their own records and, if there are different sets of records, which records they should be allowed to see.

This issue is important enough for at least sixteen states to have laws on this subject. Most require that employees be given access to the company records about them. In at least eight states the law also gives employees the right to insert rebuttal information into the file if they feel that anything is not accurate.

The question for employers in other states, and in states that require access but do not mandate employee rebuttal, is whether or not to give employees these rights through the employee handbook, even if the law does not require it. In 1977 the federal Privacy Protection Study Commission issued voluntary guidelines that it hoped employers would follow. Those guidelines recommended that all medical, test score, and reference information be kept strictly confidential. The commission also recommended that employees be given access to most, if

---

States and Employee Records

States that Mandate Employee Access to Personnel Files

Alaska	Iowa	Nevada	Pennsylvania
California	Maine	Oregon	Rhode Island

States that also Mandate that Employees be Allowed to Place Rebuttal Information in Their Personnel File

Connecticut	Massachusetts	Minnesota	Washington
Delaware	Michigan	New Hampshire	Wisconsin

---

not all, information in their records. It also felt that employees should be allowed to insert a notice of dispute if they felt that anything contained in a file was not accurate.

It is important for employers to consider these recommendations. If a policy is included in the employee handbook, then it no longer matters what the law says; the employee has been promised access and the right to rebut inaccurate information. If this promise is made, it should be lived up to.

SAMPLE EMPLOYEE HANDBOOK PROVISION

All employees of the MNO Company have the right to examine any records that pertain to them personally. If an employee feels that anything in the records is not accurate, he or she should bring it to the attention of the director of human resources. If the director refuses to remove the objected-to item, the employee has the right to place a notice in the file that the employee believes the item to be inaccurate. This notice should explain why the employee believes this to be the case.

CONCLUSION

In any personnel case, a key factor is going to be documentation. An organization with a system of written evaluations needs to make sure that the evaluations are for real. There is nothing better than accurate evaluations and nothing worse than a series of very positive but inaccurate evaluations. Supervisors should be trained in how to conduct evaluations, and evaluations should be a real attempt to both guide the employee toward improvement and evaluate the employee's past performance.

Chapter 30
Employee Benefits

During the second half of the twentieth century, more and more employers in the United States have provided more and more of their employees' compensation in the form of benefits. The main reason for this is the tax consequences. If an employer pays wages to an employee, those wages are first subject to Social Security taxes. The remainder is subject to federal, state, and in some cases city income or payroll taxes. When we combine Social Security with income and payroll taxes, the average working person seldom receives more than 70 percent of the wages he or she would have been entitled to. As Social Security and income taxes have increased, the incentive for employers and employees to find ways to avoid this large tax bite have also increased. During the 1970s and 1980s, most of what would have been wage increases was paid out in the form of employee benefits instead. In the 1990s, what would have been wage increases was generally absorbed in paying higher premiums for health insurance.

Benefits are subject to either state or federal law. The major federal law controlling employee benefits is the Employee Retirement Income Security Act (ERISA). This act controls benefit and pension plans. It preempts state law in most cases, which means that if ERISA applies, an employee must sue or file a complaint under ERISA, and any state law that might have applied will not be considered. On the other hand, if ERISA does not apply, then, in most cases, only state laws controlling contracts and other obligations will apply. This is different from most areas of employment law, such as wage and hour laws, where employers must comply with both state and federal laws.

A benefit in the general sense is anything other than wages that the employee receives from the employer. It can be anything from a free can of cola made available in the office refrigerator to a paid vacation, free lodging, or free meals. Health insurance, life insurance, and other kinds of insurance provided by the employer are also considered to be benefits. Paid leave, such as sick leave and paid vacation, is another kind of benefit.

ERISA

The Employee Retirement Income Security Act (ERISA) was passed in 1974 to regulate pension and benefit plans (29 U.S.C. sec. 1001 *et seq.*). The first important point is that ERISA does not require any employer in the United States to provide any benefits whatsoever. It does not require employers to provide any kind of pension fund or health insurance. It simply regulates these plans if they are provided.

ERISA does not apply to many things that we would generally consider to be employer-provided benefits. For example, ERISA does not apply to wages or overtime payments. These are regulated by federal and state wage and hour laws. It generally does not apply to money paid out during vacations, holidays, or other kinds of paid leaves of absence. It does not apply to employer-provided recreational facilities, holiday gifts such as free hams, sales of items to employees (whether or not the employee receives a discount), or tuition reimbursement plans. ERISA does not apply to group insurance plans if the employer does not make any payments to the plans, but simply makes them available to the employees if they wish to pay the premiums. All of these statements assume that the payments are being made out the employer's general funds and not out of a special trust fund created to provide these benefits. Once a trust fund has been created for almost any employee benefit purpose, ERISA will probably apply.

ERISA does apply to all pension plans, group insurance plans if the premiums are paid at least in part by the employer, and all trust funds created by the employer for the benefit of the employees. ERISA requires employers to provide to employees a Summary Plan Description of every pension or benefit plan. This description must describe in plain English how the plan works, what the employee's rights are under the plan, what the employee is entitled to under the plan and the procedures that the employee must follow to receive those benefits. Since most plans are subject to the supervision of both the Department of Labor and the Internal Revenue Service, copies of this Summary Plan Description and annual forms must be sent to one or both of these federal agencies. Under some circumstances, employees are entitled to an annual statement covering their individual benefits under the plan and the general state of the plan. To the extent that a plan involves insurance, it is subject to both ERISA and the relevant state's insurance laws. It may also be subject to both federal and state banking and securities laws.

GROUP INSURANCE PLANS

Group insurance plans in which the premiums are paid in full or in part by the employer are covered by ERISA. ERISA does not require employers to provide group insurance plans or define which employees must be allowed to participate in these plans. For example, an employer might offer group health and life insurance only to full-time employees, to employees who have worked for a specific period of time, such as ninety days or one year, or to a particular class of employees or a particular division within the company. Of course, these benefits should not be distributed in a way that violates the civil rights laws or any other antidiscrimination law.

The federal Age Discrimination in Employment Act and Older Workers Benefit Protection Act also apply. This means that in most cases older workers must be provided with the same benefits, including life insurance and pension benefits, as other workers. In some circumstances older workers can be offered a lower benefit level based on the fact that older workers require higher premium payments. Older workers may not be required to make up the difference between the premium required for younger workers and that required for older workers.

Employers should make it clear what insurance is provided and which employees qualify for that insurance coverage. While this can change, a summary of current insurance benefits can be included in the employee handbook.

A major concern in the 1990s has been the high cost of health insurance. A variety of methods have been used to try to control costs, including doing away with health insurance for employees altogether. Some employers have turned to managed care programs, which require approval before a medical procedure can be initiated. Others have turned to health maintenance organizations (HMOs), which focus on prevention as an answer. Still others have raised the employees' copayment and annual deductible in an effort to cut costs. The high cost of health insurance should be explained to employees along with what the company is trying to do in order to keep costs down.

SAMPLE EMPLOYEE HANDBOOK PROVISION

At the MNO Company, all full-time employees (those who work more than thirty hours a week) who have worked for at least thirty days are entitled to participate in our group health and life insurance programs. Employees must fill out the necessary forms at the human resources office. We have experienced a significant increase in health insurance premiums during the last few years, with no end in sight. In order to control costs, we have instituted a number of programs to help prevent both accidents and illness. We now participate in a health maintenance organization (HMO) instead of the kind of insurance program most of you may be familiar with. This requires you to make a nominal payment every time you use the HMO. We have also provided recreational facilities to help employees maintain their general physical health, and we encourage employees to use them. We also provide subsidies for employees who wish to participate in weight loss and stop-smoking programs as well as drug and alcohol treatment programs, and employees are encouraged to take advantage of these programs. When it comes to health, an ounce of prevention is worth a pound of cure.

FLEXIBLE SPENDING ACCOUNTS

Federal law does allow employers to establish what are called *flexible spending accounts* to help employees cover the costs of child care, health care, or both. The law allows employees to set aside up to $5,000 ($2,500 if married filing separately) to pay for child care. There is no limit on the amount that may be set aside to pay for health care. These accounts are funded with pretax dollars. The health-care flexible account can be used to pay deductibles and copayments that are not paid by the employer's group health insurance plan.

The major advantage of these plans for employees is that they can use pretax dollars to pay health and child care costs. The major disadvantage for employees is the "use it or lose it" rule. This means that under these plans, employees must forfeit any money not used during the year. The major disadvantage for employers is simply the cost of setting up and administering another employee account.

COBRA CONTINUATION

In 1985 Congress passed the Consolidated Omnibus Budget Reconciliation Act (COBRA). One of the provisions of that act required employers with twenty or more employees to make it possible for employees to continue their group health insurance coverage after leaving work. Employers are not required to pay the premiums. The employees pay the premium plus up to 2 percent more to cover the cost of administration. COBRA applies to all health insurance—type plans, including dental and vision plans.

There are a number of "qualifying events" that, if they occur, require employers to offer this continuation of insurance coverage. If an employee is fired, retires, is laid off, quits, or has his or her hours reduced below the threshold and is therefore no longer eligible for employer-paid health insurance, the employer must offer to continue the employee in the plan for up to eighteen months. If the employee becomes disabled, the employer must offer to continue the employee in the plan for up to twenty-nine months. The employee's spouse and children are entitled to continue in the group plan for up to thirty-six months if the employee dies, divorces, or goes on Medicare. If the employer goes bankrupt under Chapter 11, employees and their spouses, ex-spouses, and children may also be entitled to continued coverage under the group plan.

Summary of COBRA Provisions

1. Applies to employers with 20 or more employees.

2. Qualifying events:
    termination (other than for gross misconduct),
    reduction in hours below plan limits,
    death,
    disability,
    divorce,
    entitled to Medicare,
    bankruptcy of company.

3. Beneficiaries entitled to continuation include current or ex-spouse and children.

4. Coverage must be identical to current employer health plan.

5. Coverage must continue for 18 to 36 months depending on the circumstances.

6. Coverage not required if:
    beneficiaries fail to pay premiums,
    beneficiaries become covered by another plan or Medicare,
    widowed or divorced spouse remarries,
    employer terminates health plan for employees.

7. The employer must notify employees and spouse of continuation option when:

employee first becomes employed,
employee divorces or dies or has some other qualifying event.

8. Employee and beneficiaries have 60 days after receiving notice to decide if they will take advantage of the offer.

Employees who are discharged for gross misconduct are not entitled to a continuation of coverage, but it is not clear exactly what qualifies as gross misconduct under COBRA. Employers are required to send out a notice within thirty days after any of the qualifying events occurs, including an employee getting a divorce. In this case, a separate notice would have to be sent to the now ex-spouse telling him or her about the right to continue under the group health insurance plan. The children are also entitled to a notice, but in most cases notice to the parents will qualify as notice to the children. The employee, spouse or ex-spouse, and children have to be given sixty days to decide if they wish to continue under the group plan. Because of this notice requirement, it would be useful to notify employees of this provision in the employee handbook.

The right to continue as part of the group health insurance plan ends if any of a number of circumstances occurs. If the plan is terminated then of course those who are outside the employee group have no more right to be in the plan than the current employees do. If the outside beneficiaries stop paying the premiums, then of course they no longer have a right to coverage under the plan. If they become covered by another group health insurance plan or Medicare, then their right to remain in the group plan would also terminate. Also, if the plan is modified, the outside beneficiaries only have a right to participate in the plan currently in force.

Sample Employee Handbook Provision

Employees who quit, retire, are fired, are laid off, become disabled, or have their hours reduced, so that they no longer qualify for employer-provided group health insurance, may be entitled to continue the coverage under the group plan at their own expense. The spouse and children of such an employee may also be entitled to continued coverage under the group plan. Also, if an employee dies, divorces, or goes on Medicare, his or her spouse, ex-spouse, or children may also be entitled to continue to be covered by our group plan, at their own expense. That is why employees must inform the director of human resources when they divorce or do anything else that might trigger this eligibility.

Pension-Type Plans

If a plan is designed to provide payments after an employee cases to work, it is subject to a variety of ERISA rules and regulations. First of all, once employees reach the age of twenty-one and have worked for one year, they are generally eligible to participate in the plan. However, ERISA does not prevent employers from establishing different plans for different divisions of a company or different types or classes of employees.

ERISA requires that a plan that will pay benefits into the future have a vesting schedule that meets minimum requirements. By vesting, we mean that the employee is entitled to the benefits; they cannot be taken away. In general, there is either gradual vesting or cliff vesting. With cliff vesting, an employer may require an employee to work for up to five years before becoming vested (collectively bargained and state and local government plans may extend this to ten years). That means that if the employee leaves after four years, he or she has no rights under the plan. If the employee stays past five years, he or she has full rights under the plan. A gradual schedule is allowed in which the employee vests at least 20 percent after three years, 40 percent after four years, 60 percent after five years, 80 percent after six years, and 100 percent after seven years. Employers are free to be more generous than these requirements. For example, an employer might have cliff vesting after four years instead of five or gradual vesting that reached 100 percent after five years instead of seven.

It is important to distinguish between vesting and benefit accrual. As employees become vested, they vest only as to the benefits they have actually accrued. For example, if an employee has $10,000 worth of benefits in the account and is 20 percent vested, the employee is entitled to only $2,000 worth of benefits. As the vesting percentage goes up, the employee is entitled to more and more of the benefits that have accrued under the plan.

As a general rule, if a benefit or pension plan is set up to provide benefits in the future, the employer must set up a trust fund to take in payments every month or every year and hold that money in trust for the employees and their dependents. Before the passage of ERISA, many employers simply promised to pay a pension out of whatever money they earned in the future. There was no trust fund for retired employees. If the employer hit hard times or went out of business, the retired employees were simply out of luck. The requirement of a trust fund is one step ERISA takes in an attempt to avoid this problem.

ERISA requires that everyone who deals with the pension plan's money meet the standards of a fiduciary under the law. This means that the people who administer the funds must have only the best interests of the employees and their beneficiaries at heart when they take any action or make any decisions. They must exercise the skill and prudence of a "prudent person," and they must diversify the plan's investments to minimize risk. They must also follow the instructions contained in the plan documents.

As a general rule, a "party in interest" may not have any financial dealings with the trust that holds the money for the employees and their beneficiaries. The Department of Labor can grant an exemption to this provision if the party in interest can demonstrate why an exemption should be granted. In other words, the party can explain why the normal rules should not be followed in a particular case because the usual danger to the plan would not apply.

TWO TYPES OF PLANS

There are basically two types of pension plans, defined-benefit and defined-contribution. Defined-benefit plans are what most people think of when they hear the word *pension*. Employees are promised a fixed amount every month after they retire, determined by how high their salary was and how many years they worked for their employer. It was the failure of some large defined-benefit plans to pay the employees that were counting on the money for retirement that led Congress to pass ERISA.

Congress also created the Pension Benefit Guaranty Corporation (PBGC). This federal agency accepts premiums from defined-benefit plans to provide a fund that will pay people their pensions if their pension fund fails. There is a limit to how much the PBGC will pay to anyone in a month ($2,250 in 1991). The PBGC also regulates all defined-benefit pension plans to make sure they are solvent. Employers who have such plans are required to notify the PBGC if the plan is changed or if there are any significant changes in the number of people covered by the plan or the financial health of the trust fund that is supposed to provide benefits under the plan. The PBGC has the power to terminate a plan that is not solvent.

Under federal law, employers are allowed to terminate defined-benefit pension plans, but they must follow the procedures set down by the PBGC in doing so. They may have to make a large lump-sum payment if the plan is currently underfunded. On the other hand, if the plan is overfunded, meaning that there is more money in the trust fund than is needed to cover the projected costs of the plan, the employer may terminate the plan and take out the excess funds. However, to discourage this, Congress has imposed a series of excise taxes on the money taken out of such a plan.

The second basic type of plan is a defined-contribution plan. These plans are very different from defined-benefit plans. A defined-benefit plan tells the employee exactly how much the benefit will be (assuming that the plan is still in existence), but the employee does not have an individual account in the trust fund. The money is held as one large fund, and it is hoped that the fund's investments will provide the money needed to pay the benefits when the time comes. With a defined-contribution plan, money is placed into an individual account for each employee. The money in that account is invested in a variety of ways, with the employee having some degree of control over how it is invested in some kinds of defined-contribution plans. When it comes time for an employee to retire, he or she has an individual account with more or less money available depending on how successful the investments have been.

Which kind of plan is more advantageous for the employer depends on the circumstances. Because of the insurance premiums and PBGC regulations, a defined-benefit plan is usually more expensive to administer. Also, the amount of money needed each year to keep the trust fund solvent may be subject to large fluctuations. If the investments do well one year, the employer may not have to put much money into the fund. If they do badly the next year, the employer may have to put in a great deal. With defined-contribution plans, the regulations are simpler and the employer has a much better idea of how much money will be going into the plan each year. Which kind of plan is more advantageous to the employees involved depends on the specifics of the individual plans. A well-invested defined-contribution plan is usually better than a defined-benefit plan, which will usually be better than a poorly invested defined-contribution plan. The employee handbook should explain the basics of how the company pension plan works and notify employees that they should receive both a Summary Plan Description and an Annual Plan Report of some kind.

SAMPLE EMPLOYEE HANDBOOK PROVISION

Here at the MNO Company we have a defined-contribution benefit plan, commonly called a thrift plan or a 401(k) plan. The company matches every dollar employees contribute by contributing another dollar. The maximum amount any employee can contribute is set by law and changes from year to year to adjust for inflation. You will be asked how much you wish to contribute out of your paycheck at the beginning of each year. This program is available only to full-time employees. New employees should receive a Summary Plan Description. All employees who participate in the plan will receive an annual report covering the plan and their personal account. This plan allows employees to have some say concerning how their funds are invested. Because the money placed in the 401(k) plan is pretax and because the interest and dividends earned in the plan are also not taxed, this plan allows employees to accumulate wealth for retirement much faster than by investing on their own. Of course, when benefits are finally paid, they will be subject to income taxes. This is a voluntary plan. Employees vest 20 percent a year in this plan and will be 100 percent vested at the end of five years. Vesting simply means the extent to which the employee is entitled to receive the money paid into the plan by the employer. Employees are 100 percent vested in the funds they place in the plan at all times.

TYPES OF DEFINED-CONTRIBUTION PLANS

There are basically three types of defined-contribution plans. The first, thrift plans, allow employees to save pretax dollars for retirement. The most common of these, 401(k) plans, named after the section of the Internal Revenue Code that controls them, allow employees to place pretax dollars in their individual accounts. (These are pre-income tax dollars, but Social Security taxes will have been paid on this money.) While employers are not required to match these funds, most employers do provide some kind of match. The match might be dollar-for-dollar or some fraction. For example, for every dollar of employee contribution, the employer might contribute fifty cents. There are special limits concerning how much money can be placed in thrift plans during a year.

The second major type of defined-contribution plan is a profit-sharing plan. While it is possible to create a profit-sharing plan that simply provides a cash bonus to employees based on the profits of the company, most plans do not do this. Instead, most profit-sharing plans allow an employer to place money into the employees' individual accounts. The law used to require that a company actually make a profit in order to make a contribution to a profit-sharing plan, but that is no longer the case. This means that profit-sharing plans can be used to create defined-contribution pension plans that combine the financial power of a defined-benefit pension plan with the flexibility of a defined-contribution plan. All of the money placed in a profit-sharing plan is both pre-Social Security taxes and pre-income taxes. This means that more money can be placed in the plan than with a thrift plan.

The third major type of defined-contribution plan is an Employee Stock Ownership Plan (commonly called an ESOP). While an ESOP is like other defined-contribution plans in that each employee has an individual account, it is different in that most of the funds are invested in the stock of the company the employee works for, rather than in a large group of stocks and bonds, as would be the case with most defined-contribution plans. While that could be considered a disadvantage, it can also be an advantage if the stock does well. ESOPs will be discussed more fully in the next chapter.

Generally, an employer cannot contribute more than 15 percent of payroll to a defined-contribution plan. Also, generally, no more than $30,000 can be contributed to any employee's defined-contribution account in any one year.

QUALIFIED PLANS

The main advantage of most pension and benefit plans is that the money contributed to the plans is tax-deductible to the employer and is not taxed to the employee until the plan begins to pay benefits. For any plan, regardless of type, to be able to take advantage of this tax arrangement, it must meet the requirements of the Internal Revenue Code for "qualified plans." To be a qualified plan, the plan must meet certain criteria concerning participation, coverage, and nondiscrimination. For participation, a plan must benefit at least fifty employees or 40 percent of an employer's workforce, whichever is less, in order to be considered a qualified plan. The plan must also provide coverage for more than just the "highly compensated employees" (HCEs). This requirement prevents a plan from being used simply to benefit the highly paid employees. The rule is that either the plan must benefit at least 70 percent of the non-HCEs or the percentage of non-HCEs benefiting from the plan must be at least 70 percent of the percentage of HCEs benefiting. Finally, the plan must not discriminate in favor of HCEs. That means that if the company contributes a fixed percentage of the HCE's salary the same percentage must be contributed for other employees. While the amount of money contributed will obviously be different, the percentage must be the same if the plan is to be considered "qualified" for favorable tax treatment. There are legal limits concerning how much salary can be considered for these percentage calculations. These limits are generally only of concern to highly compensated employees.

RECEIVING BENEFITS

Generally, employees cannot begin to receive benefits from pension plans until they reach the age of 59½. If they do receive benefits before that age, they will usually have to pay a special excise tax on top of the usual federal income taxes. Also, employees must begin to receive benefits by the age of 70½.

If an employer discharges an employee in an attempt to deprive the employee of any rights protected by ERISA the employee may sue in federal court for damages. This usually occurs when an employee is very ill and causing the group health insurance premiums to go up or is about to vest in a pension plan. In both cases, if the employee can prove this was the motivation for the discharge, he or she can receive both full damages and attorney fees. Judges can order employees to be reinstated to their jobs or order the employer to pay their salary for many years into the future. For example, when John Folz was discharged from the Marriott Corporation he believed it was because they had found out that he had multiple sclerosis and would cause the health insurance costs to rise (*Folz*). John Folz convinced a judge that this was the company's motivation. The judge ordered the company to pay John Folz back pay plus the pay he would have received if he had worked until retirement. John Folz was also given all other benefits of employment including being returned to the group health insurance plan and having all rights of an employee in the pension, profit-sharing and stock option plans.

Of course all other laws concerned with discrimination would apply as well. An employer could not base the decision concerning who would be allowed to participate in a benefit plan on factors such as sex, race, or religion.

CONCLUSION

Providing employee benefits directly to employees instead of raising wages has become common in the United States because the employer is allowed to buy the benefits with pre-tax dollars. This has created a system where most people get health insurance through their employer if they get it at all. In 1995 or 1996 Congress may reform this health insurance system. In 1974 Congress reformed the pension system with the passage of ERISA. This means employees who are promised a pension have a much better chance of actually getting one at the end of the twentieth century than they did at the beginning of the twentieth century. At the same time the regulations and costs involved in complying with the federal law discourage some employers from offering a pension plan in the first place. The simplicity and lower cost of defined-contribution plans have led many employers to offer these instead of the traditional pension plan. Because of the tax advantages, even the smallest employer should consider some kind of plan for themselves and their employees.

Chapter 31

Sharing Ownership

One special kind of benefit is the opportunity to own stock in the company the employees actually work for. There is nothing new about the basic idea that workers can be owners. What the United States has done in the last half of the twentieth century is make possible a variety of methods for sharing ownership with employees. By the early 1990s, the United States had a much higher level of ownership by employees than any other country on earth.

The first issue for the owners and managers of any company considering sharing ownership with employees is fundamental: Are you really willing to treat employees to some degree like owners? Just as companies that promise to treat employees fairly are worse off if they do not do so, companies that promise to make employees owners are worse off if they provide some kind of ownership sharing and then continue to treat employees like something the cat dragged in. That does not mean that employees have to take part in every decision, and it does not mean that employees have to be given the keys to the vault. It does mean that treating employees the way the average American company treats employees will not be acceptable. While many companies do not advertise it, a large number of the good places to work in the United States also share ownership with their employees.

Once a company decides it does wish to seriously explore the idea of sharing ownership with employees, a number of options become available. (See Darien McWhirter's book, *Sharing Ownership*, for a full analysis of these options.) The advantages and disadvantages of each option can be discussed only briefly here, and you should seek legal advice to match the conditions of your company with the available ownership-sharing options.

GIVING STOCK AWAY

The simplest way to make owners out of employees is to give them some stock in the company. There are two basic types of stock, normal stock, which can be sold immediately, and restricted stock, which cannot be sold for some period of time, often five or ten years. We are assuming, of course, that the company's stock is already publicly traded. If that is not the case, then a variety of securities laws may make giving stock away either impossible or too expensive.

When Ewing Kauffman, chairman and founder of Marion Laboratories of Kansas City, wants to reward employees at the company's quarterly employee meetings (called Marion on the Move meetings), he gives them stock. He might give an employee with ten years of perfect attendance some shares, and other employees might receive stock as a reward for making a money-saving suggestion to the company suggestion plan. In 1988, when the Bank of America wanted to express appreciation to all the employees for bringing the company through difficult financial times, it decided to give every employee ten shares of Bank of America stock, worth $20.75 each at the time.

Giving stock has many advantages. It is not legally complicated if the stock is already publicly traded. It is a gift that has more meaning than merely money. Thousands of the Bank of America employees who received stock in 1988 wrote thank-you letters to the CEO telling him how much it meant to them to receive stock. It is also easy for the employee to then decide whether to keep it or sell it. The major disadvantage is that the employee will have to pay income taxes on the gift (it is income), which may force him or her to sell some or all of the shares in order to pay the tax bill.

If the owners of the company hope is that employees will keep their shares and begin to think and act differently because they are now stockholders, the owners are likely to be disappointed, as giving the employees stock will usually not have this effect. For most employees, the gift will simply be too small to make a difference in their personal financial future. Also, because they have to pay income taxes on the gift, they will have a large incentive to sell all or part of the shares immediately.

A gift of restricted stock forces the employees to keep the shares. Restricted stock is simply stock that cannot be sold for a period of time. If employees are given restricted stock that they cannot sell, and that will not be worth much in the future unless they begin to act and think like owners, it may change their outlook on the company and their job. The problem is that in some cases the employees will have to pay income taxes on this stock, just as they would if they could turn around and sell it, which can cause a financial hardship for them. This can be avoided by making a gift or bonus part in cash and part in restricted stock. The cash can be used to pay the income tax bill on the entire gift, and the restricted stock can provide a real bonus in the years ahead if the company does well.

Under American income tax laws, employees receiving restricted stock have a choice. They can wait and pay income taxes on the stock when the restrictions lapse, or they can pay income taxes when they receive the stock. This choice is controlled by Section 83 of the Internal Revenue Code. If employees decide to take the immediate tax option, then they will have to pay taxes on the stock at current market value and without regard to the fact that the stock is restricted. If the company wants employees to become long-term stockholders, this is what it wants employees to do. This way, the employee will not be forced to sell the stock when the restrictions lapse in order to pay the income tax bill at that time. As with everything else, this should be explained to the employees in the employee handbook.

SAMPLE EMPLOYEE HANDBOOK PROVISION

It is our practice at the MNO Company to pay bonuses from time to time when the financial situation allows it. Bonuses are based on a variety of factors, including the extent to which individual employees have made valuable suggestions that have improved the company. Generally, bonuses are paid half in cash and half in restricted MNO stock. "Restricted" means that the stock cannot be sold for ten years after being given to the employee (it may be left in a will). As a condition of the bonus, employees are required to pay income taxes on the restricted stock when they receive it based on the current market value of the stock. Because this will mean that the gift of restricted stock is taxed just as if the shares could be sold immediately (even though they cannot be), the cash part of the bonus is given to help pay income taxes. If employees pay income taxes at the time of the gift, they will not have to pay any further income taxes until the stock is sold. The point of giving restricted stock is that the stock will be worth something in the future only if we all continue to work harder and smarter than our competitors. We believe that to the extent all of us have that incentive, our company will be prosperous in the years to come.

STOCK OPTIONS

Another way companies can turn their employees into owners is through the use of stock options. A stock option is simply a contract between the employee and the company. The company gives the employee the option to buy a fixed number of shares for a fixed period of time at a fixed amount per share. For example, the employee might have the option to buy 1,000 shares at any time during the next ten years for $10 a share. If the shares are currently selling for $10 a share, then the employee will have an incentive to help the company prosper so that the share price will go up and the employee will be able to exercise the option and make a profit.

PepsiCo has a stock option plan for all of its employees, which it calls the SharePower plan. (PepsiCo not only makes Pepsi it also owns Kentucky Fried Chicken and Taco Bell.) The PepsiCo SharePower plan gives every employee the option on July 1 of each year to buy a number of shares (depending on the employee's salary level) at a fixed price (related to the current selling price) for ten years. The employee cannot buy more than 20 percent of the shares during the first year and 20 percent more each additional year.

While employees receiving stock options do not have to pay income taxes on the option, they will have to pay income taxes when they exercise the option if the shares they buy are worth more than they are required to pay for them. That means that while a stock option plan can encourage employees to begin to care about the bottom line and the value of the stock, in many cases they will not be able to afford to keep the shares after they exercise the option.

Section 422 of the Internal Revenue Code allows companies to set up stock option plans that avoid this "must sell" problem. Basically, (1) if the option is for ten years or less, (2) if the price the employee will pay is at least equal to the current market price, (3) if the shareholders approve the plan, which includes a maximum number of shares that can be sold, (4) if the options cannot be transferred except at death, and (5) if the amount of the stock subject to any option is less than $100,000 based on the current market price of the stock at the time the option is granted, then the employee will not have to pay income taxes until the shares are sold. Also, when exercising the option, the employee must still be an employee or have been an employee within the last three months (unless the employee has died, in which case the estate has twelve months to exercise the option). Of course, when the stock is finally sold, the increase in value over the price the employee paid will be subject to income taxes.

Stock options do provide employees with an incentive to begin to focus on the thing the stockholders care most about, the price of the stock. Employees who have stock options have an incentive to work harder and smarter to help that stock price rise so that they can make money on their stock options. On the other hand, most employees will not be able to afford to hold on to the stock once they exercise the option. They will not actually become long-term stock owners because of a stock option.

SAMPLE EMPLOYEE HANDBOOK PROVISION

The MNO General Stock Option Plan provides stock options to all employees every January 1. The option amount depends on the amount of wages earned in the preceding year. These options are for ten years, which means that for ten years the employee may exercise the option and buy shares at the price set in the option. Only full-time employees who have been employed full-time for the preceding year are eligible to participate in this plan. When you receive your stock option, please read it carefully and direct any questions to the director of human resources. Because our stock option plan meets the requirements of Section 422 of the Internal Revenue Code, employees will not have to pay income taxes on any money they make until they actually sell the stock. This means that employees may exercise their options and hold on to the stock if they wish.

STOCK PURCHASE PLANS

Another way to turn employees into stockholders is to make it easier for them to buy stock or even require that they do so. Required stock purchase plans were popular during the 1920s, but they lost their popularity after the stock market crash in 1929. Even so, some companies still operate this way. For example, America West Airlines, based in Phoenix, Arizona, requires all new employees to purchase stock in the company (except where this requirement is illegal, such as in California and Canada). Employees are required to buy shares equal to 20 percent of their first year's base salary. The company makes this purchase easier by selling the stock at 85 percent of the current market price and lending the employee the money at a low interest rate. The employees can pay back the money over five years through a payroll deduction plan.

Required stock purchase plans are not popular for many reasons, not the least of which is the fact that some companies that have instituted such plans such as America West Airlines have ended up in bankruptcy court. America West did not go bankrupt because of its required stock purchase plan, but the fact that it did go bankrupt did not help the image of this idea. The famous People Express Airline also required employees to buy stock and also ended up as a failure.

Optional stock purchase plans have been much more popular. These plans allow employees to buy stock if they want to. The plan makes it easier by saving the employees stockbrokers' commissions and even allowing them to make the purchase through a payroll deduction. Section 423 of the Internal Revenue Code allows companies to sell stock at 85 percent of the current market price if the requirements of the statute are met. Section 423 requires that the plan be approved by the shareholders, and employees who own 5 percent or more of the company's stock may not participate. The plan must be available to all employees (except new, part-time, or highly compensated employees), and all employees must be given a chance to purchase the same percentage of their salary in stock. No employee may purchase more than $25,000 worth of stock in any one year. If all the requirements of Section 423 are met, then the employee does not pay any income tax on the value over the purchase price until the stock is sold.

It is common for employees to be given an option to set aside 2, 4, or 6 percent of their pay each payday for the purpose of purchasing stock in the company. The money is placed in a special account, and every quarter the employees' money is used to purchase stock at 85 percent of the lowest market price during that quarter. The basic principles of how the stock purchase plan works should be set out in the employee handbook.

SAMPLE EMPLOYEE HANDBOOK PROVISION

We have an employee stock purchase plan at the MNO Company. This plan allows employees to set aside a percentage of their salary every payday for the purpose of buying MNO stock. The company sells the stock at 85 percent of the current market price, and employees do not have to pay a broker's commission on the purchase. Employees do not have to pay any income taxes on the difference between what they paid for the stock and what the stock is worth until the stock is sold. Anyone wishing to participate in this plan should contact the Human Resources Office for detailed information.

EMPLOYEE STOCK OWNERSHIP PLANS

The major way in which American companies share ownership with their employees is through employee stock ownership plans (commonly referred to as ESOPs). An ESOP is a special kind of defined-contribution plan that is similar in some ways to a profit sharing plan. The employer places money into the plan each payday or each quarter or each year, and the money is used to buy shares of the company for the employees (or the employer can simply place shares directly into the employees' accounts). Employees get the stock (or in some cases the value of the stock) when they retire, die, become disabled, or leave the company (within five years in the case of leaving the company).

In order to encourage employers to share ownership through the use of ESOPs, Congress has given ESOPs many tax advantages. The first is that an ESOP can borrow money and have dealings with a "party in interest." This means that an ESOP can borrow money and use the money to buy a large block of stock in the company the employees work for. As the loan is paid off, the shares are placed in the employees' individual accounts. This allows a company to borrow a lot of money and then deduct both the interest (which is always deductible) and the principal payments (which are usually not deductible) by making the loan through an ESOP. These payments are deductible because they are viewed as simply payments to an employee benefit plan. The loan can be paid off faster and more easily because of this tax advantage. Also, a company with a leveraged ESOP (an ESOP that has borrowed money) is allowed to use up to 25 percent of payroll for the purpose of paying off the principal of the ESOP loan (plus whatever is needed to pay the interest payments). This allows the value of the individual employees' accounts to rise much faster than they otherwise would. Also, dividends paid on the shares held by an ESOP are tax deductible to the company if they are paid through to the employees or used to pay off the ESOP loan. If the ESOP owns more than 50 percent of the company's stock, a bank making a loan to the ESOP can deduct half of the interest income it makes from the loan. This means that ESOPs can negotiate loans with lower interest rates than they would otherwise have to pay.

The Major Advantages of ESOPS

1. Both principal and interest payments made on an ESOP loan are deductible.
2. A company with a leveraged ESOP can use up to 25 percent of payroll to pay off the principal amount of the loan each year.
3. Dividends that are paid to an ESOP and used to pay off the ESOP loan or paid through to employees are tax-deductible to the corporation.
4. Anyone who sells shares (not publicly traded) to an ESOP may roll over the proceeds and purchase stocks and bonds of other American companies without paying any income taxes until those replacement stocks and bonds are sold. The ESOP must end up owning at least 30 percent of the stock before this rollover may be done.
5. If the ESOP owns over 50 percent of the common stock and the employees have full voting rights, a bank making a loan to an ESOP does not have to pay income taxes on half of the interest income on the ESOP loan. The loan may not be for more than fifteen years. This means that ESOP loans can be made at a lower interest rate than would otherwise be the case.

The final major advantage of ESOPs is called the 1042 rollover, after Section 1042 of the Internal Revenue Code. This provision allows the stock of a private company (a company whose stock is not traded on a stock exchange) to be sold to an ESOP with a very special advantage to the seller. The seller can take the money and roll it over (buy the stocks and bonds of other American companies) and not pay any income taxes until those new stocks and bonds are sold. The seller must have owned the shares for at least three years before the sale, and the ESOP must own the shares for at least three years after the sale. This 1042 roll-over provision can be a significant advantage for someone who owns a great deal of stock in a small company and wishes to sell some or all of these shares in order to diversify his or her investments. The ESOP must end up with at least 30 percent of the company's stock when the sale is complete. This allows the owners of small companies to sell a percentage of their stock to an ESOP and still retain control of the company.

The major advantages of an ESOP to everyone involved are related to federal income taxes. If someone buys stock through an employee stock purchase plan, he or she is using after-tax dollars. After Social Security and income taxes have been taken out, about 30 percent of the money is already gone. With an ESOP, all the money is used to buy shares. When employees receive dividends on the shares in their ESOP accounts, they do not have to pay Social Security or income taxes on the money. When this tax advantage for employees is combined with the tax advantages for employers and sellers of small-company stock, it looks like a win-win situation.

The major disadvantage of an ESOP is its complexity. An ESOP is a complicated employee benefit plan. The plan must deal with dozen of complex issues, and these issues must be explained to employees in the Summary Plan Description. If a company's stock is not traded on a stock exchange, there must be an outside stock valuation each year. In other words, an ESOP is more expensive in terms of attorney's, accountant's, and other fees. It is also important for companies that have ESOPs to take the time necessary to explain to the employees what ESOPs are and how they work. Some critics argue that ESOPs are bad because all the money goes to buy stock in only one company. These critics don't understand that ESOPs were never intended as a substitute for a pension plan. They should be seen as an addition to the other pension and benefit plans that will allow employees to have a diversified set of investments for retirement.

Sample Employee Handbook Provision

The MNO Company has an Employee Stock Ownership Plan (ESOP) that currently owns over 20 percent of the common stock of the MNO Company. This plan allows the company to borrow money and save taxes in the process. When the borrowed money is paid back, stock is placed in the individual accounts of the employees (only full-time employees participate in the ESOP). This is the most tax-advantaged way for us to arrange for employees to own stock in the MNO Company. Employees cannot get their stock until they die, retire, become disabled, or leave the company (there are restrictions on when employees who leave the company can receive their shares). Each year each employee receives an account of how many shares he or she has and how much these shares are currently worth. We strongly believe that employees should share in the financial success of the company and that this is the best way (in terms of taxes and other factors) for us to allow this to happen. We believe that the best way to ensure the long-term financial health of the company is to give every employee shares in the ESOP. Because the shares will be available for sale only many years in the future, every employee has a strong incentive to be concerned with the long-term growth of the company. Our high level of employee ownership through the ESOP allows us to develop the kind of workplace that we would all like to work in. Everyone is in the same boat, and everyone can provide everyone else with the kind of trust and flexibility that allow us to work smarter, work harder, and have fun at the same time.

CONCLUSION

During the last quarter of the twentieth century, more and more companies have found it advantageous to share ownership with their employees. The federal Internal Revenue Code has been modified a number of times to provide incentives for employers to share ownership with their employees. The hope is that employees who are also owners will work harder and smarter, and that the American economy will be stronger as a result. While sharing ownership with employees is not a guarantee of financial success, the fact is that the vast majority of companies that have shared ownership with their employees in the last half of the twentieth century have done well. Because of the financial and other advantages of the various methods of sharing ownership with employees, every company in the United States should consider doing just that.

Chapter 32

Having a Great Place to Work

Robert Levering is a coauthor of *The 100 Best Companies to Work For in America*. In 1988 his book *A Great Place to Work* was published. In it, he tried to point out in concrete terms what it is about some companies that make them great places to work. While he talked a great deal about issues such as trust and attitude, much of the book actually discussed particular personnel polices of companies that he found to be, based on the testimony of their employees, great places to work. Many of these companies have policies that go beyond the basics that we have discussed so far in this book. These policies all have potential legal problems, but these legal problems may well be countered by increased productivity. Anyone creating personnel policies should consider the examples discussed by Levering and the policies that some of America's most successful (in terms of both profits and employee satisfaction) companies have introduced.

TOTAL COMMUNICATION

Everyone agrees that communication between labor and management is a good thing. Almost everyone also agrees that there have to be limits on a good thing. A few companies don't seem to think that limits on communication are a good idea.

Communication is a two-way street. Policies should both encourage employees to communicate with management and provide employees with all the information they need to do their job and enjoy what they are doing. The Tektronix company has a weekly company newspaper that is almost unique in America. It is published by and for the employees. Management has no control over its contents. Reading this newspaper, we see employees questioning company policy and challenging management decisions. A regular column, called "Employees Are Asking," features questions from employees with answers from management. These tough questions and concrete answers can sometimes be embarrassing to some in the company, but they provide the kind of information that many employees would find advantageous.

The kind of frank communication that occurs inside the pages of Tektronix's newspaper raises the issue of free speech rights for employees. Many states have laws that protect employees who blow the whistle to government investigators. Most companies would be better off if the employees blew the whistle inside the company instead, but the laws in most states do not protect internal whistle-blowers. A company could provide these whistle-blowers with both encouragement and protection with the right kind of policy. Of course, any promise not to retaliate against an employee for what he or she says, either in the company newspaper or as part of an internal whistle-blowing policy, will have to be lived up to. Nothing would destroy morale faster than firing someone in violation of such a direct promise, not to mention that the employee could sue for breach of contract (the employee handbook) and probably win.

On the other hand, the potential benefits from policies that encourage a frank exchange of information are tremendous. A truly independent employee newspaper could actually control the flow of random rumors that abound in every company. A newspaper that employees could rely on to provide them with accurate information and responses to questions could put an end to rumors like nothing else could. A true inside-the-company whistle-blower policy could provide the kind of early warning that might save millions in fines and legal fees, not to mention the kind of negative publicity that comes when the whistle gets blown outside the organization.

Sample Employee Handbook Provision

> At the MNO Company we want to encourage the free flow of information. The MNO *Bugle* is published twice a month with no management control over its content. Employees are free to submit unsigned questions, and management is required to provide answers. Everyone in the company may use the *Bugle* as a way to express both positive and negative opinions. No employee will be punished for expressing an opinion or honestly stating facts in the MNO *Bugle*. Any employee who believes that he or she has seen a violation of law or ethics may report it to the director of human resources. The director will not reveal the reporting employee's name without the reporting employee's permission. It is important to the long-term growth and health of the MNO Company that violations of law and ethics be avoided. We will all be better off if these violations can be corrected inside the company.

No-Layoff Policies

Another policy that some of the companies Robert Levering considers to be great places to work have is a no-layoff policy. From Marion Labs to Federal Express, the policy of not laying people off when there is a slight downturn in the economy is considered to be a major benefit. Other companies do the same thing. Some, such as IBM, are famous for having once had a no-layoff policy but having been unable to sustain it in the face of competitive pressure and a falling market. Again, it is important to be specific about what it means to have a no-layoff policy, and it is important to live up this promise if it is actually made.

A no-layoff policy does not mean that people are not fired. It is important to make the distinction between being fired for misconduct or incompetence and being laid off simply because orders have been reduced. A no-layoff policy means that employees will not be laid off because of a short-term downturn in the economy or an internal reorganization that leaves some employees redundant, at least temporarily. At the same time, the policy should point out that even an IBM may have to lay off workers if that is the only way to stay in business.

Some companies simply can't afford to have a no-layoff policy, either because their business is too subject to large swings or because they simply have no idea of what the future may bring. For other companies, a no-layoff policy is easier to justify. During the recession of 1981-82, Hallmark had about 600 excess employees. Some were loaned to other departments to help with maintenance and painting. Others were loaned out to the community to do volunteer work. When the economy picked up again, these workers moved right back into their old jobs. Hallmark could be sure that the demand for its product would not stay down for too long. At Federal Express, reorganizations have meant moving hundreds of people from one job to another and working to create new opportunities.

It is important to realize the financial advantages of a no-layoff policy. It is not simply a gift to workers. Once a downturn in the economy is over, a no-layoff company does not have to spend money to hire and train new workers. It will be able to move right into the new markets ahead of competitors. A no-layoff company is also going to find that employees are more willing to experiment with new ways of doing things if they know that they will not find themselves out of a job at the end of the experiment.

Most companies with no-layoff policies would be better off discussing this in the employee handbook. If this is simply a vague "company policy" that is not written down, it can cause anxiety and legal problems when it comes time to figure out exactly what the employees who made important life decisions based on the existence of the no-layoff policy thought it meant.

SAMPLE EMPLOYEE HANDBOOK PROVISION

It is a point of pride at MNO that we are a *no-layoff* company. It is important for everyone to understand what that means. It does not mean that employees are never fired. Employees who engage in misconduct or who cannot do the job to specifications are certainly fired. It does mean that MNO will do everything possible to avoid laying off employees because the economy is in recession or our sales are down. It does mean that MNO will move people around to avoid having to lay people off because of improvements in work efficiency or because of company reorganizations. If necessary, we may impose shorter work weeks for everyone to get through a tough financial time. While this has never happened, we cannot promise that at some point in the future we won't have to lay off workers in order to save the company. We can promise that we will not do this except as a last resort.

THE ULTIMATE GRIEVANCE PROCEDURE

Federal Express has a grievance procedure that it calls the Guaranteed Fair Treatment (GFT) procedure. This is a standard grievance procedure with a twist. The twist is the use of what could be called a peer review committee at the end. If the grievance gets to the level of the vice president and the employee is still not satisfied, he or she can ask for a board of review. If the vice president refuses, the employee can ask the final appeals board, made up of the chief executive officer, the chief operating officer, and the senior vice president, to grant the request for a board of review. A board of review is made up of a nonvoting chair and five employees. The chair picks three employee members from a list of six submitted by the employee. The employee selects the other two members from a list of four employees submitted by the chair. The company and the employee agree to abide by the decision of the board of review.

It is important to recognize the potential problems and benefits of a peer review system. Under the Federal Express GFT system, the employee does not have a "right" to peer review. The vice president or the appeals board must grant the request. If a similar policy is implemented in your organization, it should be clear that this is not a question of right. If this is not made clear, some employees may find the whole process to be unfair, given the discretion management has over who gets a "fair" review. On the other hand, if management really does allow major problems to go to peer review, the existence of a peer review can solve many problems. Most employees know the difference between fair treatment and unfair treatment, and allowing them to participate in the process can give them confidence that the company has the same idea they have about fairness.

Again, once you promise to provide this kind of procedure, or make the even grander promise that people will be treated "fairly," this promise must be lived up to or legal and management problems could multiply. It is usually better to treat people fairly without promising it than to promise them fair treatment and not live up to it.

SAMPLE EMPLOYEE HANDBOOK PROVISION

> Any employee who is not happy with the result of the normal grievance procedure may petition the director of human resources to convene a "peer review panel." The director of human resources has the discretion to grant or deny this request based on factors such as the significance of the problem and the facts of the individual case. This panel will consist of six employees selected at random from all employees at the relevant location. The director will either preside over the hearing or appoint someone to preside. The vote of the peer review panel will be final, and both the employee and the company will be bound by its decision. Employees may not bring an attorney to the hearing, but they may have another employee help them to make their case.

REDUCING THE CLASS STRUCTURE

One problem at many organizations is the class division that exists between the upper-class managers and the lower-class employees. This class structure is emphasized in a dozen ways, from special parking places to executive washrooms. In some organizations the managers are called "suits" because they come to work in suits while everyone else wears "work clothes." In others the difference is played down. Managers do not wear suits and do not have special places to park, eat, or go to the bathroom. If an organization wishes not to have a class structure, this should be communicated to everyone—new managers as well as new employees.

Sample Employee Handbook Provision

The MNO Company considers all employees important. We do not have special parking spaces or dining facilities for executives because we believe that these kinds of distinctions are counterproductive. We hope that all employees, at all levels, will communicate with one another and treat one another as they themselves would wish to be treated.

The Fairness Problem

The final policy question for companies that want to be great places to work is the fairness question. This is really two different questions. Do you want to treat employees fairly? And, do you want to promise to treat employees fairly? A company can resolve to work toward treating employees fairly without making a promise to do so. A company can have management training sessions in which fairness is discussed and made concrete with specific examples of what the company would like to happen in specific situations. A company can have a variety of policies, such as a grievance policy, that help the company become more fair. All of these policies can be written without using the word *fair*.

The problem with the word *fair* is that it means many different things to many different people. It is almost impossible to define fairness in a satisfactory way, and the lack of a definition means that the company may have to go to court more often than would have been the case if this promise had not been made. At the same time, various specific policies can be written to help assure fair treatment. When the Preston Trucking Company decided to be a better and fairer place to work, it issued a statement to all employees that promised that managers would be "fair, firm and positive in correcting substandard performance and inappropriate behavior." The statement went on to say that disciplinary measures such as firing or time off without pay would be used only "as a last resort for flagrant violations" of ethical standards and work rules. The policy promised that managers would first counsel employees about a problem and give them time to improve before putting out a warning letter.

This kind of statement has many advantages. It is not just an open promise to be "fair," whatever that means. Preston Trucking went on to spell out what it meant by fairness. It talked about discharge and discipline for substandard performance and inappropriate behavior. The policy spelled out the kind of discipline policy that many companies have. If a company is going to talk about fairness, it should talk about it in the context of discipline, not as a general concept that will affect all aspects of the organization.

Sample Employee Handbook Provision

The MNO Company prides itself on being a fair company. What does that mean? It means that managers do not discipline or discharge employees without first providing a warning whenever that would be appropriate. It means that employees are counseled about a problem before a written warning or notice of discipline is placed in their personnel file. It means that employees are allowed to tell their side of the story before any decision is made to discharge or discipline them. It means that employees may file a grievance if they believe that they have been treated wrongly. The MNO Company does not promise never to make a mistake. It does promise to try to treat employees fairly as far as discipline and discharge decisions are concerned.

Conclusion

Being a "great place to work" has both costs and benefits. A company that decides it wants to reap the benefits of being a great place to work must also be prepared to pay the costs. That means that promises will be made and must be lived up to. However, the benefits can be great, and the costs can be kept low if everyone in the company understands what it means to be fair.

Chapter 33

Arbitration, Mediation, and Contracts

Much of the discussion in this book has centered around the concept of lawsuits and the prevention of lawsuits. Of course, lawsuits have many disadvantages for everyone involved. They tend to be expensive and time-consuming for both employers and employees. There are alternatives, and in the area of employee-employer relations, it is usually going to be up to the employer to decide if some alternative method of dispute resolution will be used.

ARBITRATION

Modern arbitration goes back to the Middle Ages, when merchants in Europe agreed to submit their disputes to a neutral arbitrator rather than suing in court. Because these merchants had developed their own rules for dealing with one another, it seemed sensible that they should also have their own judges to resolve disputes. In the Jay Treaty of 1794, the United States and Great Britain agreed to submit a variety of disputes to arbitration, including disputes over the boundaries of the new United States. The New York Stock Exchange provided for arbitration of disputes between members in its 1817 constitution. This principle was later expanded to include disputes between members and others outside the Exchange.

The basic idea of arbitration is that a dispute can be handled much more quickly and at less expense if both sides submit their dispute to an arbitrator rather than going to court. The arbitrator, as someone familiar with the particular business, should be able to make a decision much more easily than a judge who might not have any notion of what is considered to be normal practice in a particular trade or business. In the United States, it was a difficult question of law whether two parties could agree in a contract to submit a dispute over the interpretation of that contract or other disputes between the parties to arbitration. New York passed the first modern arbitration statute in 1920, making it clear that agreements to arbitrate would be binding in New York. Congress followed with a federal law in 1925, and most other states passed similar legislation in the decades that followed.

In the world of employers and employees, it became common in the twentieth century to place an arbitration clause in most collectively bargained agreements between employers and labor unions. These clauses set out what kinds of disputes would be submitted to arbitration and how the arbitrator would be chosen. Generally, these arbitration agreements required the union or the employer to submit a dispute under the contract to the decision of an arbitrator rather than suing in court. In general, this meant that if the union believed that an employee had been discharged, or otherwise disadvantaged, in violation of the contract, this dispute went to an arbitrator rather than a judge. This allowed both the union and the employer to save money and avoided some of the time and expense involved in going through the usual court procedure. In most cases, an employee is required to file a grievance and go through the company grievance procedure before asking for arbitration.

Another advantage of arbitration is that the decision of the arbitrator is final. Neither side may appeal the decision. Participants may ask a court to overturn the decision if they can show that the arbitrator was biased or that some gross violation of procedure makes the whole process void, but this seldom happens. While in theory an arbitrator has the same power to order the parties to do things and pay damages as a judge, arbitrators are generally considered to be more conservative in their damage awards than a judge and jury would be.

In the 1980s, some employers tried to argue that because employees covered by union contracts were required to submit disputes to arbitration, that should include all disputes, even disputes over whether or not the employee had been discharged in violation of law. These employers argued that once an employee had taken the issue of his or her discharge through to a final decision by an arbitrator, that employee should not then be allowed to sue and argue that he or she had been fired in violation of civil rights laws or other laws controlling wrongful discharge. In 1988 the Supreme Court dealt with this issue in the *Lingle* case. The employee sued for wrongful discharge under Illinois law, and the employer argued that this issue should be dealt with exclusively by arbitration under the union contract. The Supreme Court disagreed. The Court pointed out that all the union contract said was that disputes concerning the interpretation of that contract would be submitted to arbitration. It did not say that all disputes between employer and employees would be submitted to arbitration. In this case, this was not a dispute concerning the interpretation of the union contract. The employee was not arguing that the discharge was in violation of the contract. Instead, the employee was arguing that the discharge violated Illinois law, which is a very different thing.

The decision in *Lingle* left open the question of whether an employer and employees could agree to submit all disputes to arbitration, including issues of illegal discharge. The Supreme Court answered that question in the affirmative in 1991 with its decision in the *Gilmer* case. In that case, the employee had agreed to submit all "controversies arising out of employment or termination" to arbitration. The employee wanted to sue for age discrimination under federal and state law, but the Supreme Court ruled that this could not happen. The employee had agreed to arbitrate "all controversies," and this certainly fell within that category. The employee would have to submit to arbitration instead. Some people hoped that Congress would set some guidelines on the issue of when employers and employees might agree to submit to arbitration disputes on questions such as whether a discharge violated a civil rights law in the Civil Rights Act of 1991. Congress did not. That appears to mean that employers who wish to may ask their employees to agree to submit controversies relating to "employment or termination" to arbitration.

Can employers require employees to submit disputes to arbitration through a clause in the employee handbook? In 1990, the Ohio Supreme Court ruled that an employee suing under the employee handbook had to follow the dispute resolution procedure set out in that handbook (*Nemazee*). While it is not clear how other courts might rule, this and other decisions suggest that, at least in states that consider employee handbooks to be employment contracts, an arbitration clause would be enforced.

The next question for any employer is whether or not this would be a good idea. On the one hand, arbitrators generally make much lower damage awards than judges and juries. On the other hand, it is much less expensive for an employee to take a dispute to arbitration. That means that more disputes might be taken to arbitration than would have reached the courts. When an attorney considers whether or not to take an employee's case, the main considerations are the probability of success and the time and expense that will be involved in taking the case through the legal process. Because arbitration takes much less time and expense, some cases will be accepted that would not have been taken to court.

There is another consideration that any employer must consider. One advantage of arbitration is that it brings a dispute to an end quickly and in a very final way. An employee who feels that he or she has been wronged by an employer but cannot convince an attorney to take the case to court because of its complexity or because of a low probability of victory may decide to take the law into his or her own hands. The leading cause of death in the American workplace is now homicide. How many of these killings might have been avoided if simple disputes had not been allowed to get out of hand, or to fester until someone exploded?

Any employer considering placing an arbitration section into an employee handbook must realize that for arbitration to be successful, the arbitrator must both be impartial and be perceived as being impartial. It is doubtful that some of the arbitration services that have sprung up will be seen as impartial by either employees or the courts. One way to deal with this is for the employer and the employee to each name someone to a two-person committee charged with picking an arbitrator. This procedure guarantees that both sides will feel that justice has been done.

For a large company, another option might be to hire a full-time arbitrator for the company. This would have to be someone who was above reproach and who could serve out a term of office free from fear of discharge. A retired judge might be a good candidate. The company arbitrator might be given a contract for several years that could not be renewed. The outgoing arbitrator might submit a list of three people to a committee made up of three randomly selected employees and three randomly selected managers, who would make the final choice. The advantage of having a full-time arbitrator would be that all grievances that were not handled to the satisfaction of any employee could be taken to the arbitrator for a final decision. All charges of discrimination or wrongful discharge could also be handled by the in-house arbitrator. Because the person would be familiar with the company and its procedures, he or she would be in a better position to deal with all kinds of grievances than someone brought in from the outside to deal with only one dispute.

In fact, the arbitrator could also arbitrate disputes between shareholders and the company, or shareholders and anyone inside the company. This could mean that a large number of potential disputes could be handled quickly and inexpensively, with everyone feeling that he or she had had a fair day in court. If we imagine that the MNO Company is a pioneer in this area, its employee handbook provision might look like this.

SAMPLE EMPLOYEE HANDBOOK PROVISION

At the MNO Company we want to provide a process for dealing with all disputes between employees and the company. By coming to work at MNO or staying at MNO, all employees agree that all controversies and disagreements between them and the company will be submitted to binding arbitration through the company arbitrator. Any issues concerning discharge will also be submitted to the arbitrator, including questions of whether or not civil rights laws have been violated as well as violations of other statutes, the common law, or contract. Any issue relating to employment at the MNO Company must be submitted to the arbitrator and may not be taken to a court of law for resolution. The MNO arbitrator is appointed for a five-year term by a committee made up of three randomly selected managers and three randomly selected employees. Every five years a new MNO arbitrator is chosen from a list of three names submitted by the outgoing arbitrator. The MNO arbitrator is paid exactly the same salary and benefits as the director of human resources and has an office and staff support to help us reach amicable resolutions of disputes quickly and with as little expense as possible to both sides. We are fortunate to have Judge Watson, retired from the California Supreme Court, currently filling that role. Anyone who is not happy with a final decision in the grievance procedure may take the issue to the arbitrator. Anyone who has been discharged may take the issue of whether or not that discharge violated any contract or law to the arbitrator. These issues may not be taken to court and must be taken to the arbitrator for resolution. The decision of the arbitrator is final and binding on all employees and the MNO Company. Employees who have disputes with one another are invited to use the offices of the MNO arbitrator if they wish to do so by agreement between the parties.

MEDIATION

Arbitration is binding on the parties. Mediation is not. A mediator is brought into a dispute to help the two sides work out a compromise. The mediator tries to find out what the parties can agree on and where they disagree. He or she tries to help both sides articulate what it is they believe the facts to be and what they hope to get out of the resolution of the dispute. Many states are trying to encourage parties to make use of mediation, although in too many cases this is simply turning into another delay in the already delayed judicial process.

Mediation has a long history in helping to solve labor-management disputes in the United States. The federal Mediation and Conciliation Service is an independent federal agency that provides mediation services when unions and employers cannot resolve their differences short of strikes and lockouts. The hope is that by providing a neutral mediator, the disruption of the economy caused by strikes and lockouts can be kept to a minimum.

Should an employer place a required mediation clause in an employee handbook? Again, there are pros and cons. If employees are required to take a dispute to mediation before bringing a lawsuit, it may help to resolve the dispute and save both sides the time and expense of a court proceeding. On the other hand, it may not, and it may simply force everyone to go through a process that will not be binding on anyone and will not solve any problems. Such clauses are certainly not yet common in employee handbooks in the United States.

CONTRACTS

Something that many employers in the United States should consider is giving real contracts for a definite term of years to some of their employees. An actual written contract for, let's say, two years has a number of advantages for everyone. It lets the employee know that he or she has a job for a definite period of time. While the employee under such a contract can, in most cases, quit, most people do not. They feel duty bound to stay. The contract can be written to allow the employer to fire the employee during the term of the contract for good cause or if revenues fall below past levels. Having a written term contract forces the employer to review these employees every two years when deciding to sign another term contract.

Any employer who has employees inventing things, creating things, or working under complex commission or bonus schemes should seriously consider using a written term contract. The same is also true for any employee the employer feels it necessary to ask to sign an agreement not to compete after leaving the job. In fact, an employer might well create two types of employees, those with term contracts and those without, and set up the company policies to provide different benefits to these two different groups.

One major advantage of giving an employee a written term contract is that it will impress a jury if a case ever comes to trial. Most people do not get term contracts where they work. They will probably feel that any employer willing to do this must be a pretty good employer. In any trial over the discharge of the employee, the fundamental question is: Why was this person fired? Because the person's term contract ran out! is a very good answer.

Any employer considering using term contracts with employees should contact an attorney skilled in writing employment contracts. Clauses that were considered enforceable a few years ago are now probably not enforceable, so care has to be taken in writing a contract. It should be written, as much as possible, in plain English so that employees cannot say they did not understand what they were getting into when they signed it.

Another problem comes up when an employee is already working and the employer decides to ask him or her to sign a written contract preventing him or her from competing with the employer for a period of time after leaving the company. Some judges will require that the employee be given something special in return for this promise or they will not enforce it. A very small raise or bonus will qualify, but this is something that too many employers ignore. It is impossible to know in advance whether the judge that hears your case will ask for this "new consideration," but it is easy to provide an employee with something if you know this might become an issue in the future. Just as with a gift, it is not the amount but the "thought" that counts. You are asking the employee to do something new, and you have to give something new in return.

It is also important to realize that over the last quarter of the twentieth century, more and more judges have decided that they simply will not enforce agreements not to compete with the employer unless the employee has really been given something special, such as special training or access to very important trade secrets. Employers should consider having employees who deal directly with customers sign an agreement not to solicit the customers they worked with if they leave the company. This is much less of an inconvenience for the employee than a real agreement not to compete, and judges are much more willing to enforce these "no solicitation" agreements.

A Private Civil Service System

There is another option that employers should consider. The main advantage employees have if they work under a civil service system or a union contract is that they cannot be fired except for good cause. These systems set up a probationary period, which may be as short as thirty days or as long as six years. In more and more states judges and juries are becoming more and more willing to find in favor of employees who are discharged after working for the same employer for several years. In their minds, such an employee should not be fired except for a good reason. Also, many employers find that their main competition for good employees is a government that offers a civil service system. These private employers have to either pay higher wages or accept less qualified employees and watch as their more qualified employees leave for the protection of the government civil service system whenever an opening comes up. Hospitals are one example of private employers faced with this dilemma. The Supreme Court of Illinois decided that handbooks are enforceable contracts when it came across a handbook of a private hospital that gave employees the equivalent of civil service protection after a ninety-day probationary period (*Duldulao*). The Illinois Supreme Court reasoned that the private hospital got a benefit from such a system—namely, it was able to compete with government hospitals for qualified employees.

Any private employer can use its employee handbook to create its own civil service system. The probationary period can be as long as the employer feels is necessary to determine if this is an employee worth keeping. Judges and juries are impressed with these kinds of systems and are much more likely to give the employer the benefit of the doubt if such a system has been put in place. Or a private civil service system can be combined with a requirement of binding arbitration (or the use of the retired judge in-house arbitrator). This means that employees get the basic benefit of a union contract, protection from unreasonable discharge, without having to pay union dues. The employer avoids all the work rule and other limitations that unions have become famous for.

A private civil service system with binding arbitration can also provide that "all disputes," including claims of wrongful discharge or civil rights violations, have to be handled by the civil service arbitration system. This means that the long list of possible hearings and court trials can be combined into one hearing in front of an arbitrator.

Montana has passed a statute that requires all private employers to set up a private civil service system (Mont. 39-2-901). The employer must declare a "probationary period," and after employees have completed the probationary period, they can be discharged only for "good cause." It is too early to tell how this statute is working out.

One of the problems with the current system is that an employee, regardless of how good his or her case is, can run an employer through a long series of hearings and trials over the basic issue of the real reason for his or her discharge. These might include a hearing at the unemployment compensation agency, a hearing before the EEOC, a union arbitration hearing, a trial in state court under state wrongful discharge laws, and a trial in federal court under federal civil rights laws. It would be better for everyone if all of this could be handled at one hearing, perhaps before the unemployment compensation agency. What if state law allowed employers and employees to agree to submit any dispute concerning a discharge to a final decision on "all matters of fact and law" to the decision of the unemployment compensation hearing officer? Then both the employee and the employer could get on with the business of living without a great deal of time and expense. So far, no state has seen fit to offer this kind of solution to employers and employees.

CONCLUSION

Arbitration, mediation, and written contracts should all be considered by any employer that wishes to save money and improve performance. Each of these options has advantages and disadvantages that should be considered. Whether or not arbitration is right for a particular company may depend on how much the company wants to spend on dispute resolution and how much the advantages of arbitration seem worth the cost. The benefits of a quick and simple end to a dispute with an employee can be very great. However, it remains to be seen how judges will view mandatory arbitration provisions in employee handbooks.

APPENDIX: Reasons Generally Considered to be
Good Cause for Dismissal

1. Falsification of records, including employment applications
2. Theft, fraud, gambling, carrying a weapon, or otherwise violating the law on the employer's premises
3. Willful or repeated violations of safety precautions
4. Fighting, throwing things, or engaging in horseplay or disorderly conduct that endangers the employee or others
5. Insubordination or refusal to comply with instructions
6. Unauthorized use of company material or equipment
7. Willful or repeated failure to comply with policies
8. Drunkenness or excessive use of alcoholic beverages or illegal use of drugs
9. Substandard performance of the work
10. Immoral or indecent conduct on company property
11. Verbal or physical conduct constituting sexual harassment
12. Excessive absenteeism or tardiness
13. Threatening or coercing fellow employees
14. Engaging in outside activities that constitute a conflict of interest

Chapter 34
Avoiding Lawsuits

While it may seem obvious, the first step in avoiding lawsuits of all kinds is to know and obey the law. With employment law, that is easier said than done. While this book provides some basic guidance, it should be obvious to every reader that each new state legislative session brings some new interference in the employment relationship. Employment law is one area where one bad apple really can spoil the barrel, and there is, unfortunately, more than one bad apple. All it takes is publicity about one employer doing something outrageous to bring calls for new legislation to make sure that never happens again.

As new employment laws are discussed, the cost of insubstantial lawsuits is seldom considered. While federal law tries to limit liability for small employers, these limits can usually be overcome by suing under state law. There really is no way for even the smallest employer to avoid being sued for wrongful discharge or discrimination under either state statutes or state common law as interpreted by the courts.

Simply obeying the law is not enough. A company should have a reputation for obeying the law as well. When any attorney decides whether or not to bring a lawsuit against any company, the first thing he or she will consider is what the average juror is probably going to come into the jury box thinking about this particular company. If the company is not liked in the area, then it is a much easier target for a lawsuit. If it has a reputation for not caring much about laws designed to protect either consumers or employees, the jurors will probably assume that the company is guilty until proven innocent.

THINKING ABOUT THE TRIAL THAT MAY NEVER COME

Even though most lawsuits are settled out of court, everyone involved in the process is considering what a judge and jury will probably do with the case. For a company, this means thinking about how executives will look on the witness stand before making decisions concerning promotion to top executive positions. If a company is sued by a woman for discrimination or harassment, it doesn't help if all the company's top executives are men. If the jury is made up of several races, it doesn't help if all the executives are of one race. In a major lawsuit, the way the CEO comes across on the witness stand may be the most important factor. Several large lawsuits have been lost because the CEO came across as an arrogant "boss" rather than as a caring person. Also, as you would expect, it doesn't hurt if the CEO has a reputation in the community for being a caring person.

One defense that should be raised in many lawsuits is that the employee who did the wrong thing was acting contrary to express company policy. While that employee should be sued, the company should not be liable. That is where a well-written employee handbook can come in handy. While juries are not impressed by company policy statements that sit in a drawer in the CEO's desk, they are impressed by policies that are published and communicated to everyone in the organization. That is exactly what an employee handbook is. It provides the company with a record of its having ordered everyone to behave in particular ways. In some cases, such as sexual harassment, what the company handbook said may be as important as what actually happened to the injured employee.

TREAT EMPLOYEES FAIRLY

We have worked throughout this book to avoid making a promise that employees will be treated "fairly" by the company. That is because the concept of what is "fair" is too difficult to define. At the same time, companies should try to treat people fairly whenever possible. Again, the reputation within the company and the community for fairness can be invaluable. There is nothing worse for an attorney representing an employer than to find that most of the employees will be testifying against the company they work for.

If a company works to be a "good place to work," word gets around. Very few attorneys would want to sue Federal Express in Memphis, Tennessee. It has a reputation for treating its employees well, and it is large enough that almost everyone in the city knows someone who works there or has a relative or friend who works there. Given that reputation, the average juror is going to give Federal Express and hundreds of other companies with similar reputations across America the benefit of the doubt. In most lawsuits by employees, it comes down to the employee's word against the employer's. It is up to the jury to decide who is telling the truth. There is no forensic scientist, no fingerprints, and no report from a laboratory pointing to the murder weapon, as there is on television. The employee claims to have been treated badly, and the company says this did not happen. If the company has a bad reputation, the employee gets the benefit of the doubt. If the company has a good reputation, then the company gets the benefit of the doubt. It is just that simple in many cases.

AN OUNCE OF PREVENTION

Employment law is one area in which an ounce of prevention is worth a pound of cure. Most employers know when they have a potential legal problem in this area, and there should be an attorney that routinely gets called in before potential problems become real ones. While the attorney may not be able to head off every lawsuit, there is usually a better way to handle most situations. Also, if the attorney knows about the problem early on, he or she will be in a much better position to deal with it if it becomes a legal case in the future.

It is also going to be much cheaper to have managers attend a workshop or read a book than it will be to defend just one major lawsuit. Because it is often not what managers do that counts so much as how they do it and what they say while they are doing it, it is important to give them some warning about common mistakes that can be avoided. It is the manager who cannot bring himself to tell the older worker that she is simply not doing a good job that causes the age discrimination lawsuit.

As we have seen throughout this book, damages in many cases would have been much less if an attorney had been called in to negotiate a settlement and if the employee had signed a release. Employees know that they may or may not actually get something from a lawsuit and it will take years to get to a jury in most cities. Even a very small percentage of what they might get is going to sound pretty good in most cases. It will also be better for the company's reputation. If people hear that a company is sued often by its employees or former employees, it is natural to assume that something is wrong. Again, reputation is half of the battle.

PUBLIC IMAGE IS IMPORTANT

Many stockholders question the need to spend money helping the local public television station or the local hospital. The real answer is that these kinds of well-publicized efforts to help make the community a better place to live really can be worth their weight in gold when it comes time to pick a jury in that city. People do remember that they heard about the company project to help crippled children. They do remember when their favorite public television show is sponsored in part by the company. They do remember the large group of employees helping to clean up the environment or helping to paint the school after vandals turned it into a mess.

LOOSE LIPS SINK COMPANIES

Another lesson that runs throughout this entire book is that what you say can often mean more than what you do. It is the oral promise that cannot be lived up to that causes more problems that the written term contract entered into by both parties. It is the oral promise that "everyone has a job for life" that causes more problems than an employee handbook that spells out when people can and cannot be discharged. It is the defamatory statement, the unthinking negative comment, the off-hand racial or sexual slur that poisons the workplace and makes a lawsuit much more likely.

When it comes to bonus plans, suggestion plans, complex commissions, and other promises of special compensation, it is the vague oral promise that causes problems. The written plan, which is summarized accurately in the employee handbook, is seldom a cause for legal dispute. An employee handbook that is well written and reliable can prove to be the best defense against loose lips in a thousand and one situations.

GOOD PLACES TO WORK HAVE THEIR ADVANTAGES

In his book *A Great Place to Work*, Robert Levering points out many of the obvious advantages of having a great place for your employees to work and some not so obvious advantages. His research suggests that people who invested in the "100 best companies to work for" in the 1970s made significantly more money in the 1980s than they would have by simply investing in the S&P 500. One of the undiscussed reasons for this is that most of the companies that are good places to work do not get sued. That means they spend a lot less time and money defending against lawsuits and can use those resources to make the company more productive.

Good places to work have other advantages. The modern company spends a great deal of time on training and recruiting. Even when the job market seems filled with applicants, the really good employees are not easy to find. Once you find one, it is a lot cheaper to keep him or her than to spend the money necessary to find another. The reality is, low turnover and low absenteeism can also significantly affect the bottom line.

EMPLOYEES REALLY DO COME COMPLETE WITH A BRAIN

Employees really can make a big difference in the long-term health of any organization. If they are allowed to put their ideas through a real suggestion plan, they may just find the solution to the problem. Policies that really do allow for full communication and participation can have a major impact on the bottom line.

The other side of that is the issue of how much time employees have to spend worrying about company procedure. If the policies in the handbook allow all employees to know exactly where they stand and what to expect, many potential problems can be avoided. There is nothing worse than making a promise to an employee that is not kept. The company is usually better off if it does not make the promise in the first place. That means that a careful review of both the employee handbook and actual company practices with outside help from an attorney or a consultant can often spot problems before they become significant. Energy burned up "hating the company" is energy that is not available to get work done. This is particularly true of work that demands high levels of quality. Total quality is not possible in an organization filled with distrustful employees.

CONCLUSION

Avoiding employee lawsuits is much more complex than simply obeying the law. That and fifty cents might buy you a cup of coffee. Much more is required. An employer must be seen by both its employees and the community at large as a good citizen, a good employer, and a good company. Not only must good employers be good employers, they must be seen to be good employers. An employee handbook that can be given to the jury with some pride will help a great deal. Managers who understand the need to treat people fairly can mean the difference between success and failure both inside and outside the courtroom.

Chapter 35
Conclusion

The goal of this book has been to provide basic information about employment law in a form that will be useful to the average employer. In an attempt to make the information as relevant and useful as possible, it has been discussed in the context of writing an employee handbook. However, we come at the end to the basic question we asked at the beginning: Should employers have an employee handbook? Handbooks make promises, and those promises must be lived up to or they will be enforced in most courts. This is a disadvantage only if employers do not intend to live up to their promises. On the other hand, handbooks provide employees with a great deal of information in a quick and easy way. They can also be valuable for defense against many different kinds of lawsuits. An employer who decides to write an employee handbook should make sure to have an attorney look it over before printing.

FINISHING THE EMPLOYEE HANDBOOK

The appendix to this book contains most of the sample employee handbook provisions contained in the previous chapters. The last provision may the most important. The handbook should explain how and when the employer plans to revise the handbook and reserves the right to make revisions. This can be done in a variety of ways. The handbook might have a date, such as the "1994-5" Handbook, with a statement that the employer will revise the handbook every two years. This lets everyone know that the handbook will be revised and that everything is subject to revision. However, this suggests that the handbook will not be changed during that period. Another option is to simply state that the handbook is subject to revision at any time. Whatever option an employer chooses, there must be some discussion of this in the handbook.

While many of the most basic employee handbook provisions have been discussed in this book, there are certainly dozens of other provisions that might be considered and that might be appropriate for particular employers. A employer might consider having a dress code provision in the handbook. In a few cities, such as the District of Columbia, the law requires that there be a written and enforced dress code before employees can be disciplined or discharged because of their dress. A good dress code is difficult to write. To give fair warning to employees, it must say something more than that employees will be expected to "dress appropriately." At the same time, it is difficult to write a policy that covers everyone and does not say something as vague as this. The dress code can at a minimum require employees to be "clean and neat" and state the kinds of clothing that are not acceptable, such as "halter tops" or "sandals."

The handbook might be more specific about issues such as when breaks may be taken and what employees may do on their breaks. Do breaks come at a special time, or are employees expected to take breaks on their own schedule? Is everyone supposed to take a morning and afternoon break, or is this simply left up to the individual employees? Are employees expected to clock off on the time clock when they go to lunch? All of these issues might be covered in the handbook.

Many employers in the United States drug test their employees. Any employer with a drug testing program should discuss that program in the employee handbook. Is it a random program or is there a schedule that is followed? Are all employees subject to testing or only some groups of employees, such as those who work with dangerous equipment? What kind of safeguards are used to help make sure that an employee is not falsely accused of being on an illegal drug? What effort will be made to keep the results of the tests confidential?

Many employers will have some employees who are authorized to use company vehicles. The handbook might deal with who is authorized to use company vehicles and the need to be safe and courteous drivers. Traffic accidents and citations should be discussed, with a procedure for dealing with these inevitable problems. Do employees pay any traffic fines, or does the employer? What happens if an employee loses her driver's license? Who is in charge of company vehicles? These and other questions should be answered in the employee handbook.

There may be a variety of promises an employer wishes to make to employees. For example, the employer may wish to promise some kind of severance pay to all employees. A written severance pay plan has advantages in that it avoids the appearance, and the practice, of discrimination. If a company is going to give some employees some kind of severance pay, then a written policy should be developed. There are many reasons for a severance pay plan. Many union contracts provide for severance pay, and an employer who hopes to prevent unionization might wish to put some kind of plan in the handbook to show that employees can get the same benefits without calling in a union.

There are some provisions that a large company might have that will not be relevant to a small organization. For example, a large company with many locations might have a policy on how and when employees may transfer from one facility to another. A small employer will not need such a policy. A large employer might provide a wider variety of employee benefits, such as tuition reimbursement, that most smaller employers will not wish to provide. An employer who does work for the Defense Department might need to go into greater detail concerning security and background checks, while most employers will be satisfied with the provisions discussed in this book.

Using the Handbook to Best Advantage

Once an employer has a well-written, legally reviewed employee handbook, it should form the basis of relations with all employees. The new employee should be given a copy and told to read it cover to cover before coming to the new employee orientation. Even the smallest employer should have some kind of new employee orientation, even if it is simply going through the employee handbook and asking if there are any questions. The person who handles this task should make a note of any questions that employees ask that are not already answered in the handbook. This orientation period is a good time to find out if any employees have been promised things the employer did not intend, such as lifetime employment. All the new employee forms can be filled out with someone there to help with this process. Information that would not have been appropriate when hiring, such as number of children and their ages, can now be obtained.

Courts want to know if the handbook was simply handed out, or was it discussed. This is particularly true of policies such as sexual harassment. New employee orientation is a good time to cover sexual harassment and other issues to emphasize the employer's desire to obey the law. It is also a good time to emphasize that the communication policy is for real. Special procedures, such as a "peer review" system, should also be discussed at some length to make sure there are no misunderstandings about what the employer is promising to do.

OBEYING THE LAW

One thing should be clear after reading this book: No matter how hard an employer tries, it will be difficult to know about and obey every law that affects the workplace. That is simply a fact of life. In many cases it will be enough that the employer tried to know and obey the law. The state labor commissioner and the U.S. Department of Labor should be contacted from time to time for updated information about the laws and regulations. If safety is a concern, OSHA should be asked to make an inspection in some circumstances rather than waiting for a serious accident or illness. A cooperative attitude goes a long way with most agencies charged with regulating the workplace.

CHANGING THE LAW

Anyone who is trying to run an expanding private company should be disgusted after reading this book. Every time the company expands into another state, a new set of laws and regulations comes into play. In most areas of employment law, both the states and the federal government provide legislation and court decisions that employers must be aware of. This is not a problem for a large company with an army of attorneys or a very small company that only operates in one state. It is a serious problem for anyone who wants to expand a business. The time is fast approaching when employers in the United States will simply be buried under laws and regulations that contradict or overlap. There is no reason why we should not have one federal labor code to cover almost everything discussed in this book. An employer would turn to one agency, the U.S. Labor Department, for information. Instead, we are moving in the opposite direction. Two decades ago most employers worked with the federal OSHA. Now half the states have their own OSHA with different rules and regulations on workplace safety. Almost every state has its own civil rights agency, its own laws on wrongful discharge, and its own regulations on everything from employee breaks to proper pay periods.

The need for one modern unemployment agency at the federal level is the greatest need of all. Employers should be able to punch into a national data bank with information about all unemployed workers. Employers should be able to interview those workers over closed-circuit television and have them take specific tests at the location they happen to be at. None of this is possible under today's system.

WORKING WITH EMPLOYEES

The philosophy that underlies this book is that employers will be better off if they work with their employees, rather than against them. That means providing information about company policies to all employees through the use of an employee handbook. That means having an employee orientation to answer questions. That means having policies that encourage communication and employee ownership. Many employers feel they do a good job of working with employees, but they prefer to keep those employees in the dark about a great deal. This causes far more problems than most employers realize.

Many of the employee handbook provisions that have been suggested in this book attempt to make it clear to employees what the law requires. Most employees will not be familiar with these laws. In many cases it is to the employer's advantage to help employees to understand both the employer's and the employee's obligations under the law. Employees need to understand that in many areas of company policy, the employer is not free to do anything it wishes.

The first few chapters of this book dealt with trying to provide basic information to employees in the handbook that would allow the average employee to feel like they really were a part of the company. Let them in on the private jokes and private words that mean so much to some and nothing to others. Even the smallest company needs to consider the desirability of doing this.

PLAN AHEAD

This book is intended for anyone who has employees, but particularly for employers who plan to expand over time. Even the smallest employer should begin to consider which laws do apply or will soon apply to them and make plans for dealing with that inevitable fact. Small employers do not have to provide family and medical leave under the federal Family and Medical Leave Act, but they certainly can if they want to, and their employees will be grateful if they do. Small employers may not yet be covered by the federal Civil Rights Act, but they may be covered by state laws or court decisions that have the same effect. Sexual harassment is something even the smallest employer can be sued for if the employee's attorney is creative enough and calls it something like intentional infliction of emotional distress or assault. A statement about sexual harassment will be helpful even in these situations.

GET LEGAL ADVICE

This book begins and ends with the same warning: The law is constantly changing, as are interpretations of the law by judges. No one can expect to take a book like this one and simply copy the suggested employee handbook provisions. Every state is different, and over time federal law will also change. In every region of the country a different federal circuit court controls how federal law will be interpreted in that region, and they do not always agree. Every state supreme court has a different idea of its role in regulating the employer-employee relationship, and the members of these courts change over time. That does not mean that employers should give up. Far from it. It means that employers must make an effort to stay current in the law by attending seminars or working with an employment attorney. In most cases judges and juries will take into consideration the fact that an employer was trying to obey what in reality are far too complex legal provisions.

This really is one area where many problems can be prevented with a phone call to an attorney and some effort to use preventive medicine. It is hoped that by reading this book the average employer now has a better idea of when to make that phone call and what to ask.

A Sample Employee Handbook for the MNO Company

WELCOME

Welcome to the MNO Company. Employees at the MNO Company are at-will employees. That means that employees can be dismissed at any time for any reason or no reason and that employees can leave at any time for any reason or no reason. No one in the MNO Company has the authority to promise any employee that he or she will be employed for a particular or indefinite period of time except the president and she must do so in writing. Any employee who feels that he or she has been promised that he or she will be employed for a particular length of time, or be fired only for good cause, should contact the human resources director immediately.

A LITTLE COMPANY HISTORY

Welcome to the MNO Company. On behalf of myself and everyone here at MNO, let me say that after two decades of company growth, we are glad you are here. As the founder and current CEO of the company, I want to explain in a few pages where this company has been and where I hope it is going.

This company really began one day when Sue Jackson and I were sitting in a café discussing how crazy the company we worked for at the time was. We honestly believed that a few changes would result in major savings and much greater productivity. I had just inherited some money from my aunt, and Sue had saved a little over the years. We had heard that the company was going to discontinue a product line because it no longer felt it could keep up with foreign competition. Sue and I felt that it was a golden opportunity to begin a new business. We offered to buy the product line along with its trademarks and patents. The company had expected to just write it all off, so it was glad to help us. Our former employer also realized that if we could make a go of it, they it would make money selling us some of the key components. That is part of the reason why we continue to buy those parts only from that company. While we might be able to save a little money if we shopped around, I feel duty-bound to continue to buy from that company as long as its prices are in the ballpark and its quality remains high.

When word got out that Sue and I were going to begin our own business, a dozen other women in the organization came to us and asked to be a part of the new venture. Some had money to invest, and others were willing to quit or retire and come with us for lower salaries so that the new business could have a fighting chance. We did not set out to exclude men during that initial period; it just turned out that our first two dozen employees were women. Of course, now many of our employees are men.

We leased an abandoned warehouse and set out to move the production out of the other company. There were a lot of problems, as you might imagine. The long-distance phone company gave us hell, and that is why we no longer take advantage of that particular company's services. We also needed to purchase a computer early on, and when the salesmen came around we were offended by their attitude toward us as women businesspeople. That is why we purchased the computer we have today and why we continue to use only that company's products. It was the only company that seemed to take a women's company seriously.

Sue was our computer genius. She set up the passwords and purchased the software. Two years after Sue and I started the company, Sue was killed in a car accident. That is why we call our headquarters "the house that Sue built" and why the computer is still referred to as "Sue's monster." Only Sue could tame it in the early days.

When we realized that we needed a larger facility, we began looking around for a new location. While we were doing that, Boston had the worst winter in history, and everyone expressed a willingness to move to a warmer climate. North Carolina seemed like the best location for many reasons, and that is why we ended up in North Carolina. The newspaper called us the "Babes from Boston" when we first arrived, and we decided to take that with pride instead of being offended. That is why when I address the troops, I call everyone "guys and babes." It is an inside joke. Since we became profitable six months after the move and soon put a major competitor out of business, we felt the babes were doing pretty well during those first few years.

The first time we sent a group to Washington, D.C. to make a sales pitch for a large contract, all of us showed up in blue suits. We did not plan it; it just worked out that way. The big brass in the Pentagon thought we must have a kind of uniform and, being people who spend their lives in uniform, thought that was a good idea. We got the contract. That is why the uniform of the day for salespeople is the basic blue suit and why we still expect everyone who represents the company to do so in basic blue. I guess it is a kind of superstition, but who can argue with success?

One of our competitive advantages in the beginning was our willingness to make full use of computer technology. It sometimes led us down rat holes, but we are still willing to work with computers because in the past we ended up saving a great deal of time and money in the long run by getting everything into the computer. We were the first company in town to put all new product development into workstations with high level graphics capabilities, and when our workstation supplier was in financial trouble, we invested in that business. We are proud of its continued success. It turned out to be a good investment from our point of view.

We now have locations in six countries and over 400 employees, but we still consider ourselves a bunch of transplanted New Englanders no matter where we go. When we first came to North Carolina, we found people expecting us to do strange things like have four o'clock tea, and we did not want to disappoint them. We still take a four o'clock tea break and try to have everyone sit down together for twenty minutes and talk about the day's work before getting ready to shut down. Some of our best ideas have come at tea time, and that is why even if we have to stay late and pay overtime to meet a deadline, I insist that we continue with the tradition.

Everyone in our organization during those early days was fond of travel. When we instituted our suggestion plan program, we decided to reward good suggestions with trips that would allow the person to combine business with pleasure and allow us to deduct the trip as a business expense. That is why to this day the suggestion plan winners get trips to places where they can see the sights and talk to possible new suppliers or customers at the same time. We found early on that some customers felt honored that we sent a delegation instead of just a salesperson, so we didn't tell them it was a kind of vacation. It's one of our best-kept secrets.

Because so many of the early employees were also investors, we tried to take advantage of the tax laws as much as possible. That is why lunch is free (subsidized by Uncle Sam) and why trips are made that combine business with pleasure. That is also why we currently have both a stock purchase plan and an employee stock ownership plan. You will read more about these plans later in this employee handbook.

We named the company the MNO Company because someone said that if a group of women thought they could manufacture such a complex product and meet defense department specifications for quality, they must be headed for La-La Land. We thought about naming the company La-La, but we decided that that would put some customers off. MNO are the initials of my aunt, the one who died and left me the money to start the company. We work hard to avoid sexual harassment because many of us had experienced it in our lives before we began the company and felt that this was one problem we could solve right away. When the policy says that anyone who feels he or she has been the victim of sexual harassment should feel free to bring the problem directly to me, I mean it. I won't stand for it!

Of course, now we produce for both the public and private sectors and are continuing to expand into related products. We figure that if one new idea in ten pays off, we are ahead of the game. That is why we go to such lengths to get new ideas out of employees. Our most profitable product, the POPO machine, was literally the result of a dream Sue had one night right after we began the business.

During those early days we all had to perform every task at one time or another. It gave us a competitive advantage. That is why we spend so much time on cross-training. We don't have a union because our employees have felt they did not need one, not because we have done anything to prevent unionization. Many of our personnel policies are unique, but we stand behind them. Our goal is to have fun and make money at the same time.

We opened our second plant in Arizona because we couldn't afford California and our third in Ireland because of special tax breaks from the government. We decided on Australia instead of Indonesia for the fourth plant because none of us could speak anything but English. The plants in Turkey and Chile came on line next, and I hope we can move into South Africa in the near future. While we are a business, not a charity, we consider ourselves to be citizens of the world at this point, and we hope that we are good citizens. Every facility has adopted a local public school, and we mean it when we say that the future of the world begins in the classroom.

I hope this little history helps you understand us a little better. We do things a little differently around here because of who we are and how we got our start. I am proud of us, and I know I will be proud of you as you become part of our group.

Sincerely

MARY WONDERLY
Founder and CEO

A CORPORATE PHILOSOPHY

There can be no better time than our hundredth anniversary to reflect on where we have been and where we are going. As is painfully clear to everyone, our once-great company has gone through some hard times recently. We have completed the elimination of over 100,000 employee positions and almost half of our product lines during the last decade. It is now time to focus on the future.

Our short-term goal is to show a profit during the coming years, although we may not show a profit every quarter. Our long-term goal is to return to a position of dominance in the industry. We recognize some major mistakes of the past. We hired far too many employees in anticipation of growth that was not forthcoming. We can only hope to avoid this by making more realistic predictions in the future. We created new competitors by contracting out work that we could have done ourselves, only to find that our subcontractors had jumped into the competitive world that we once dominated. We hope to do more work in-house to avoid this happening in the future. We did not listen to our customers when they told us they wanted major changes in our product mix.

Our major goal for the long term is to become *the listening company*. We intend to listen more to our customers and to seek out their advice about possible new products. We intend to listen more to our employees when they tell us how our products can be produced for less money with higher quality. We intend to listen to our stockholders when they tell us the kinds of financial returns they expect over the long term. We intend to listen to our competitors when they tell us what they are doing better than we are. We intend to listen to our suppliers when they tell us we have unrealistic ideas concerning what they can produce and at what cost. Management at this company has been too isolated in the past and we hope to end that isolation.

In order to be more competitive in the world market, we intend to move more of our production and research facilities to other countries and to make more strategic alliances with other companies. These have proved successful for us in the past, and we expect them to help us regain profitability in the future. We hope this can be accomplished without further layoffs in the United States, but we will have to see what the future brings.

For too long this company rested on its past achievements. This led to complacency and a refusal to look at new possibilities. We hope to move forward by turning to our world-famous research centers for new innovations. Dozens of new products are in the testing stage as I write this statement of corporate philosophy, and we hope to bring many of them to market in the near future.

During the company's recent history we relied too much on centralized decision making. This led to long time delays that made it impossible for us to take advantage of innovations that we discovered. In order to avoid this problem in the future, we intend to decentralize decision making wherever possible. That means giving managers and employees more authority to act on their own.

As everyone knows, we spent millions of dollars on consultants' fees in an attempt to become a "total quality company," with little to show for it besides a few banners and silly signs. As the chief executive officer, I take full responsibility for that mistake. I was completely taken in by a group of con artists, and I can only hope that I won't make that mistake again. That does not mean that quality is not still at the top of our agenda. It does mean that we in upper management realize that a few slogans and pep rallies are not the way to achieve quality products. Quality products come only from highly trained and motivated employees.

As we enter the second century of this company's existence, we have a great deal to be proud of. We have played a major role in bringing the cold war to a close, and our defense work will continue, although at a lower level than in the past. Our innovations have become industry standards over the course of this last century, and I hope that will continue to be the case in the future.

Many of you remember my grandfather, the person who really built this business into the global giant it has become. He had a few principles that he tried to live by, and I can only hope that in the future we can remember those principles. He believed that salespeople are the eyes and ears of any company and should be given the chance to provide input wherever possible. He believed that the greatest product is not worth a dime if no one can afford it. He believed that research pays off only if researchers are given a chance to dream the impossible. Finally, he believed that if people are treated with respect, they will respond in kind. These were good principles in his day, and they are good principles today.

I hope we will return to the days when we set the industry standard. I hope we will return to the days when people looking for a job in this industry come to us first because they know how well we treated our employees. I hope we will return to the days when every quarter meant a dividend for our shareholders and a bonus for our employees. I hope we will again be the company my grandfather and thousands of others worked to build over the decades and that people will once again say, "Don't worry, it's a sure thing" when they talk about our products. I know it will take hard work and patience on the part of everyone involved in the company, but I think we will find the golden age again.

PERSONNEL POLICY

Welcome to the MNO Company. As president, I want to assure you that my door really is always open to you. The most difficult problem I face as president is getting information that is accurate and timely. If there is something you feel I should know, please tell me.

Here at MNO we face some tough competition, both here in the United States and from other countries. Sometimes this means cutting costs or trying to improve efficiency. I know, as someone who started on the shop floor, that you know more about the production process than anyone else. I want to hear your ideas. We have an extensive employee suggestion plan that you will read about in this handbook, and I just want to say that I am committed to getting as many good ideas from the employees as possible. Our three most profitable products all resulted from employee suggestions.

I wish I could promise you that we would never find it necessary to lay off employees, but I can't. The reality of the market is that if we are beaten in quality or price, we may have to lay people off. It is really up to you and to me to work hard to make sure we never have to face that prospect.

You will read in this handbook about our policies against harassment and discrimination. I want to assure you that I am committed to making sure that every employee in this organization treats every other employee as an individual and with the respect all people deserve, regardless of race, sex, or color. If you see any behavior that does not live up to that goal, I expect you to follow the procedures set out in this handbook to bring it to the attention of the Human Resources Department.

You know without my telling you that the name of the game is quality, and quality is the job of everyone in this company, from me, the president, right down to every man and woman on the shop floor. I expect you to do everything you can to help us maintain our high standards of quality. In this company, everyone on the shop floor has the power to pull the plug and shut down the facility if he or she sees a quality problem that warrants that action. While I don't always agree that this is the right course, I promise you that no one has ever been punished in any way for doing just that, and no one will be as long as I am president of this company.

Throughout this handbook you will read about our policies on everything from holidays to sick leave. Every even-numbered year we conduct an employee poll and ask everyone to provide input before we produce the next employee handbook. I hope you will give us your opinions when asked.

I try to make this a fun place to work, but I don't always succeed. I hope you will help me to keep a smile on everyone's face. We all know that the same task can be fun or boring depending on the attitude of the people doing it. I try to keep a smile on my face, and I hope you too will have a sense of humor as you become a part of our team.

Welcome to the company.

ON DISCRIMINATION

The MNO Company is committed to providing equal opportunity to all qualified employees without regard to race, color, religion, sex, national origin, age, physical or mental handicap, or status as a military veteran. All personnel decisions, including hiring, promotions, and compensation, should be made without regard to these factors. Anyone who believes that he or she, or anyone else in this corporation, has been the victim of discrimination should contact the human resources director immediately.

JOB DESCRIPTIONS

At the MNO Company we try very hard to develop a written job description for every position and to keep these job descriptions up to date. Every employee will be expected to help the human resources department keep job descriptions current and to make sure that job descriptions are accurate. It is important that job descriptions accurately reflect the work being done and that the essential functions of the job be listed.

SEXUAL HARASSMENT

The MNO Company hires both women and men. We recognize that this can cause problems, and it is our hope that these problems can be avoided by having every employee make reasonable efforts to be sensitive to other employees. Sexual harassment is a violation of both law and company policy. Sexual harassment comes in many forms. It may be a supervisor promising to do an employee a favor in return for a sexual favor. It may be behavior that is unreasonable, such as touching someone in familiar and unwanted ways. It may be using language that causes offense to someone. Both men and women can be victims of sexual harassment.

The MNO Company usually will not be able to do anything about sexual harassment until it is brought to the company's attention. Any employee who is the victim of sexual harassment, or who witnesses what he or she believes to be sexual harassment, should contact the director of human resources immediately. This is true regardless of who the harasser is, including suppliers and customers. Our employees should not have to tolerate inappropriate behavior at the hands of supervisors, suppliers, customers, or fellow employees.

Every effort will be made to conduct an investigation as quickly and as confidentially as possible. All employees will be expected to cooperate with any investigation of sexual harassment. No one bringing a sexual harassment complaint to the attention of the human resources director will be punished in any way, even if it is decided that that person was mistaken. The human resources director will decide what action to take if sexual harassment is found to exist.

We expect everyone working for the MNO Company to recognize that what one person sees as harassment may have been innocent and unintentional. Nevertheless, behavior that makes a fellow employee uncomfortable should be avoided. We expect employees to bring any problems in this area to the attention of the director of human resources rather than trying to solve the problem themselves. While it may simply be a case of misunderstood communication, the director of human resources is trained in this area and needs to know of any potential problems.

SUPERVISOR-EMPLOYEE ROMANCE

Charges of sexual harassment often arise because of romantic relationships between supervisors and subordinates. Such relationships are strictly forbidden here at MNO Company. Anyone who is aware of such a relationship should report it at once to the director of human resources.

RACIAL AND RELIGIOUS HARASSMENT

The MNO Company hires people of all races, colors, places of national origin, and religions. We recognize that this can cause problems, and it is our hope that these problems can be avoided by having every employee make reasonable efforts to be sensitive to other employees. Any kind of harassment is a violation of company policy, regardless of the reasons for it. Harassment comes in many forms. It may be a supervisor or employee using a racial term that is generally considered offensive. It may be telling jokes that belittle or intimidate the members of some group. It may mean making fun of particular religious practices. Anyone can be the victim of harassment.

The MNO Company usually will not be able to do anything about harassment until it is brought to the company's attention. Any employee who feels that he or she has been the victim of harassment, or who witnesses what he or she believes to be harassment, should contact the director of human resources immediately. This is true regardless of who the harasser is, including suppliers and customers. Our employees should not have to tolerate inappropriate behavior at the hands of supervisors, suppliers, customers, or fellow employees.

Every effort will be made to conduct an investigation as quickly and as confidentially as possible. All employees will be expected to cooperate with any investigation of harassment. No one bringing a harassment complaint to the attention of the human resources director will be punished in any way, even if it is decided that the person was mistaken. The human resources director will decide what action to take if harassment is found to exist.

We expect everyone working for MNO Company to recognize that what one person sees as harassment may have been innocent and unintentional. Nevertheless, behavior that makes a fellow employee uncomfortable should be avoided. We expect employees to bring any problems in this area to the attention of the director of human resources rather than trying to solve such problems themselves. While it may simply be a case of misunderstood communication, the director of human resources is trained in this area and needs to know of any potential problems.

AFFIRMATIVE OUTREACH

The MNO Corporation is an affirmative outreach company. We try whenever possible to advertise any job openings widely throughout the region. We notify the state employment commission and advertise in a number of periodicals when we have job openings. We also post all job openings on the bulletin boards. We encourage our employees to help us in this effort. Any suggestions concerning ways in which we can publicize job openings to the widest possible audience will be considered to the extent that they are cost-effective. We also encourage our employees to notify anyone they feel might be interested in working here at the MNO Corporation about relevant job openings.

DIVERSITY AS A PLUS

The MNO Corporation believes that it can benefit from having employees with diverse backgrounds. While we of course seek only qualified employees, when many candidates are qualified for a position, we do take factors such as race, sex, and life experience into account. We provide goods and services for a very diverse population, and we believe that it is to our advantage to have a workforce that reflects that diversity. We do not have quotas, and we do not consider people for positions for which they are not qualified.

AFFIRMATIVE ACTION

The MNO Company is a contractor with the federal government and several states that require affirmative action in the areas of race and sex. In conjunction with the Office of Federal Contract Compliance Programs, we have developed an affirmative action plan, which is available in the Human Resources Department for any employee who wishes to read it. It contains goals and a timetable for meeting those goals. It does not require us to hire people who are not qualified for any job. It does require us to make reasonable efforts to reach out to women and minorities in job categories where we have a low percentage of women or minorities and to offer them the job if they meet the minimum qualifications. We are also required to reach out and hire the disabled and Vietnam veterans.

RELIGIOUS DISCRIMINATION AND ACCOMMODATION

The MNO Company is required by federal and state civil rights laws to avoid discrimination against people because of their religion and to reasonably accommodate any employee who cannot otherwise perform the job because of his or her religion. This most often means allowing some employees to take their Sabbath day off and allowing them to observe their religious holidays. The MNO Company is able to accommodate diverse religious practices only to the extent that our employees are willing to switch shifts and work overtime on occasion. The MNO Company hopes that all employees will be understanding when they are asked to make it possible for other employees to observe their religious practices.

REASONABLE ACCOMMODATION FOR THE DISABLED

The MNO Company, as part of a general effort in American society, is trying to provide reasonable accommodation for disabled individuals. All employees are expected to help with this effort. This may mean restructuring a job or altering a work process if it does not affect the quality or quantity of the work performed. It may mean altering a work schedule or asking for help from fellow employees.

AFFIRMATIVE ACTION FOR THE DISABLED

As a contractor with the federal government, the MNO Company is required to provide affirmative action and reasonable accommodation for handicapped individuals who can perform jobs here at MNO. The written affirmative action plan is in the Human Resources Department and can be read by any employee or job applicant who is interested. We believe that we have a good record of hiring and accommodating the handicapped here at the MNO Company, but we are always trying to improve on our past performance. Employees here at MNO are expected to work with the Human Resources Department when a handicapped individual is hired to help with accommodation and possible job restructuring. We are confident that all of our employees will use their best efforts to make accommodation successful.

AFFIRMATIVE ACTION FOR VIETNAM VETERANS

As a contractor with the federal government, the MNO Company is required to provide affirmative action and reasonable accommodation for Vietnam-era veterans who can perform jobs here at MNO. The written affirmative action plan is in the Human Resources Department and can be read by any employee or job applicant who is interested. We believe that we have a good record of hiring and accommodating Vietnam-era veterans here at the MNO Company, but we are always trying to improve on our past performance. Some veterans may be disabled and require accommodation or job restructuring. We are confident that all of our employees will use their best efforts to make accommodation successful.

A DRUG-FREE WORKPLACE

As a federal contractor, the MNO Company is required to comply with the federal Drug-Free Workplace Act. This act requires us to notify you that the manufacture, distribution, dispensation, possession, or use of controlled substances is illegal and is prohibited at any of our facilities. If an employee is found to be manufacturing, distributing, dispensing, possessing or using any controlled substances either at work or while on company business, he or she will be subject to disciplinary action, which may include termination. The MNO Company cannot afford to pay for a drug rehabilitation program, but the Human Resource Department will provide any employees who request it with a list of available rehabilitation and counseling services in the community. Any employees who are convicted of violating the drug laws while at work or on company business are required to notify the director of human resources within five days after the conviction. If you must manufacture, distribute, dispense, possess, or use controlled substances, please do so somewhere else besides work so that we do not lose our federal contracts, which could result in layoffs of employees for lack of business. Because of this potential terrible consequence, we expect all of our employees to be on the lookout for the violation of this policy and to report such violations immediately to the director of human resources or their immediate supervisor. We also hope that anyone currently manufacturing, distributing, dispensing, possessing, or using any controlled substance will stop and seek help immediately.

PHYSICAL EXAMINATIONS

The MNO Company conducts physical examinations before hiring new employees and requires regular physical examinations of all employees. Medical information is kept in a confidential file separate from other personnel information. This information is released only to supervisors to the extent that they need to know about job restrictions that might apply and to health services and safety personnel so that they may respond appropriately in the case of an emergency. It is also released to government officials who investigate our compliance with law. Employees who have a medical condition that should be brought to the attention of emergency personnel are urged to inform the appropriate person in the Department of Human Resources. Employees who have a physical or mental condition that may affect their ability to do their job are also urged to inform the appropriate person in the Department of Human Resources. The MNO Company does not discriminate against disabled people. However, we cannot accommodate disabilities we do not know about, and we cannot be responsible for emergency treatment in situations where employees have withheld information about their physical condition.

OLDER WORKERS

The MNO Company does not have a mandatory retirement age for any of its employees. Employees in safety-related occupations may be tested on a uniform basis to make sure that they are able to perform their jobs, regardless of age. Employees who are planning to retire should inform the director of human resources as soon as possible after making that decision. The MNO Company expects all employees to treat all other employees with respect, regardless of age. At the same time, all employees are expected to report any employee who is a danger to himself or herself or to other employees because of an unwillingness or inability to perform job tasks in a safe way.

FAMILY AND MEDICAL LEAVE

The MNO Company is subject to the provisions of the federal Family and Medical Leave Act. This act allows employees to take up to twelve weeks of unpaid leave a year because of the birth or adoption of a child; because of the serious health condition of a child, parent, or spouse; or because of their own serious health condition. For the purposes of this policy, a year will be a calendar year. Only employees who have been employed for at least a year may take unpaid family and medical leave. Employees are asked to provide notice as soon as possible if unpaid leave will be required. Employees will be required to take any accumulated paid vacation leave and paid sick/personal leave before taking unpaid family and medical leave. Health insurance coverage will be continued through the leave period. Employees returning from family and medical leave will be returned to the same or an equivalent position unless a reduction in force or other layoff has eliminated their job.

SUPERVISION OF RELATIVES

The MNO Company does not prevent people who are related to each other or married to each other from working here. However, no one may directly supervise his or her spouse or relative. If a supervisor and a subordinate get married, one of them must resign if there is no reasonable way to transfer one of the two to a different division. If they cannot decide between them which will go, then the lower-paid employee will be fired.

COMMERCIALS

Here at the MNO Company we are constantly taking pictures and making commercials of various kinds. Anyone coming to work for us consents, by accepting the job, to participate in these commercials and agrees that the MNO Company may use his or her name and picture for the purposes of commercial advertisement. We consider making commercial advertisements for the company to be part of everyone's job description, and part of everyone's pay is compensation for this activity. While in some cases we may undertake to pay employees who must spend a great deal of time in this activity a special bonus, whether or not we do so is strictly up to the discretion of the MNO Company. Anyone coming to work for the MNO Company agrees to allow the company to continue to use his or her name and picture for commercial purposes even after he or she leaves the company if such pictures were taken or advertisements constructed while the person was employed by the MNO Company.

CONFIDENTIAL INFORMATION

While you are employed at the MNO Company, you may have reason to provide confidential personal information about yourself to your supervisor, medical personnel or the Human Resources Department. All supervisors, managers, and employees are expected to keep such information confidential and reveal it only to those who need to know it. At the same time, it is important for all employees to realize that this kind of information must be revealed in some circumstances and will be revealed in situations in which some employees will feel it should not have been revealed. By coming to work for the MNO Company, you agree to leave the question of when personal information known by those in the company will be revealed to others in the company and to whom it will be revealed to the discretion of the company and its managers and employees. The MNO Company expects all of its managers and employees to use good judgment in this regard. Generally, confidential information concerning medical issues and disabilities should be revealed only to supervisors and others who must know in order to work effectively with the person involved or to accommodate a disability, to emergency and medical personnel who may be called upon to provide emergency treatment, and to government officials investigating our compliance with law.

INFORMATION ABOUT EMPLOYEES

Because of the problem of making potentially defamatory statements about current and former employees, it is the policy of the MNO Company not to give out any information about current or former employees except to government officials who are authorized to receive such information. Any manager or employee who is approached for information about any current or former employee should refer the matter to the Human Resources Department.

SEARCHES AND INSPECTIONS

The MNO Company engages in a significant amount of confidential research, both for itself and for the United States government. Also, the MNO Company has experienced a significant amount of theft over the last few years. Every employee coming to work at the MNO Company is on notice that anything inside a company facility is subject to search at any time for any reason or no reason. This means that all company property, such as desks and lockers, is subject to search at all times. It also means that the personal belongings of employees, such as purses and briefcases, are also subject to search, as is the clothing of employees. All automobiles on company property are also subject to search by the company at any time. Anyone entering or leaving an MNO facility is subject to inspection and search. We are a drug-free workplace, and we have a responsibility to maintain a drug-free atmosphere, which can be accomplished only by periodic searches. All employees are expected to cooperate with any manager or security guard who is conducting a search.

MAIL

It is the policy of the MNO Company to assume that all mail arriving at an MNO facility is related to company business. All employees should know that any mail arriving at an MNO facility may be opened by someone other than the particular person it is addressed to. Employees are expected to receive personal or confidential mail at their homes, not at work.

ELECTRONIC MONITORING

In an effort to maintain quality in relationships with both suppliers and customers, the MNO Company routinely monitors all phone conversations on company phone lines. An employee who wishes to be sure that a personal conversation is private should make use of one of the pay phones located in several areas. The MNO Company also uses video surveillance cameras to enhance the effectiveness of our security personnel. The cameras are in plain sight for everyone to see. There are no hidden cameras, and there are no cameras in restrooms. The MNO Corporation does not routinely monitor the electronic mail network but reserves the right to do so. The MNO Company does not use bugs or hidden microphones. If any employee believes he or she has been electronically bugged or finds what he or she believes might be a hidden microphone, the employee should report this immediately to security.

PUBLIC STATEMENTS BY EMPLOYEES

We at the MNO Company recognize that our employees have the right to speak out on issues of concern to the general public. At the same time, we expect our employees to recognize that some statements may cause disharmony among coworkers or interfere with the employee's ability to perform his or her duties. We ask employees who are planning to make a public statement that might have these negative effects to discuss their statement with the director of human resources before making it. Also, whenever an employee of the MNO Company makes a public statement, it is possible that those hearing it might believe this statement to be a statement of the MNO Company's official position on the topic under discussion. We expect all employees to either clear such statements with the appropriate company official or make it clear that they are not speaking for the company. We also expect that employees making statements concerning the activities or policies of the MNO Company will check their facts with the appropriate company official before making a statement that might turn out to be false and place the company in a bad light. All of us at the MNO Company recognize that our success depends on our maintaining our positive image with the general public, and we hope that our employees will help us to continue to enhance that image whenever possible.

VIOLATIONS OF THE LAW

The MNO Company is involved in a number of areas where the company is required to obey complex legal provisions. The MNO Company is a law-abiding citizen, and every employee at every level is instructed to obey the law at all times. Any employee who believes that the MNO Company is not obeying the law should bring that concern to the appropriate manager or, if in doubt, to the director of human resources. While employees have the right to take their concerns to government officials, the MNO Company hopes that these issues can be solved internally before it is necessary to bring in government law enforcement officials. If a legal violation can be dealt with internally that will save time and money and help prevent negative publicity.

OUTSIDE EMPLOYMENT

The MNO Company expects that professional and managerial employees are devoting their full time and effort to fulfilling their duties with the company. The MNO Company also expects that all other full-time employees are not engaged in activities outside of work that will prevent them from doing their best when they are working at the MNO Company. Any employee, full-time or part-time, who is employed for wages outside of the time spent at the MNO Company is required to inform the director of human resources about this outside employment and provide the director of human resources with phone numbers and addresses so that we can contact you if necessary while you are at your other place of employment.

CONFLICT OF INTEREST

The MNO Company is engaged in a large number of projects and does work for governments around the world. We expect our employees to do everything they can to help us maintain and expand our business and to refrain from doing any-thing that might interfere with our success. It is often difficult for employees to know if something they are doing might constitute a conflict of interest, and that is why we spend time on this subject as part of our new-employee orientation. Generally, it is a conflict of interest to provide information to a competitor or deal with a competitor in any way without discussing it first with the director of hu-man resources or some other appropriate executive of the MNO Company. We expect employees who see business opportunities that MNO might be interested in to inform the company before taking advantage of them. We also expect em-ployees who have personal financial or other interests that might color their judg-ment when dealing with either customers or suppliers to inform the appropriate executive at MNO before continuing to engage in conduct that might raise issues of conflict of interest.

CRIMINAL ACTIVITY

Every employee at the MNO Company is required to inform the director of hu-man resources if he or she is charged with any crime, including traffic violations, and to keep the director informed about the outcome of the case. We expect our employees to obey all laws, both at work and away from work, and to recognize that their actions, even away from work, can reflect on the reputation of the MNO Company.

POLITICAL OPINIONS

We at the MNO Company believe that everyone should be allowed to hold and express political opinions without interference from an employer. It is the policy of the MNO Company not to take a person's political affiliation into account when making personnel decisions. At the same time, we recognize that the ex-pression of strong political opinions at work can be disruptive. We expect all our employees to spend their time at work working and to save their political ac-tivities and political arguments for after working hours and away from MNO facilities.

EMPLOYEE CLASSIFICATION

Here at the MNO Company we have full-time and part-time employees. Part-time employees are generally not entitled to any company benefits, such as health insurance and paid vacations. The director of human resources will inform every employee whether he or she is full-time or part-time. Also, we have three basic types of employees based on the federal Fair Labor Standards Act. Our em-ployees are classified as either salaried exempt, salaried nonexempt or hourly nonexempt. An exempt employee is exempt from the overtime provisions of the Fair Labor Standards Act. A nonexempt employee is entitled to overtime pay re-gardless of whether he or she receives a paycheck calculated for the hours worked each week or a regular salary. Because of this, salaried nonexempt em-ployees are given a statement showing what their regular rate of pay is and guar-anteeing them overtime pay whether they work overtime or not. This practice is to avoid potentially open-ended liability under the law. If you are a salaried non-exempt employee, this practice will be explained to you when you are hired. No hourly nonexempt employee should ever work overtime without express orders to do so from his or her supervisor.

CHILD LABOR AND IMMIGRATION LAWS

The MNO Company intends to comply with all laws, including the child labor and immigration laws. This means that we hire only people who are old enough and eligible to work under both federal and state statutes. Generally, if there is any doubt about age, proof of age should be required. Every employee hired by MNO is required to complete an I-9 form and prove that he or she is either a U.S. citizen or an alien eligible to work under U.S. immigration laws. All employees are expected to comply with these laws and to inform the director of human resources if they have any reason to believe that a coworker is either under age or an alien who is not eligible to work under U.S. Immigration laws.

WAGE PAYMENT AND GARNISHMENT

The MNO Company has a variety of types of employees, and different classifications of employees may receive their pay on different days or at different intervals. To avoid problems, the MNO Company will not make advance payments or release a paycheck to anyone other than the employee or his or her representative (who must have a signed authorization from the employee). In the event that employees have their wages garnished or assign their wages, the MNO Company will comply with the law and make the payments as required by law. We expect all employees to cooperate in this process if it becomes necessary. Any questions concerning pay or wage garnishment should be directed to the director of human resources.

LEAVE TO VOTE

The MNO Company realizes that some employees will not be able to vote before or after work. We ask such employees to inform their supervisor or the director of human resources at least one week before an election in which such an employee wishes to participate during regular working hours. Full-time hourly employees will be given a reasonable amount of time off without pay to vote. Full-time salaried employees will be given a reasonable amount of time off to vote with pay. The MNO Company expects all employees to time their trip to the polls in a way that causes the least disruption to the smooth functioning of the company. In most cases, it is assumed that employees can vote before or after work.

JURY AND MILITARY DUTY

Salaried employees who are summoned to participate in a court proceeding as either a juror or a witness will be given paid leave of up to five days in any one calendar year in order to fulfill this obligation. Any amount received by the salaried employee for these services will be deducted from the employee's pay for this period. Hourly employees will be given unpaid leave in order to fulfill these obligations.

Salaried employees who are called to temporary military duty will be given up to two weeks' paid leave in order to fulfill this obligation. Anything over two weeks will be considered not to be temporary. Any amount received by the salaried employee for this service will be deducted from the employee's pay for this period. Hourly employees will be given unpaid leave in order to fulfill temporary military obligations.

Any employee, salaried or hourly, full or part-time, who is called to active duty with the U.S. military for a period of less than four years will be entitled to reinstatement to his or her old position to the extent required by federal and state laws and regulations.

SICK/PERSONAL LEAVE

Full-time salaried employees at the MNO Company receive one day of sick/personal leave for every two months of work completed. Employees may accumulate up to twenty days of sick/personal leave. An accumulation over twenty days will be lost. This is paid leave, paid at the employee's regular salary. Full-time salaried employees who are eligible for Family and Medical Leave under our Family and Medical Leave policy and the federal Family and Medical Leave Act must use up their paid sick/personal leave before taking unpaid leave. Employees who have accumulated sick/personal leave days when they terminate their employment with MNO Company will receive payment for those accumulated days up to the twenty-day limit allowed by this policy.

VACATION LEAVE

Full-time salaried employees at the MNO Company receive one day of paid vacation for every month worked at the company. Employees may accumulate up to twenty days of paid vacation. An accumulation over twenty days will be lost. Requests for vacation times must be made to the employee's direct supervisor and will be scheduled to take into account the work process at MNO Company. Generally, most vacations will be scheduled during the summer. Vacation must be taken in increments of at least one week at a time. If a company holiday falls during an employee's paid vacation, the employee may add a day or days at the beginning or end of the vacation period to take this into account.

COMPANY HOLIDAYS

Each year the MNO Company surveys employees concerning which holidays to take during the coming year. Generally twelve days are taken as holidays and the facilities of MNO Company are shut down. A list of the holidays for the coming year is posted on bulletin boards in December after the employee survey. Full-time salaried employees are paid during these holiday periods as if they were performing regular service.

CLOSED FACILITIES

All MNO facilities are closed except to employees and authorized guests of the company. We expect all employees to follow security procedures, including informing their friends and relatives that as a general rule they will not be allowed past the security gate. No solicitation is allowed on company property, including the parking lots.

UNIONS

The MNO Company does not currently have any contracts with any unions. It is against company policy to discriminate against anyone because he or she belongs to a union. It is also against company policy to discriminate against anyone because he or she does not belong to a union.

COMMUNICATION

The MNO Company got where it is today, in part, because of a willingness to listen to employees. It is the policy of the MNO Company to encourage employees to express their ideas and concerns to their supervisors. The MNO Company tries to keep employees informed about changes in the company and the world that might affect them, and the company expects the employees to do the same thing. Employees are instructed to report any violations of law or company policy to the director of human resources as quickly as possible. It is the policy of the MNO Company to obey all laws, and if an employee believes that a law is being violated by either the MNO Company or someone with whom the MNO Company interacts, this should be communicated as quickly as possible.

SUGGESTIONS

We have two kinds of suggestion plans at the MNO Company. The first is our ongoing suggestion plan. Any employee may submit a suggestion in writing to the director of human resources at any time. The director will forward these suggestions to the appropriate company officials for consideration and possible implementation. Every year, in March, the director will appoint a committee made up of three managers and three employees to review the last year's suggestions. The three employees will be chosen at random from among all employees. The director shall act as chair of this committee. This committee will decide what awards will given for suggestions. The top award will be an all-expenses-paid trip to Europe for three weeks for the winner and his or her immediate family. At least one top award will be given out every year. The committee may decide to give out more than one top award. The committee may also decide to make cash awards of $5,000 or less. The decision of the committee is final, and both the company and the employees will be bound by its decision.

Second, here at the MNO Company, we do have a special employee suggestion contest from time to time. These contests are separate and apart from the usual suggestion plan process. These contests involve group entries, and only groups of at least five employees may participate in the contest. Prizes will be announced for each contest as the contest is announced.

Participation in the ongoing suggestion plan process and the special suggestion contests is strictly voluntary. We at MNO hope that all employees will want to take part. Many important improvements have been the result of employee suggestions.

SAFETY

The MNO Company has a very good record in the area of safety, and we intend to keep it that way. Every employee is expected to ask for and receive safety training before beginning any new job. Supervisors are expected to make sure that every job is performed safely and that all employees are wearing proper safety equipment. Anyone in the MNO Company who believes that a task could be performed more safely should discuss that idea with the director of human resources. The director of human resources is responsible for all aspects of safety at the MNO Company, and anyone who has any questions, comments, or complaints about safety should contact the director.

ACCIDENT AND ILLNESS REPORTS

If anyone sees an accident, he or she should report this immediately to a supervisor or the director of human resources and to the emergency office. Every employee is also expected to report any illness that might in any way be related to work to the director of human resources as quickly as possible. Employees are given emergency training from time to time in order to keep minor injuries from turning into major injuries.

HAZARDOUS MATERIALS

Hazardous materials are used in some facilities of the MNO Company. A file of Material Safety Data Sheets is kept in all facilities in which hazardous materials are used. Employees who come into contact with hazardous materials will be trained in their safe use and should consult the Material Safety Data Sheets if they are in doubt about the proper safety precautions that should be taken with a particular substance. Employees who do come into contact with hazardous materials are expected to participate in the Hazardous Materials Communication Training Program. Any employee who wishes to may see the Hazardous Materials Communication Plan for the facility where he or she works. Employees are expected to handle all hazardous materials with caution and to be sure that they are trained in the proper safety and use guidelines before using any hazardous material.

REPETITIVE MOTION INJURY PREVENTION

One of the major health problems in the American workplace today is repetitive motion injuries, sometimes called repeated trauma injuries. These injuries are caused by performing the same tasks over and over again in the same way for long periods of time. Backs, wrists, elbows, and shoulders are the most vulnerable. These injuries can be prevented by the use of braces or supports, changing the way some tasks are performed, taking breaks, or performing a variety of tasks to avoid long periods of repeated motion. Early warning signs include numbness or tingling in an arm, leg, or finger or persistent and recurring pain from movement or pressure. Any employee who experiences any early warning sign should report that fact immediately to a supervisor or the director of human resources.

STRESS AND STRAIN PREVENTION

The MNO Company is aware that workers are likely to suffer from repetitive motion injuries, eyestrain from video display terminals, and job stress without proper breaks and exercise periods. That is why we have an extensive program of breaks and exercise periods for people subject to these kinds of injuries. There is a tendency to get busy and forget to take these breaks and do these exercises, but it is very important for everyone that these precautions be taken. Job stress can often be avoided by simply taking a break when needed. Employees who feel that they are suffering from high levels of stress should contact the director of human resources about the problem.

SMOKING

Smoking is not allowed inside any MNO facility or building. This is a strict policy, and it is strictly enforced. Employees who must smoke may do so outside the building during a break from work. Smoking is hazardous both to the person smoking and to those who breath the smoke secondhand. The MNO Company will pay half the cost of programs designed to help our employees stop smoking. Employees who wish to quit should contact the director of human resources for information about approved programs.

ALCOHOLIC BEVERAGES

No alcoholic beverage of any kind is allowed in any MNO building or facility. Alcoholic beverages are not to be served at any MNO company function, including a picnic, dance, or party. While employees are of course free to consume alcoholic beverages on their own time away from work, employees who come to work unable to perform their job because of alcohol will not be provided with any accommodation. The MNO Company will pay half the cost of some alcohol treatment programs. Interested employees should contact the director of human resources for information about approved programs.

BLOOD AND CONTAGIOUS DISEASES

Employees with AIDS and other diseases are protected by the Americans with Disabilities Act. This means that they will be allowed to work if they can do so with reasonable accommodation. All employees should realize that diseases such as AIDS and hepatitis are carried by blood or in other body fluids. When helping an injured coworker, gloves and other protective gear should be worn if the person is bleeding. Any employee who becomes ill with a contagious disease should report this to the director of human resources so that proper precautions can be taken and emergency personnel can be warned. All medical information is kept confidential and revealed only to company officials who need to know.

WORKERS' COMPENSATION INSURANCE

At the MNO Company we have workers' compensation insurance for all our employees. It is important that every employee report any accident or illness that might be in any way job-related to the director of human resources as quickly as possible. It is important for all employees to realize that the more we have to spend on premium payments for workers' compensation insurance, the less money we have to pay our employees. As an incentive for everyone to work more safely, we budget a certain amount every year to cover workers' compensation premiums and the cost of temporary workers who are needed to replace injured workers. If we spend less than the budgeted amount in a year, that money will be used to fund a safety appreciation party at the end of the year.

EMPLOYEE DUTIES

Under American law, employees are considered to have a series of duties that they owe their employers. We at the MNO Company expect our employees to live up to those duties.

The first duty is the *duty to work to the best of your abilities*. Employees expect us to pay them. In return, we expect employees not only to come to work on time but to do their very best. We hope that employees who do not feel that they can do their very best because of some factor that can be corrected will discuss that with their supervisor or the director of human resources. We spend a lot of money on training and equipment, and we hope that our employees will help us to make the most of that investment.

The second duty is the *duty of care*. At MNO Company, employees are entrusted with machines worth a great deal of money. We expect employees to treat these machines, and all MNO property, with the utmost care. The more we have to spend on maintenance and repair, the less we have to pay employees.

The third duty is the *duty of loyalty*. If employees see a business opportunity that they think the MNO Company might take advantage of, they are duty bound to inform the company about it. Also, employees are not allowed to compete with MNO Company in any way. Employees who act as suppliers or customers or who own or work for suppliers, customers, or competitors are expected to inform the director of human resources of this as quickly as possible.

The fourth duty is the *duty of good conduct*. We have a right to expect our employees to conduct themselves away from work in a way that brings credit on the MNO Company and to avoid acting in a way that might bring ridicule or disrepute on the company. Employees who feel that they might have done something that violated this duty are expected to discuss this with the director of human resources as quickly as possible.

The fifth duty is the *duty of confidence*. Employees are expected not to reveal confidential information to anyone outside the company. This includes information about trade secrets, pay, product specifications, software, customers, vendors, marketing or business plans, price information, product formulas, recipes, blueprints, production processes, or our employees. This duty extends to employees who no longer work for MNO Company. Also, all books, reports, files, and records kept or developed by an employee belong to the MNO Company, not to the employee.

EMPLOYEES WHO WORK DIRECTLY WITH CUSTOMERS

Employees who work directly with customers are prohibited from soliciting those customers for another company for a period of two years after leaving the MNO Company. Anyone coming to work for the MNO Company agrees to abide by this provision and to not, directly or indirectly, seek to do business with any person or company that he or she worked with or serviced while working at the MNO Company.

EMPLOYEES WHO INVENT, CREATE OR WRITE AT WORK

Employees who invent, write, or create things while at work agree that these inventions and creations belong to the MNO Company. Employees agree to help the MNO Company patent and copyright inventions and creations made while they are employed at the MNO Company and to assign patents or copyrights to the company if that is necessary. Employees also agree to cooperate with the MNO Company in obtaining patent and copyright protection for their inventions and creations. If the MNO Company decides not to seek a patent but to keep the invention a secret, employees agree not to divulge any information to anyone else about any inventions they created or worked with while at the MNO Company.

LAID-OFF EMPLOYEES

Any employee who is laid off for any reason should leave his or her address with the director of human resources. During the next two years, the laid-off employee will be notified if any jobs come open that he or she might be qualified for. We have a large investment in our employees, and, when possible, we try to hire them back. However, the MNO Company does not promise to hire back laid-off employees. The laid-off employee will be given an interview and will be hired if he or she is judged to be the best candidate for the job.

UNEMPLOYMENT COMPENSATION AGENCIES

The only person authorized to deal with state and federal unemployment compensation agencies is the director of human resources. If anyone in the MNO Company receives a request for information about a former employee, from an unemployment compensation agency or anyone else, he or she should refer the person making the inquiry to the director of human resources. Anyone who receives any kind of written request for information about a former employee should forward that request to the director of human resources also. From time to time employees may be requested to testify at an unemployment compensation hearing. We expect them to tell the truth. The decision whether or not to challenge a request for unemployment compensation by a former employee will be made by the director of human resources after appropriate fact finding and consultation.

DISCIPLINE

At the MNO Company we recognize that in some cases employees will violate rules or engage in actions that do not justify dismissal but do justify some other disciplinary action. In those situations, supervisors are required to write a report and place a copy of that report in the personnel file of the employee involved. Any employee who feels that he or she has been unfairly treated by this process may file a grievance.

GRIEVANCE

At MNO Company we realize that there will be times when a complaint cannot be resolved without some formal grievance procedure. An employee who cannot resolve a problem informally should file a written grievance (on a grievance form obtained from the Human Resources Office) with his or her immediate supervisor. The supervisor will investigate the matter and attempt to resolve the problem. If that is not possible, the supervisor will file a written response, and both the complaint and the written response will be sent to the director of human resources. The director will investigate the matter and attempt to solve the problem. If the employee is not happy about the director's resolution of the problem the employee may appeal the director's decision to the president of the MNO Company. The president's decision will be final. While it is our hope that most problems can be solved informally, we also recognize that some issues are complex and can be resolved only if problems and responses are put in writing and submitted to someone who is not directly involved. Employees who use the formal grievance procedure will not suffer in any way as long as they have filed their grievance with a good-faith belief that something is wrong that could be corrected by the actions of someone higher up in the company hierarchy. The only decision that is not subject to the grievance procedure is the dismissal of an employee.

EVALUATIONS

The MNO Company believes that everyone in the organization needs, and deserves, feedback concerning his or her performance. That is why periodic performance evaluations are conducted for everyone. The evaluations will look at everything from quantity and quality of work done to attendance and relations with coworkers. The purpose of these evaluations is to help employees improve and to guide personnel decisions. Every employee is expected to participate in the evaluation process with an eye toward improving his or her own performance and the performance of the entire organization.

PERSONNEL RECORDS

All employees of the MNO Company have the right to examine any records that pertain to them personally. If an employee feels that anything in the records is not accurate, he or she should bring it to the attention of the director of human resources. If the director refuses to remove the objected-to item, the employee has the right to place a notice in the file that the employee believes the item to be inaccurate. This notice should explain why the employee believes this to be the case.

HEALTH AND LIFE INSURANCE

At the MNO Company, all full-time employees (those who work more than thirty hours a week) who have worked for at least thirty days are entitled to participate in our group health and life insurance programs. Employees must fill out the necessary forms at the human resources office. We have experienced a significant increase in health insurance premiums during the last few years, with no end in sight. In order to control costs, we have instituted a number of programs to help prevent both accidents and illness. We now participate in a health maintenance organization (HMO) instead of the kind of insurance program most of you may be familiar with. This requires you to make a nominal payment every time you use the HMO. We have also provided recreational facilities to help employees maintain their general physical health, and we encourage employees to use them. We also provide subsidies for employees who wish to participate in weight loss and stop-smoking programs as well as drug and alcohol treatment programs, and employees are encouraged to take advantage of these programs. When it comes to health, an ounce of prevention is worth a pound of cure.

CONTINUATION OF GROUP HEALTH INSURANCE

Employees who quit, retire, are fired, are laid off, become disabled, or have their hours reduced, so that they no longer qualify for employer-provided group health insurance, may be entitled to continue the coverage under the group plan at their own expense. The spouse and children of such an employee may also be entitled to continued coverage under the group plan. Also, if an employee dies, divorces or goes on Medicare, his or her spouse, ex-spouse, or children may also be entitled to continue to be covered by our group plan, at their own expense. That is why employees must inform the director of human resources when they divorce or do anything else that might trigger this eligibility.

401(k) PLAN

Here at the MNO Company we have a defined-contribution benefit plan, commonly called a thrift plan or a 401(k) plan. The company matches every dollar employees contribute by contributing another dollar. The maximum amount any employee can contribute is set by law and changes from year to year to adjust for inflation. You will be asked how much you wish to contribute out of your paycheck at the beginning of each year. This program is available only to full-time employees. New employees should receive a Summary Plan Description. All employees who participate in the plan will receive an annual report covering the plan and their personal account. This plan allows employees to have some say concerning how their funds are invested. Because the money placed in the 401(k) plan is pretax and because the interest and dividends earned in the plan are also not taxed, this plan allows employees to accumulate wealth for retirement much faster than by investing on their own. Of course, when benefits are finally paid, they will be subject to income taxes. This is a voluntary plan. Employees vest 20 percent a year in this plan and will be 100 percent vested at the end of five years. Vesting simply means the extent to which the employee is entitled to receive the money paid into the plan by the employer. Employees are 100 percent vested in the funds they place in the plan at all times.

BONUSES

It is our practice at the MNO Company to pay bonuses from time to time when the financial situation allows it. Bonuses are based on a variety of factors, including the extent to which individual employees have made valuable suggestions that have improved the company. Generally, bonuses are paid half in cash and half in restricted MNO stock. The stock is restricted, meaning it can not be sold for ten years after being given to the employee (it may be left in a will). As a condition of the bonus, employees are required to pay income taxes on the restricted stock when they receive it based on the current market value of the stock. Because this will mean that the gift of restricted stock is taxed just as if the shares could be sold immediately (even though they cannot be), the cash part of the bonus is given to help pay income taxes. By paying income taxes at the time of the gift, employees will not have to pay any further income taxes until the stock is sold. The point of giving restricted stock is that the stock will be worth something in the future only if we all continue to work harder and smarter than our competitors. We believe that to the extent all of us have that incentive, our company will be prosperous in the years to come.

STOCK OPTION PLAN

The MNO General Stock Option Plan provides stock options to all employees every January 1. The option amount depends on the amount of wages earned in the preceding year. These options are for ten years, which means that for ten years the employee may exercise the option and buy shares at the price set in the option. Only full-time employees who have been employed full-time for the preceding year are eligible to participate in this plan. When you receive your stock option, please read it carefully and direct any questions to the director of human resources. Because our stock option plan meets the requirements of Section 422 of the Internal Revenue Code, employees will not have to pay income taxes on any money they make until they actually sell the stock. This means that employees may exercise their options and hold on to the stock if they wish.

STOCK PURCHASE PLAN

We have an employee stock purchase plan at the MNO Company. This plan allows employees to set aside a percentage of their salary every payday for the purpose of buying MNO stock. The company sells the stock at 85 percent of the current market price, and employees do not have to pay a broker's commission on the purchase. Employees do not have to pay any income taxes on the difference between what they paid for the stock and what the stock is worth until the stock is sold. Anyone wishing to participate in this plan should contact the Human Resources Office for detailed information.

EMPLOYEE STOCK OWNERSHIP PLAN

The MNO Company has an Employee Stock Ownership Plan (ESOP) that currently owns over 20 percent of the common stock of the MNO Company. This plan allows the company to borrow money and save taxes in the process. When the borrowed money is paid back, stock is placed in the individual accounts of the employees (only full-time employees participate in the ESOP). This is the most tax-advantaged way for us to arrange for employees to own stock in the MNO Company. Employees cannot get their stock until they die, retire, become disabled, or leave the company (there are restrictions on when employees who leave the company can receive their shares). Each year each employee receives an account of how many shares he or she has and how much these shares are currently worth. We strongly believe that employees should share in the financial success of the company and that this is the best way (in terms of taxes and other factors) for us to allow this to happen. We believe that the best way to ensure the long-term financial health of the company is to give every employee shares in the ESOP. Because the shares will be available for sale only many years in the future, every employee has a strong incentive to be concerned with the long-term growth of the company. Our high level of employee ownership through the ESOP allows us to develop the kind of workplace that we would all like to work in. Everyone is in the same boat, and everyone can provide everyone else with the kind of trust and flexibility that allow us to work smarter, work harder, and have fun at the same time.

THE FREE FLOW OF INFORMATION

At the MNO Company we want to encourage the free flow of information. The MNO *Bugle* is published twice a month with no management control over its content. Employees are free to submit unsigned questions, and management is required to provide answers. Everyone in the company may use the *Bugle* as a way to express both positive and negative opinions. No employee will be punished for expressing an opinion or honestly stating facts in the MNO *Bugle*. Any employee who believes that he or she has seen a violation of law or ethics may report it to the director of human resources. The director will not reveal the reporting employee's name without the reporting employee's permission. It is important to the long-term growth and health of the MNO Company that violations of law and ethics be avoided. We will all be better off if these violations can be corrected inside the company.

NO-LAYOFF POLICY

It is a point of pride at MNO that we are a *no-layoff* company. It is important for everyone to understand what that means. It does not mean that employees are never fired. Employees who engage in misconduct or who cannot do the job to specifications are certainly fired. It does mean that MNO will do everything possible to avoid laying off employees because the economy is in recession or our sales are down. It does mean that MNO will move people around to avoid having to lay people off because of improvements in work efficiency or because of company reorganizations. If necessary, we may impose shorter work weeks for everyone to get through a tough financial time. While this has never happened, we cannot promise that at some point in the future we won't have to lay off workers in order to save the company. We can promise that we will not do this except as a last resort.

PEER REVIEW PANEL

Any employee who is not happy with the result of the normal grievance procedure may petition the director of human resources to convene a "peer review panel." The director of human resources has the discretion to grant or deny this request based on factors such as the significance of the problem and the facts of the individual case. This panel will consist of six employees selected at random from all employees at the relevant location. The director will either preside over the hearing or appoint someone to preside. The vote of the peer review panel will be final, and both the employee and the company will be bound by its decision. Employees may not bring an attorney to the hearing, but they may have another employee help them to make their case.

NO SPECIAL PRIVILEGES

The MNO Company considers all employees important. We do not have special parking spaces or dining facilities for executives because we believe that these kinds of distinctions are counterproductive. We hope that all employees, at all levels, will communicate with one another and treat one another as they themselves would wish to be treated.

FAIRNESS

The MNO Company prides itself on being a fair company. What does that mean? It means that managers do not discipline or discharge employees without first providing a warning whenever that would be appropriate. It means that employees are counseled about a problem before a written warning or notice of discipline is placed in their personnel file. It means that employees are allowed to tell their side of the story before any decision is made to discharge or discipline them. It means that employees may file a grievance if they believe that they have been treated wrongly. The MNO Company does not promise never to make a mistake. It does promise to try to treat employees fairly as far as discipline and discharge decisions are concerned.

ARBITRATION

At the MNO Company we want to provide a process for dealing with all disputes between employees and the company. By coming to work at MNO or staying at MNO, all employees agree that all controversies and disagreements between them and the company will be submitted to binding arbitration through the company arbitrator. Any issues concerning discharge will also be submitted to the arbitrator, including questions of whether or not civil rights laws have been violated as well as violations of other statutes, the common law, or contract. Any issue relating to employment at the MNO Company must be submitted to the arbitrator and may not be taken to a court of law for resolution. The MNO arbitrator is appointed for a five-year term by a committee made up of three randomly selected managers and three randomly selected employees. Every five years a new MNO arbitrator is chosen from a list of three names submitted by the outgoing arbitrator. The MNO arbitrator is paid exactly the same salary and benefits as the director of human resources and has an office and staff support to help us reach amicable resolutions of disputes quickly and with as little expense as possible to both sides. We are fortunate to have Judge Watson, retired from the California Supreme Court, currently filling that role. Anyone who is not happy with a final decision in the grievance procedure may take the issue to the arbitrator. Anyone who has been discharged may take the issue of whether or not that discharge violated any contract or law to the arbitrator. These issues may not be taken to court and must be taken to the arbitrator for resolution. The decision of the arbitrator is final and binding on all employees and the MNO Company. Employees who have disputes with one another are invited to use the offices of the MNO arbitrator if they wish to do so by agreement between the parties.

REVISIONS

This employee handbook is subject to revision at any time by the MNO Company.

Table of Cases

Index